The Europa Library of Business Biography
Series Editor: Neil McKendrick

Herbert Austin

The British Motor Car Industry to 1941

Herbert Austin (1866–1941).

Herbert Austin

The British Motor Car Industry to 1941

Roy Church

London
Europa Publications Limited

Europa Publications Limited
18 Bedford Square, London, WC1B 3JN

British Library Cataloguing in Publication Data

Church, Roy Anthony
Herbert Austin (The Europa Library of Business Biography: 4).
1. Austin, Herbert. 2. Automobile industry and trade—Great Britain—Biography.
3. Businessmen—Great Britain—Biography
338.7'62'922220924 TL140.A9
ISBN 0 905118 29 4

Printed and bound in England by
Staples Printers Rochester Limited
at The Stanhope Press.

Contents

List of Plans and Graphs

List of Tables in the Text

List of Plates

GENERAL INTRODUCTION

The Enemies of Technology and the Self-Made Man

Neil McKendrick

IN ITS ATTITUDES to men of business English society has heeded for too long the Blakean view that 'the tigers of wrath are wiser than the horses of instruction'. It has followed its heart, not its head. And its heart has been more moved by the anger of poets and novelists than its head has been convinced by the reason of economists or business historians. When one compares the verbal brilliance of some of the tigers with the honest plodding of most of the horses, it is difficult not to sympathize with society's choice.[1]

Anger and dismissive contempt have inspired more memorable prose – and more purple passages – than have the quieter voices of justification through practical need.

As a result our society's instinctive response to business and technology has been deeply influenced by the view that mills are characteristically 'dark' and 'Satanic', that merchants are the 'fiends of

[1] This introduction is a further attempt to explore and explain what I have called *The Luddite Interpretation of History: the Enemies of the Entrepreneurial Ideal.* It is based on the belief that social and cultural forces can often have as important an effect on economic growth as can the more strictly economic elements. Earlier contributions to this theme can be found in Neil McKendrick, General Introduction to R. J. Overy, *William Morris, Viscount Nuffield* (1976), pp. vii–xliv; Neil McKendrick, 'In Search of a Secular Ideal', the General Introduction to Clive Trebilcock, *The Vickers Brothers: Armaments and Enterprise, 1854–1914* (1977), pp. ix–xxxiv; and Neil McKendrick, 'Literary Luddism and the Businessman', the General Introduction to P. N. Davies, *Sir Alfred Jones: Shipping Entrepreneur Par Excellence* (1978), pp. ix–lvi. These three volumes, together with Professor R. A. Church, *Herbert Austin*, are the first fruits of *The Europa Library of Business Biography*.

commerce', that the businessman's historic role has been to serve as little more than the mahout to Dickens's 'melancholy mad elephants', the machines which trampled humanity to death in search of private profits. Invited by Wordsworth to share his 'just disdain', the majority response has been to accept.

Blake and Wordsworth and Dickens were not, of course, alone. They were lead singers to an impressive chorus of disapproval and condemnation of the men who presided over and profited from the introduction of technology. The businessman has rarely been able wholly to rid himself of this indictment. Partly, of course, he has been convicted of guilt by association – his association with pollution and profit and the inhuman efficiency of the machine. He has incurred the wrath of a society which has held him responsible for the destruction of the world we have lost, for the pollution of our environment, for the exploitation of human greed. Even those who concede that we are living a material triumph, often argue that it is at the cost of a spiritual disaster. They feel that man has handed over his destiny to 'sorcerers who are totally blind to the meaning of the human adventure',[2] to a totalitarian technology which is 'a power unto itself, absorbing men and society to its necessities',[3] conditioned by nothing but 'its own calculus of efficiency'.[4]

The anti-technology movement is as powerful as it is pervasive. It is a formidable adversary alone, and its many influential allies make it even more formidable. But much derives from its spontaneous emotional appeal to so many of our most deeply ingrained prejudices – so well absorbed as to masquerade as natural instincts. For what is hated and feared and despised 'is a kind of force that gives rise to technology, something undefined, but inhuman, mechanical, lifeless, a blind monster, a death force'.[5]

To its enemies it is 'something hideous they are running away from but know they can never escape'.[6] They instinctively feel that it is dangerous and threatening. They are profoundly out of sympathy with those who run it and understand it:

[2] Jacques Ellul, *The Technological Society*, (New York, 1964), p. xxxi.

[3] Paul A. Gagnon, 'La Vie Future: Some French Responses to the Technological Society', *Journal of European Studies*, vi (1976), p. 177.

[4] Jacques Ellul, op. cit., p. 435.

[5] Robert M. Persig, *Zen and the Art of Motorcycle Maintenance: An Inquiry into its Values* (1974), p. 16.

[6] Ibid.

> Somewhere there are people who understand it and run it but those are technologists, and they speak in inhuman language when describing what they do. It's all parts and relationships of unheard-of things, that never make any sense no matter how often you hear about them. And their things, their monster keeps eating up land and polluting their air and lakes, and there is no way to strike back at it, and hardly any way to escape it.
>
> That attitude is not hard to come to. You go through a heavy industrial area of a large city and there it all is, the technology. In front of it are high barbed-wire fences, locked gates, signs saying 'NO TRESPASSING', and beyond, through sooty air, you see ugly strange shapes of metal and brick whose purpose is unknown, and whose masters you will never see. What it's for you don't know, and why it's there, there's no one to tell, and so all you can feel is alienated, estranged, as though you didn't belong there. Who owns and understands this doesn't want you around. All this technology has somehow made you a stranger in your own land. Its very shape and appearance and mysteriousness say, 'Get out'.[7]

The emotional sense of alienation is far stronger than any logical explanation of industry's purposeful role. The instinctive dislike is the dominant response:

> You know there's an explanation for all this somewhere and what it's doing undoubtedly serves mankind in some indirect way but that isn't what you see. What you see is the NO TRESPASSING, KEEP OUT signs and not anything serving people but little people, like ants, serving these strange incomprehensible shapes. And you think, even if I were a part of this, even if I were not a stranger, I would be just another ant serving the shapes. So the final feeling is hostile, and I think that's ultimately what's involved in this otherwise unexplainable attitude. . . . Anything to do with valves and shafts and wrenches is part of *that* dehumanized world, and they would rather not think about it. They do not want to get into it.[8]

These feelings may be spontaneous, instinctive and personal, but, argues Persig's hero, they are part of a mass response which permeates much of our society. Those who arrive at a personal, instinctive hatred of industrial technology 'are not alone':

> There is no question that they have been following their natural feelings in this and not trying to imitate anyone and the natural feelings of very many people are similar on this matter; so that when you look at them collectively, as journalists do, you get the illusion of a mass movement, an anti-technological mass movement, an entire political anti-technological left

[7] Ibid., p. 16.
[8] Ibid., pp. 16–17.

> emerging, looming up from apparently nowhere, saying, 'Stop the technology. Have it somewhere else. Don't have it here.' It is still restrained by a thin web of logic that points out that without the factories there are no jobs or standards of living. But there are human forces stronger than logic. There always have been, and if they become strong enough in their hatred of technology that web can break.[9]

In Persig's vision of modern society, even the technologists are natural Luddites. Even the mechanics 'butcher' the machine. They are no more than 'spectator' technologists.[10]

> There was no identification with the job. . . . They were already trying not to have any thoughts about their work *on* the job. . . . [They were] living with technology without really having anything to do with it . . . their own selves were outside of it, detached, removed. They were involved in it but not in such a way as to care.[11]

Persig's picture of those within industry as psychologically alienated from technology, and those outside it as instinctively and profoundly hostile to it, is all the more effective because his novel is almost unique in English speaking literature in being a brilliant imaginative enquiry into the beauty and values of technology. His eloquently deranged hero thinks that 'flight from and hatred of technology is self-defeating. The Buddha, the Godhead, resides quite as comfortably in the circuits of a digital computer or the gears of a cycle transmission as he does on the top of a mountain or in the petals of a flower. To think otherwise is to demean the Buddha – which is to demean oneself. That is what I want to talk about in this Chautauqua.'[12]

Why quote Persig at length when there are so many other voices, so eloquent in their denunciation of industry, technology and its human manipulators? There is no shortage of writers convinced that industrial technology perverts the meaning of life and work, shatters silence and privacy, poisons the air and the land and the rivers and the sea, devours land and lives and resources, debases culture, degrades minds, and sears the nerves of men held captive in cities organized wholly in the interest of quick profit and power. It is not difficult to find writers who see the impact of industrial technology on the world's surface as 'a case of terminal acne'.[13]

[9] Persig, ibid., p. 17.
[10] Ibid., p. 25.
[11] Ibid., p. 26.
[12] Ibid., p. 18.
[13] Lisa Alther, *Kinflicks* (1976), p. 19.

One major justification for citing Persig lies in the fact that he is not writing the standard polemic but attempting the delicate task of persuasion and reconciliation. And by portraying so precisely the attitude of mind of so many opponents of technology, Persig highlights the difficulties of trying to communicate with them. The clash of values is so profound, the sense of distaste so powerful, the gulf in feeling so unbridgeable, that an attempt at mutual understanding has to fight not only ignorance and suspicion, but a powerful desire *not* to hear arguments, a positive wish *not* to face the facts. Persig's opponents of technology 'want *not* to understand it. Not to *hear* about it.'[14] In Persig's words 'it is as though two old friends, a Catholic and a Protestant, were sitting drinking beer, enjoying life, and the subject of birth control somehow came up. Big freeze-out.'[15] The conversation cannot fruitfully continue in the face of a fundamental 'conflict of faith, of faith in empirical social planning versus faith in the authority of God as revealed by the teaching of the Catholic Church. You can prove the practicality of planned parenthood till you are tired of listening to yourself and it's going to go nowhere because your antagonist isn't buying the assumption that anything socially practical is good *per se*. Goodness for him has other sources.'[16]

In Persig's novel the two sides of the technology debate are as profoundly divided as such age-old political and religious antagonists. The opponents can barely communicate. Facts and opinion can no longer be freely exchanged and discussed. 'After two sentences on the subject his eyes go completely glassy and he changes the conversation or just looks away. He doesn't want to hear about it.'[17] In such circumstances minds seem closed to persuasion, ears deaf to argument, and the possibilities of instruction seem discouragingly small.

Such attitudes have a long history and few have suffered more from them than the self-made businessman who introduced or promoted or profited from the new technology. He was the leading human agent in the advance of technology and so he has borne the brunt of the opposition to it. Schumpeter caught this attitude precisely when he wrote:

> From the fact that the criticism of the capitalist order proceeds from a critical attitude of mind, i.e. from an attitude which spurns allegiance to

[14] Persig, ibid., p. 12.
[15] Ibid., p. 11.
[16] Ibid., p. 11.
[17] Ibid., p. 11.

> extra-rational values, it does not follow that rational refutation will be accepted. Such refutation may wear the rational garb of attack but can never reach the extra-rational driving power that always lurks behind it ... capitalism stands its trial before judges who have the sentence of death in their pockets. They are going to pass it, whatever defence they may hear. [18]

In Schumpeter's view, the call for credentials is not addressed in a judicial frame of mind which would accept the possibility of a satisfactory answer. The black cap is ready for the businessman before the evidence has been heard.

Such attitudes have not always existed – at least not in the same form – and it is the historian's duty to explain how and why and when they grew up. For their existence is of great significance in understanding the course of Britain's economic fortunes and the changing entrepreneurial contribution to those fortunes. They provide in my opinion a major explanation of the mandarin career choice of British graduates and a consequential failure of business to recruit the ablest products of our society.[19] They also provide a significant part of the explanation of the defensive and suspicious attitude to management which characterizes much of the British labour force. Together those explanations help one to understand Britain's relative failure in terms of modern economic growth.

* * *

Why then has there existed in Britain, in the last hundred years or so, such a widespread and deeply entrenched distaste for the self-made businessman? Why has he so rarely achieved popularity? Why has he so rarely been rewarded with widespread esteem? Partly it is because he carries with him too many unlovely associations inherited from an unenviable past. Those who feel that the criticism of the businessman 'has passed beyond rationality'[20] also feel that the critics are still tilting against targets which no longer exist outside the folk memory of past events and personalities. Certainly few of their historical and fictional predecessors achieved unalloyed hero-status as they fought their way up into positions from which they could challenge the political and economic, if very rarely the social, power of the traditional ruling

[18] Joseph A. Schumpeter, *Capitalism, Socialism and Democracy* (1943), p. 144.

[19] See Neil McKendrick, 'In Search of a Secular Ideal', op. cit., pp. xxi–xxiv; and 'Literary Luddism and the Businessman', op. cit., pp. xliii–xlvi.

[20] John Atkins, *Six Novelists Look at Society* (1977), p. 39.

classes. Those who achieved arch villain status have imprinted themselves far more indelibly on British cultural attitudes.

That imprinting goes a long way to explain the instinctive distaste which so many commentators have identified as the characteristic British reaction to the self-made man. When Mrs Trollope visited America she was stupefied by the pride that leading Americans took in the fact that they were self-taught and self-made, which, as she acidly remarked, meant to her only that they were badly taught and badly made.[21] Such failings were to grow stronger in late Victorian Britain, as Carlyle and Ruskin and Arnold triumphed over Samuel Smiles in the battle of opinions over the self-made man of business. In the long term the results have been unmistakeable. So much so that the self-made businessman has come to be regarded as an offence against taste, tradition, civilized values, educated standards, even against religion – although in this last respect it was more in the type than in the want of faith that he gave offence. Whether the Unitarian of the eighteenth century, the Quaker of the nineteenth century, or the Jew of the twentieth century, he was rarely held to conform to the accepted canons of society. His beliefs, like his social origins, all too often confirmed his position amongst the minorities or socially marginal groups.

Society, in fact, refused to concede that he was 'a gentleman', and, even more damning than that capsule verdict, society usually held that he could never really become one. His descendants – when properly processed through suitable civilizing and educative channels – could be accepted, even married, and allowed to live down their past. The realistic response to the *nouveaux riches* was nicely caught when one Elizabeth Bowen character said of another (revealingly called Lady Latterly), 'She was *nouveau riche*; but, as Anthonia says, better late than never.'[22] If the wealth was impressive enough and had newly acquired estates and titles as an acceptable camouflage, most, if not all, could be forgiven. Time and the balm of money can heal most wounds, and disguise most origins. But the need for disguise is very real, the balm has often to be very liberally spread, and, as a result, the origins are very rarely given the credit that is their due.

[21] See John G. Cawelti, *Apostles of the Self-Made Man* (Chicago, 1965), p. 3; Irvin G. Sylie, *The Self-Made Man in America* (New York, 1954); A. Whitney Griswold, 'The American Cult of Success', *American Journal of Sociology* (1934); Donald McConnell, *Economic Virtues in the United States* (New York, 1930).

[22] Elizabeth Bowen, *A World of Love* (1955).

Few Englishmen boast of being in trade, or indeed of the fact that their wealth and standing came from their father's and grandfather's being in it. Some of the most memorable criticism of the business world has come from those like Ruskin, the son of a rich tradesman, whose financial independence was based on the system he so effectively and so damagingly chose to attack. As a result we are remarkably uninformed about many of the families who controlled the great industrial complexes of Victorian Britain – the Peases, Backhouses, Lambtons and Bells of the north-east coast; the Guests and Crawshays of South Wales; the Tennants, Dixons and Bairds of Scotland; the Rathbones, Forwards, Booths, Holts of Manchester; the Illingworths of Bradford and Halifax; the Forsters, Baines and Kitsons of Leeds. In their own towns these were the great merchant princes of their day, but these provincial élites have not greatly troubled the pens of those chronicling the course of British history.

If they or their descendants had made a contribution to politics, rather than to business, then their names would have made a far greater impact on our history. Samuel Whitbread's contribution to brewing and Robert Owen's to cotton would be far less celebrated but for their political importance. Robert Peel and Gladstone both came from entrepreneurial families, but it is the fact that they devoted their abilities to politics, not to industry and trade, that has kept their family name alive. Joseph Chamberlain was a screw manufacturer who retired from business with a comfortable fortune by the age of thirty-eight, but it is doubtful if many would have known of this fact without his later political career to draw attention to it. His political ally John Morley, son of cotton manufacturers on one side and shipowners on the other, saved his parents' business activities from complete anonymity by going into politics.

The anonymity of so many men of business is both the product of the British society's disdain for them, and also partly the cause of it. The pervasive ignorance is both a consequence of the characteristic wish *not* to know, not to understand, and a partial explanation of it. Cause and effect are deeply interlocked.

Both the disdain and the ignorance can be, and have been, explained in terms of social snobbery, political hostility, religious prejudice, plain xenophobia, humanitarian revulsion, and moral superiority – and all these have contributed to the adoption of these characteristic attitudes. But a potent further cause is the instinctive dislike which feeds on this ignorance, and the instinctive suspicion which ignorance breeds –

especially when it is nurtured and sustained by a folk memory peopled with the villains and monsters and demon-kings of literature.

British fiction is an instructive source for this attitude of mind and also, in part, an explanation for its survival. For its propaganda effects have been both potent and hostile – more potent than the alternative tradition of the apostles of the self-made man, and characteristically hostile in its balance of malign to benign portraits of businessmen – and enviably effective in promoting a lasting image of the former. For not only has the general verdict of the English on their self-made men of business been strongly negative, many of the individual verdicts have been memorably cruel.

English businessmen rose, in Cobbett's dismissive phrase, 'from the dunghill to the chariot', and to judge from their later social, and in particular their literary, reception, they were held by many to carry with them the tell-tale odour of those humble origins. Those origins, however, were rarely allowed to be so humble as to arouse admiration for their ability to emerge successfully from them. Those who tried to extract sympathy for their early sufferings, or admiration for the efforts they had made 'to better themselves', faced effective and easily accessible antidotes specifically designed to counteract such appeals.

The most famous and most influential of all is that provided by Dickens in *Hard Times* (1854). His caricature of Josiah Bounderby was a brilliantly effective counterblast to the admired characteristics of the self-made businessman, the claimed virtues of self-help and self-improvement, the current idealizations of the early captains of industry. For not only was Bounderby odious, he was also a fraud. His much vaunted poverty was wildly exaggerated, his education through adversity a self-congratulatory fantasy, his much trumpeted early suffering almost wholly counterfeit.

Few would in any case have reacted to Bounderby's account of his own life with much sympathy. The details, which he so remorselessly rehearses, are impressive enough at first sight – born in a ditch, abandoned by his mother, abused by his drunken grandmother, with a pigsty (or at best a paving stone) for his bed, it is a picturesque rags-to-riches story, but Bounderby is so boastful, so self-satisfied, such a 'Bully of humility'[23] that he forfeits all but the most grudging acknowledgement of his self-proclaimed achievements: 'Vagabond, errand-boy, labourer, porter, clerk, chief-manager, small partner,

[23] Charles Dickens, *Hard Times* (1854), p. 12.

Josiah Bounderby of Coketown. Those are the antecedents and the culmination.'[24] Once Mrs. Pegler, a village shopkeeper, is revealed as his mother, and once she indignantly reveals the truth ('Josiah in the gutter! . . . No such thing, Sir. Never! For shame on you!'), and once she catalogues his loving parents, his widowed mother sacrificing herself for her son, his apprenticeship to a kind master who helped him on the road to prosperity, then Bounderby stands revealed as the vulgar, ignorant, self-interested liar that Dickens intended him to be. His lack of education, his lack of refinement are real enough, but they are now stripped of the justifications and excuses he had so often put forward on his own behalf. Dickens has skilfully turned the self-made businessman's special pleading against him.

By first making this pleading so insistent and so unsympathetic, and by then revealing it as false, he makes what would have been a conventional and straightforward social ascent through business seem particularly dishonourable. In doing so he provided a remarkably effective answer to the attractions of the self-made man. He inoculates British society against the appeal of the self-help legend. He undermines what in other societies has been a potent and much-loved myth. Match Bounderby against the worthy heroes of Smilesian sermons on *Self-Help*, and it is Bounderby who will inevitably imprint himself on our unconscious prejudices. Once absorbed, this vivid image has proved remarkably difficult to dislodge. From the first moment that Dickens introduces him, it is difficult to forget the unappetizing image of the balding, bloated, braying bully-boy:

> He was a rich man: banker, merchant, manufacturer, and what not. A big, loud man, with a stare and a metallic laugh. A man made out of a coarse material, which seemed to have been stretched to make so much of him. A man with a great puffed head and forehead, swelled veins in his temples, and such a strained skin to his face that it seemed to hold his eyes open and lift his eyebrows up. A man with a pervading appearance on him of being inflated like a balloon, and ready to start. A man who could never sufficiently vaunt himself a self-made man. A man who was always proclaiming, through that brassy speaking-trumpet of a voice of his, his old ignorance and his old poverty.

And its indelible qualities have been intensified and deepened by other Dickensian characters bearing the same message. For Bounderby is not alone in being an unfortunate Victorian advocate for the self-made man.

[24] Ibid., p. 14.

Dickens is not looking for a sympathetic response when he has Mr. Merdle in *Little Dorrit* (1855–57) indignantly justify his right to 'go into Society' with the words 'And yet will you tell me that I oughtn't to go into Society? I, who shower money upon it in this way? I, who might be almost said to – to – to harness myself to a watering-cart full of money, and go about saturating Society every day of my life?'[25] Any doubts one might have about Dickens's didactic intentions, any doubts about where his sympathies lay (and where ours should lie) are dispelled by his comment that people 'prostrated themselves before [Merdle], more degradedly and less excusably than the darkest savage creeps out of his hole in the ground to propitiate, in some log or reptile, the Deity of his benighted soul'.[26]

Dickens was not, of course, alone. Trollope's Melmotte in *The Way We Live Now* (1874–75) provides further reinforcement for the case against the businessman, and Mrs. Hurtle's defence of Melmotte provides, and was intended to provide, further evidence for the prosecution. Her craven acceptance of his dishonesty and her uncritical commitment to Mammon merely confirms *his* guilt and *her* credulity:

> Such a man [she argues] rises above honesty . . . as a great general rises above humanity when he sacrifices an army to conquer a nation. Such greatness is incompatible with small scruples. A pigmy man is stopped by a little ditch, but a giant stalks over the rivers.[27]

With advocates of Mrs. Hurtle's moral stature, Melmotte and his like scarcely had need of attackers. But attacked they were and their critics were given better lines and better arguments than Mrs. Hurtle.

When one is looking for the prevalence of the view that the self-made businessman was a bounder seeking to grind the faces of the poor and to screw from society the fattest possible profits, one does well to take note of the accusing resonance which rings from the names of Dickens's Bounderby and Merdle, or Disraeli's Shuffle and Screw, or the doubtful company owned by Meredith's Major Strike, or George Eliot's Sir Gavial Mantrap, or Samuel Warren's Sir Sharper Bubble or Charles Lever's Davenport Dunn. Our prevailing social values echo all too clearly the condemnation encapsulated in those names. Indeed the forces hostile to industry and the businessman have done more than

[25] Charles Dickens, *Little Dorrit* (1855–57), Book 1, ch. 33.
[26] Ibid., Book 2, ch. 12.
[27] Trollope, *The Way We Live Now* (1874–75), vol. 1, ch. 26.

merely *reflect* those elements in the literary tradition which they have found emotionally and politically satisfying. They have distorted others to suit their case. For by a curious transference of guilt, the cold, systematic reasoning of the utilitarian M.P. Gradgrind has been taken as symptomatic of the profit-maximizing, mechanical, rational businessman and his name is all too often taken to symbolize heartless industrialists rather than insensitive fact-besotted educationalists.[28]

That real life Bounderbys, Merdles, and Melmottes existed in Victorian society as well as in Victorian fiction is not in doubt. They existed, but so did authentic prototypes of Mrs. Gaskell's John Thornton, of Mrs. Craik's John Halifax, of Mrs. Stone's Mr. Ainsley, of Miss Meteyard's admirable fictional heroes, of Disraeli's Mr. Trafford, or, indeed, of Dickens's Cheeryble brothers. Examples of both extremes were specifically based on actual businessmen.

In fact fictional examples of both types existed precisely because in high-Victorian England there *was* a vigorous debate over the virtues and vices of 'the new captains of industry, free, in their phase of vigour, from pseudo-aristocratic conventions, motivated by drives that were highly personal, intensely obscure, enormously powerful, and sustained by the will to dominate'.[29] The emergence of such men inevitably set up tensions. They posed both a powerful threat and an enticing promise. To many of their contemporaries these symbols of the new commercial middle class were 'the hero-villains of the nineteenth century scene. They were heroic in renovating society, in sponsoring new wealth, in increasing man's capacity to manipulate his physical surroundings, in filling the ancient gap between workers and owners of land, in sponsoring a political system with an ever-broadening franchise, and in constituting themselves an element of society sensitive to new possibilities, yet remaining robustly pragmatic. As villains they were responsible for embarking themselves and everyone else on an irreversible course leading no one knew where, the unperceiving liberators of forces that could be neither understood nor controlled,

[28] This point is elaborated and further exemplified, in Neil McKendrick, 'Literary Luddism and the Businessman', General Introduction to *Sir Alfred Jones: Shipping Entrepreneur Par Excellence* by P. N. Davies (1978), pp. xxxiii–xxxiv. Admittedly, Gradgrind has 'retired from the wholesale hardware trade', but Dickens was satirizing him as the typical Utilitarian M.P., 'the arithmetical figure in Parliament', 'the eminently practical father', the didactic pedant running his own school.

[29] See S. J. Checkland, *The Rise of Industrial Society in England, 1815–1885* (1964), pp. 290–304.

creating a society maturing toward an unprecedented vulnerability to manipulation, consolidating in their own hands the elements of wealth and power, seemingly indifferent to the effects of their actions in bringing pain and even destruction, and too often philistines or imitators, unable to develop their own cultural expression to fill the gap left by the destruction of agrarian society.'[30]

They were hero-villains, then, precisely because of the powerfully conflicting effects of their virtues and their vices. The very reason why so many novelists mocked and satirized the self-made businessman was because so many in contemporary society were so uncritically in his thrall. Arnold's Philistines were attacked so bitterly because he felt that they were overwhelmingly in the majority. He and many other influential critics were attacking an unquestioning commitment to Mammon; and, of course, were right to do so. Unfortunately they succeeded so well that an attitude of mind, which needed correcting and refining and improving, has instead been well nigh eradicated. Few would wish to see the pursuit of profit at the head of any list of human values, but any society which disparages it to the point of ignoring it will possess little of the surplus wealth which is so necessary to maintain the values which are, or should be, at the top of that list.

If the Luddite attack is wholly successful, if the technologist and the self-made businessman become merely figures of fun or objects of suspicion, then it can have very damaging effects on our attitudes to industry. It can produce a pervasive distrust of business and the businessman. It can breed disdain and suspicion and ignorance which can in turn profoundly damage our economy.

For some men in business this happened very early. And some have hardly ever escaped the disdain felt for trade. The lesser men of business – the small manufacturer, the local brewers, millers, coal merchants and the like – have rarely received much admiration. They were ever the victims of snobbery. And they were often the victims of mere size.

Small business is currently fashionable – at least with Schumacher and his supporters.[31] In the 1970s, the beauty of smallness has suddenly been perceived, just as, in contrast, in the 1920s the call was all for big business, and economies of scale. But small has not always been beautiful.

[30] S. J. Checkland, op. cit.

[31] E. F. Schumacher, *Small is Beautiful* (1973).

In high-Victorian Britain, and for most of the last two hundred years, the small-scale businessman has faced powerful disapproving prejudices. They were 'involved in a triple opprobrium. Dealing in small quantities, being in intimate contact with, and even touching the goods themselves, and directly receiving money payments from hand to hand, constituted a trinity of shameful acts. These criteria, derived from an agrarian aristocracy, however devoid of ethical content, were a sufficient basis of judgment for those whose opinions determined who was on the right side of the prestige gap that separated tradesmen from others.'[32] Not that they lacked their own social hierarchy complete with its own snobberies! What after all, asked Carlyle sarcastically, is suburban society, but 'retired wholesalers looking down on retired retailers'. Carlyle, of course, felt fully justified in looking down on both. In fact, snobbery alone was enough to settle the fate of the small businessman. Merely being 'tainted with the stain of trade' was bad enough. Actually being a tradesman was almost unforgiveable.

Such attitudes were at times so characteristic and so ubiquitous in England that, at least through 'the camera eye' of an American observer, John Dos Passos, even English animals were expected to show their powers of social discrimination – by accepting 'nice people' and by biting tradesmen:

> She was a very fashionable lady and adored bull terriers . . . and there were white lilies in the hall . . . the bull terriers bit the trades people. . . . No, my dear, they never bite nice people and they're quite topping with friends.[33]

The self-made businessman's problem was that he had, almost inevitably, to start in the foothills, and if he succeeded in avoiding the shame of remaining small, then he had to face the threatening dangers of plutocratic prominence. If he escaped being ignored (and bitten by bullterriers) by growing large, he had then to face not only a different form of social condescension but a sharper political attack.

Rich businessmen have not often handled their wealth discreetly, and when businessmen behave like stereotypes from socialist posters it provokes more than one class to react. For if plutocracy provokes socialism, it also provokes an affronted reaction from the landed aristocracy and the 'decent' gentry whose position as leaders of society it inevitably threatens.

[32] S. J. Checkland, op. cit., pp. 198–9.

[33] John Dos Passos, *U.S.A.* (Penguin edition, 1966), p. 192. *The 42nd Parallel* (1930), *Nineteen Nineteen* (1932) and *The Big Money* (1936) were first published as a collective trilogy in 1938.

On the few occasions that rich 'outsiders' have burst into social and political prominence in Britain, the social reaction of established society has been as bitter as the predictable fury from the political left. When, for instance, men like Cassel, Lever, Northcliffe, Lipton, Beit, Barnato, Sassoon and Cowdray, burst into prominence in Edwardian England they were not well received outside the royal circle. Such social prominence for 'new' wealth was an exceptionally rare happening in English life, and its novelty did not make it any the more welcome.

As Professor Vincent wrote recently, 'these, the Edwardian rich, were names which would have meant little to Gladstone, and have meant even less, as a group in their own right, since 1922. They belong to a specific place, time and circle: that of King Edward's plutocracy. They did not long outlast the old King. . . . A few self-made plutocrats reached prominence in Lloyd George's Government of businessmen, only to disappear with him in 1922. Only Mond, the founder of ICI with his slogan of "Vales for the Velsh" remained, a mournful survivor in Baldwin's England. The plutocrat was not a success: he was a target no one could miss.'[34]

Vincent's description of the Edwardian plutocrats gives some clues to the motives which lay behind the hostile reception of the self-made man in Britain:

> London became a democracy of millionaires. . . . Sir Thomas Lipton, an unknown grocer, had only to buy a yacht and give £100,000 for Alexandra's soup kitchens to become a royal intimate. Unlike in Parisian society, no appearance of cultivation of mind was necessary for acceptance. It was enough to make oneself useful, like Arthur Sassoon 'the Jew page boy' who gets up after each course to make bets for the King and the others while they are at lunch.[35]

There neatly encapsulated is the hostility to those who emerge from social anonymity merely through wealth, the hostility to conspicuous consumption, and the characteristic anti-semitism of the period which is enshrined in the novels of John Buchan and the polemics of Hilaire Belloc. The gruesome details of opulent self-indulgence were not confined to the newly rich as a study of Edwardian menus makes clear; any lack of cultivation could be more than matched in the landed shires of the rural gentry; and their great houses differed only in age.

[34] J. R. Vincent, 'Conspicuous Consumers', a review of Jamie Camplin, *The Rise of the Plutocrats: Wealth and Power in Edwardian England* (1978), in *The Observer*, 16 July 1978, p. 26.

[35] J. R. Vincent, loc. cit.

It was as the *nouveaux riches*, especially the Jewish *nouveaux riches*, that they were attacked. When Hillaire Belloc called the House of Lords 'a committee for the protection of the Anglo-Judaic plutocracy',[36] or immortalized Beit as the Randlord, the anti-semitism is as unmistakeable as was the disgust inspired by their wealth.

It mattered little that Beit began a new era of benefaction with his medical research fellowships, or that Lever gave not only his Leverhulme Trust, but the Port Sunlight Art Gallery, or that Cassel ('Windsor Cassel' as he was mockingly known) was lavish in his medical and educational bequests. The traditional rich were never as creatively charitable as the new millionaires. But the generosity of the newly rich seems to have confirmed their guilt rather than assuaged it. Their generosity was evidence of their excessive riches. The traditional aristocracy's traditional parsimony was evidence of their elegant sufficiency. Only time could cure the difference because the plutocrat's wealth was new, and, as new, deeply suspect.

Most significantly of all, it mattered even less to their critics that Lever, Lipton and Northcliffe were men of entrepreneurial genius in marketing, that the Jewish scientist Mond built up one of the great industrial giants in the fast growth sector in which Britain most urgently needed to grow, that Cowdray revolutionized the transport system of Mexico, or that the new wealth of the Jewish financiers was essential to oil the wheels of more significant areas of the economy than the King's lavish social life.

Even this acceptance by the King proved a mixed blessing, because as always admiration, or even acceptance, of the successful self-made businessman evoked a sharp literary response to satisfy the social prejudices which their success inspired. Where Buchan and Belloc appealed to anti-semitism, H. G. Wells appealed to anti-commercialism. His *Tono-Bungay* published in 1908 was a direct attack on the dynamic marketing of consumer goods which Lipton and Lever had so brilliantly exploited. But Edward Ponderovo's rise and fall through the marketing of patent medicine and the unscrupulous use of advertising was held to symbolize not only the decay and imminent collapse of England, but of all Western culture.[37] It was not enough to identify the moral bankruptcy of such methods, it was necessary to indicate the road to decadence along which they would inevitably lead.

[36] Quoted in J. Camplin, op. cit.

[37] See John Reed, *Victorian Conventions* (1975), p. 192.

The same technique of writing about *future* perils rather than *present* ones was even more heavily employed when discussing technology. It is still a standard technique today and it has a long pedigree. The exploitation of the fear of what machines *might* do, rather than what they actually do, stretches back at least as far as Samuel Butler's *Erewhon* of 1872. In 'The Book of Machines' we read that 'there is no security against the *ultimate* development of mechanical consciousness', and we are invited to reflect not only upon 'the extraordinary advance which machines have made during the last few hundred years', but also to imagine what they will '*in the end become*'.[38] The present anti-technology movement has much in common with the question put in Butler's 'Colleges of Unreason': 'Is it not safer to nip this mischief in the bud and to forbid [the machines] further progress? . . . I fear none of the existing machines; what I fear is the extraordinary rapidity with which they are becoming something very different to what they are at present. No class of beings have in any time past made so rapid a movement forward. Should not that movement be jealously watched, and checked while we can check it? And is it not necessary for this end to destroy the more advanced machines which are in use at present, though it is admitted they are in themselves harmless?'[39]

In *Erewhon* the argument is against the potential and future danger. But more potent because more immediate and because more read, was Dickens's picture of the present results of industrial technology in Coketown in *Hard Times*. Its honourable place in Leavis's *The Great Tradition* is in itself sufficient to explain its extraordinary influence on the consciousness of educated men of the mid-twentieth century.

Leavis's verdict is uncompromising. The novel is a 'masterpiece. . . . Of all Dickens's works it is the one that has all the strength of his genius, together with a strength no other of them can show – that of a completely serious work of art . . . in *Hard Times* he is for once possessed of a comprehensive vision, one in which the inhumanities of Victorian civilisation are seen as fostered and sanctioned by a hard philosophy, the aggressive formulation of an inhumane spirit.'[40] The spirit is represented by Gradgrind and Bounderby. And although 'what Gradgrind stands for is, though repellent, nevertheless respectable; Bounderby is Victorian "rugged individualism" in its grossest and most

[38] Samuel Butler, *Erewhon* (1872), Signet edition, 1960, p. 173. [My italics.]
[39] Ibid., pp. 173–7.
[40] F. R. Leavis, *The Great Tradition* (1948), p. 227.

intransigent form . . . concerned with nothing but self-assertion and power and material success.'[41]

It is a damning verdict on industry and industrialists which other critics have been very ready to confirm.[42] It encapsulates a verdict on industrial society which has been frequently refreshed and confirmed by later vivid pictures of the ugliness of its characteristic products. D. H. Lawrence's verdict on Tevershall is a twentieth-century echo of the 'spirit quenching hideousness' of Coketown:

> The long squalid straggle of Tevershall, the blackened brick dwellings, the black slate roofs, glistening at their sharp edges, the mud black with coal-dust, the pavements wet and black. It was as if dismalness had soaked through and through everything. The utter negation of natural beauty, the utter negation of the gladness of life, the utter absence of the instinct for shapely beauty which every bird and beast has, the utter death of the human instinctive faculty was appalling. The stacks of soap in the grocers' shops, the rhubarb and lemons in the greengrocers'! the awful hats in the milliners all went by ugly, ugly, ugly. . . .[43]

Dickens's verdict on *Coketown* was, of course, even more explicit in its condemnation of technology and the men who profited from it. If the *personal* image which haunts *Hard Times* is a hideous amalgam of Bounderby and Gradgrind, the *industrial* image is 'of machinery which runs itself, as though without the volition of the human beings it nevertheless compels to attend it'.[44]

> Time went on in Coketown like its own machinery: so much material wrought up, so much fuel consumed, so many powers worn out, so much money made . . . the piston of the steam-engine worked monotonously up and down like the head of an elephant in a state of melancholy madness . . . all the melancholy-mad elephants, polished and oiled up for the day's monotony, were at their heavy exercise again. . . . The whole town seemed to be frying in oil. There was a stifling smell of hot oil everywhere. The steam-engines shone with it, the dresses of the Hands were soiled with it, the mills throughout their many stories oozed and trickled it . . . and their inhabitants, wasting with heat, toiled languidly in the desert. But no tem-

[41] Ibid., p. 228.

[42] David Craig's Introduction to *Hard Times* (Penguin edition, 1969), p. 36: '. . . the masters cried out to be satirised . . . in so far as he excels in [this], it succeeds, and thereby earns the currency which has made "Coketown" the classic name for the early industrial city.'

[43] Quoted by F. R. Leavis, op. cit., p. 232.

[44] David Craig, op. cit., p. 24.

> perature made the melancholy-mad elephants more mad or more sane. Their wearisome heads went up and down at the same rate, in hot weather and cold, wet weather and dry, fair weather and foul. The measured motion of their shadows on the walls, was the substitute Coketown had to show for the shadows of rustling woods; while, for the summer hum of insects, it could offer, all the year round, from the dawn of Monday to the night of Saturday, the whirr of shafts and wheels.[45]

The imagery is vivid and meaningful. For 'the comparison of the factory to "melancholy mad elephants" is more than a verbal flourish. It suggests that their exhaustless energies are as misused as the lives of the workers by the social-economic system which set them in motion.'[46]

The impact of technology on the Coketown environment was all pervading. Coketown was 'a town of machinery'. Machinery dominated everything. Machinery turned its canal black. Machinery's effluent so polluted its river that it 'ran purple with ill-smelling dye'. Machinery's smoke defeated even the sun. It produced such 'a blur of soot and smoke' that Coketown 'lay shrouded in a haze of its own, which appeared impervious to the suns rays'. But although Dickens allowed the climate to remain fairly neutral, admitting that 'there was such a thing [as] a sunny mid-summer day . . . sometimes, even in Coketown', he was merciless in his mockery and condemnation of those whose machinery blocked out its life-giving rays in their remorseless pursuit of profit and self-interest.

> Surely there never was such fragile china-ware as that of which the millers of Coketown were made. Handle them never so lightly and they fell to pieces with such ease that you might suspect them of having been flawed before. They were ruined, when they were required to send labouring children to school; they were ruined when inspectors were appointed to look into their works; *they were ruined, when such inspectors considered it doubtful whether they were quite justified in chopping people up with their machinery*; they were utterly undone, when it was hinted that perhaps they need not always make quite so much smoke. Besides Mr. Bounderby's gold spoon which was generally received in Coketown, another prevalent fiction was very popular there. It took the form of a threat. Whenever a Coketowner felt he was ill-used – that is to say, whenever he was not left entirely alone, and it was proposed to hold him accountable for the consequences of any of his acts – he was sure to come out with the awful menace, that he would 'sooner pitch his property

[45] Dickens, *Hard Times*, ch. 5.

[46] *Industrialisation and Culture, 1830–1914* (1970), ed. Christopher Harris, Graham Martin and Aaron Scharf, p. 378.

into the Atlantic'. This had terrified the Home Secretary within an inch of his life, on several occasions.[47]

Little wonder that for so many the triumphs of industrial technology and the achievement of the self-made man meant, and mean, little more than greed and pollution, deprivation and disease, ugliness and profit. Yet Manchester, the shock-city of Victorian society, could inspire Victorian novelists to extravagant praise. Disraeli may have taken many of his wicked industrialists straight from the Blue Book reports of the worst factory owners; and when illustrating such abuses as the truck system, the tommy shop system, or the cottage system, he may have achieved his powerful sense of verisimilitude by adding only a minimum of art to the material he obtained from parliamentary reports;[48] but he was also capable of redressing the balance by seeing Manchester, as its contemporary admirers did, as 'a symbol of all that was most dazzling in Victorian industrialism . . . a signpost to future glories'.[49] For the hero of Disraeli's *Coningsby* (1844) Manchester is a revelation of the dynamic energy which properly harnessed could carry England to a new perfection of civilization. It provided evidence of the gigantic creative power of modern technological man:

> What Art was to the ancient world, Science is to the Modern; the distinctive faculty. In the minds of men the useful has succeeded to the beautiful. Instead of the city of the Violet Crown, a Lancashire village has expanded into a mighty region of factories and warehouses. Yet rightly understood, Manchester is as great a human exploit as Athens.
>
> The inhabitants indeed are not as impressed with this idiosyncracy as the countrymen of Pericles and Phidias. They do not fully comprehend the position which they occupy. It is the philosopher alone who can conceive the grandeur of Manchester, and the immensity of the future.[50]

In *Sybil* too Disraeli could produce a fictional idealization of the industrialist, but revealingly his ideal Mr. Trafford is the younger son of an aristocratic family and his virtues serve only to highlight the vices of Joseph Diggs, or the millowners, Shuffle and Screw.

47 Dickens, *Hard Times*, Book 1, ch. 5. My italics.

48 C. R. Fay, *Great Britain from Adam Smith to the Present Day* (1928), p. 378, points out that the tommy shop scene in *Sybil* comes straight out of the Midland Mining Commission Report of 1843, 'sentence for sentence, with Joseph Diggs in place of a certain coal proprietor in the Report named Banks'.

49 Stephen Gill, Introduction to Elizabeth Gaskell's *Mary Barton: A Tale of Manchester Life* (1848), Penguin edition, 1972, p. 14.

50 Benjamin Disraeli, *Coningsby* (1844).

Just as Carlyle's Plugson of St. Dolly Undershot (although 'a Captain of Industry, born Member of the Ultimate genuine Aristocracy of this Universe', a potential 'Captain of the World', and England's hope for the future) was still represented as the creature of this 'melancholy creed' of Mammonism, who still needed to be converted from his belief in the 'Cash-Gospel'; so Disraeli's Millbank ('an infernal manufacturer' to his son's schoolmates at Eton) is allowed to achieve his apotheosis as the symbol of the *working* aristocracy only when his daughter ('untainted by the gospel of Mammon') marries Coningsby, the symbol of the *landed* aristocracy.[51] The ambivalence was real. The excuses for, and the justification of, the industrialists were often very necessary. But technology and its masters could be praised in Victorian fiction. If posterity has chosen to remember mainly the negative verdict, its choice is understandable given the memorable portraits on the black side and the critics' predilection for publicizing them.

What is less forgiveable is the improvement of what Leavis called 'the moral fable'. For in condemning the materialism of industrial society, the critics have often gone further than the evidence allows. Take the moralizing connection between money and dirt which so many critics have seen in the dust heaps in *Our Mutual Friend.* The simple verdict that the message of the book is (in Dr. Daleski's words) that 'Money is dust' has understandably proved too straightforward for some critics. So the dust heaps have been given a richer psychological significance, and the moral message has been strengthened and made more vivid, by critics grafting their own curious faecal preoccupations on to Dickens's. Humphrey House added an extra touch of squalor (and, in so doing, improved the symbolism) by pointing out, as Dickens did not, that the Victorian dust heaps regularly contained human excrement. One critic having provided the excrement which Dickens neglectfully forgot to include, another provides the interpretation which Dickens would doubtless have intended had he (which he did not) included the excrement in the first place. We are indebted to Dr. H. P. Sucksmith for the remarkable insight that Dickens 'intuitively' equated wealth with excrement; and also for the information, which he generously adds, that this is 'a genuine correspondence (as we know today) since the acquisition of gold is partly motivated by an anal complex'. If so, as John Carey has wryly pointed

[51] See Reed, op. cit., pp. 124–5.

out, Dickens's 'understanding of the anal complex was first hand',[52] for it should not be forgotten that Dickens himself was 'a highly successful businessman who amassed a fortune of £93,000'[53] – no small sum by Victorian standards.

To charge the heaps with any moral message teaching the worthlessness of material wealth is critically simplistic (and ignores a great deal of evidence to the contrary in Dickens's own work)[54] but it is unquestionably a popularly accepted verdict. To impose on the verdict any further faecal significance is to add psychological fantasy to critical misinterpretation. But such crude besmirching is in line with the most influential literary traditions.

It is often forgotten, for instance, that Dickens could admire industry. It is often deliberately overlooked that he could admire the urban environment it produced, the people who manned it, and the 'money-wealth' it gave rise to. Many critics are surprised to learn, considering the picture of industrialism in *Hard Times*, that Dickens should have paid tribute at a public banquet, the year before the novel appeared, to:

> . . . the great compact phalanx of the people, by whose industry, perseverance, and intelligence, and their result in money wealth such places as Birmingham and many others like it, have arisen.[55]

This was not simply an act of public courtesy on Dickens's part. It reflected attitudes which can be clearly detected in his novels. For although posterity has largely chosen to ignore the fact Dickens was no more consistent in his attitudes to industry and industrialists than he was to poor relief, to the trade unions or to 'independent self-reliance'. His sympathies were prodigal and they were fluid. He 'reflected the popular mind in that he [was] able to espouse diametrically

[52] John Carey, *The Violent Effigy: a Study of Dickens' Imagination* (1973), p. 110. Carey has no doubt about Dickens's intentions: 'There can be no doubt about his presenting money as dirt in *Our Mutual Friend*'; 'We can dismiss the notion that the dust heaps are charged with any moral message about the worthlessness of material wealth'; 'Heaps were not horrible for Dickens, nor was money, and the presence of the dust heaps in *Our Mutual Friend* is the richer because they won't submit to be catalogued under any moral platitude.'

[53] Ibid.

[54] To see it most ably marshalled see John Carey, op. cit., pp. 109–11. To him Dickens's view of the heaps is at times romantic, and the heaps themselves 'life-enhancing' – a view which I do not share.

[55] John Carey, *The Violent Effigy* (1973), p. 9.

opposed opinion with almost equal vehemence'.[56] The quality of his poetic character should not be measured by his consistency as a social theorist, for he took, to use Keats's beautifully apposite phrase, 'as much delight in conceiving an Iago as an Imogen' – and vice versa; his creative imagination could encompass the Cheeryble brothers as well as Mr. Dombey or Josiah Bounderby. Partly, of course, this is a reflection of the richness of that imagination, his 'great, careless prodigality' to use Kafka's phrase. But, more significantly to the historian, it is evidence of Dickens's capacity to perform what T. S. Eliot calls the poet's business – that is, to express the greatest emotional intensity of his time based on whatever the time happens to think. Victorian England was ambivalent in its thoughts about businessmen – it could worship them uncritically and despise them wholeheartedly.

If the hatred came to dominate in this love-hate relationship, that is probably a fair reflection of the prevailing attitude amongst the more culturally aware observers. But later critics (responding eagerly to the emotional demands of *their* time) have made sure that the adverse message predominates. The literary tradition has fixed the image of industrialism as intrinsically hostile to humanity; and has often improved on the evidence to underline the moral message of the worthlessness of material wealth.

An uncritical admiration of industrialism needs its critics. When the productive powers of industry become a fetish, when what is no more than an essential means of maintaining and enriching our society comes to be praised as the central and overriding end, then a corrective voice becomes vital. It has certainly not been lacking in Britain. Just as Dickens – and so many other Victorian novelists – rightly railed at the uncritical worship of Mammon, so the twentieth-century critics – historical as well as literary – have underlined the limitations of materialism and the dangers of industrialism.

Tawney's voice – in the direct line of descent from Arnold and Ruskin – has been more influential than most. In *The Acquisitive Society* he warned in 1921 that 'the essence of industrialism . . . is not any particular method of industry, but a particular estimate of the importance of industry, which results in it being thought the only thing that is important at all, so that it is elevated from the subordinate place which it should occupy among human interests and activities into being the standard by which all other interests and activities are

[56] Ibid., p. 8.

judged'.[57] Never afraid to repeat his message, he went on to exemplify what he called the 'perversion' of industrialism:

> When a Cabinet Minister declares that the greatness of this country depends upon the volume of its exports, so that France, which exports comparatively little, and Elizabethan England, which exported next to nothing, are presumably to be pitied as altogether inferior civilizations, that is Industrialism. It is the confusion of one minor department of life with the whole of life. . . . When the Press clamours that the one thing needed to make this island an Arcadia is productivity, and more productivity, and yet more productivity, that is Industrialism. It is the confusion of means with ends.[58]

Having dealt with the ends and the means, he demolished some five years later the pretensions of the men who congratulated themselves on achieving them. 'Few tricks of the unsophisticated intellect', he wrote, 'are more curious than the naive psychology of the businessman, who ascribes his achievements to his own unaided efforts in bland unconsciousness of a social order without whose continuous support he would be as a lamb bleating in the desert.'[59]

Unfortunately the social order has been less inclined to share the blame when its lack of such continuous support has coincided with a decline in the businessman's achievements. Englishmen of all parties and persuasions have listened so attentively to Tawney's richly justified indictment of the folly of confusing the means with the ends, that they have neglected the means to such an extent that they can no longer afford the ends. They have turned their backs so successfully on the self-made man that he has had to operate with a workforce and deal with a society trained to despise him, and to fear him, or at best to ignore his efforts.

An awareness that the businessman is not solely responsible for his success has too often led on to a feeling that he is hardly responsible at all. A belief that productivity is not the supreme aim, has too often bred a feeling that it is of little value. A conviction that profits are often excessive has too often bred a distrust of all profit. In a determination to dethrone the gods of profit, productivity and entrepreneurship, it is all too easy to destroy a proper awareness of the benefits they can offer.

[57] R. H. Tawney, *The Acquisitive Society* (1921), pp. 47–8.

[58] Ibid., pp. 48–9. Remove the word 'minor' and it would be difficult to disagree with this.

[59] R. H. Tawney, *Religion and the Rise of Capitalism* (1926), p. 221.

Once again the American contrast is revealing. Where the American legend of the self-made man has been sustained by the pervasive belief that 'this is a country of self-made men than which nothing better could be said of any state of society',[60] the British legend has been less well endowed with support. Nor is it simply a question of admiration. In American fiction the businessman is still pilloried because he is thought to be an important target, and his central role in society is as readily acknowledged as it is heatedly discussed. In Britain he has largely disappeared from the concerns of the novelist. Whether self-made or made by inheritance, whether triumphing through marketing or technological inventiveness, he simply does not figure. It is entirely predictable that it should be an American novelist, Robert Persig, who should both state the case against technology, and attempt its defence. It is entirely predictable that some of the most memorable attacks on the entrepreneur should emerge from the States.[61] 'Apart from the concept of Catch 22 itself, Joseph Heller's other great contribution to contemporary thought is the character of the classic entrepreneur, Milo Minderbinder, the archetype of American human relations – "It's all in the syndicate and everybody has a share".' Milo took the solidarity ethic to its logical conclusions; 'it is all right to bomb your own base, provided it can be done profitably and everybody has a share'.[62]

But literary Luddism has not yet triumphed in America. The businessman is still a hero-villain, and so the controversy still rages as it did in Victorian Britain. Technology, industry, and the self-made businessman are still large, important and worthwhile targets because they have large, important and worthwhile support.

Americans still admire them in sufficient numbers to provoke repeated attacks. They still preoccupy even the *avant-garde*. Even the latest sensation of American theatre, David Mamet, concentrates on the 'intensely American gods – money, success and power: how to acquire them, hold on to them and defend them'.[63] He describes his recent work *The Water Engine* (1977) as 'a play about the American myth'. It describes the progress of a man who invents a motor fuelled

[60] Calvin Colton, *Junius Tracts* (1844), quoted in John G. Cawelti's *Apostles of the Self-Made Man* (Chicago, 1965), p. ii.

[61] This is as true of American historiography as it is of fiction. See McKendrick, 'In Search of a Secular Ideal', op. cit., p. xiv.

[62] Alistair Mark, *The Rise and Fall of the British Manager* (1977), p. 31.

[63] S. Lawson, 'Language Equals Action', *Horizon* (November 1977), vol. 20, no. 3, p. 43.

by water. Although the conclusion is that the inventor gets destroyed by the greedy money men, it is a specific investigation of the 1930s' preoccupation with the perfectability of mankind through the perfection of its machines. The American tradition of the self-made businessman triumphing through his exploitation of traditional moral virtues and the mastery of technology is still sufficiently strong to provoke even the most fashionable authors.

Horatio Alger is by no means dead. Popular culture has preserved him despite all attempts to bury him.[64] The epitaphs on American businessmen, and American judgements on the world's self-made technologists, make up a massive anthology of eulogy compared with the thin trickle of praise in Britain, so meagre in the last hundred years that it has often threatened to dry up altogether. When Andrew Carnegie compiled his list of the twenty greatest men in the history of the world, it was unashamedly meritocratic and the area in which those on the list displayed their merit was unambiguously that of applied technology. The list included Bessemer, Watt, Stephenson, Bell, Franklin and Neilson (the last two specifically for their technologically useful inventions rather than for any other achievements the world might have admired). 'All these began as manual workers', wrote Carnegie. 'There is not one rich or titled leader in the whole list. All were compelled to earn their bread.' The fact that Carnegie has included some famous Britons does not disguise the fact that it is a characteristically American list.

Where else could one of the most popular strip cartoons – *Little Orphan Annie* – survive for fifty years in the Sunday newspapers (at her peak in 500 newspapers!) with the protection of only her dog and her adopted protector, the bald, irascible billionaire (Oliver 'Daddy' Warbucks), the magnate whose avowed intent was to make and sell arms and to amass profits. He must have enjoyed spectacular success for he was billed as the richest man in the world.[65] Since Harold Gray, Annie's and Warbucks's creator, was politically on the extreme right, and since he explicitly used his strip as a platform for his reactionary political views, his choice of Warbucks as the apotheosis of the old-

[64] For some of the reasons see Neil McKendrick, 'In Search of a Secular Ideal', the General Introduction to Clive Trebilcock, *The Vickers Brothers: Armaments and Enterprise, 1854–1914* (1977), pp. xiv–xix.

[65] When in the 1930s Annie's dog went missing, the concern was so great and so widespread that Henry Ford, doubtless feeling a brotherly sympathy for Warbucks, sent an anxious telegram.

fashioned American virtues is scarcely surprising. What is significant is that millions of Americans could happily sympathize and identify with him. The very existence, much less the popularity of a protective father figure called Warbucks is sufficient testimony to the survival of sympathy for wealth however acquired and an admiration for those who acquired it. To have openly and massively profited from war under such a blatant soubriquet would have ensured a very different cultural fate in England. Think only of George Bernard Shaw's odious armaments king, Andrew Undershaft.

Little wonder that American authors still feel as Dickens, and Trollope, and Lever and others felt in Victorian England that such sympathies deserved a powerful corrective. There is some evidence that the Luddite view is beginning to triumph even in the USA. Popular psychologists assure us, 'Things are changing. Every day swells the tide of men who are trying to shake the habit of competitive climbing up through the narrow grid of the technocracy.'[66]

But there is a very long way to go before the businessman is reduced to being little more than a mild example of the niceties of British snobbery.[67] In Britain the novelist no longer bothers to attack salesmen or industrialists or businessmen. They hardly bother to mention him. A study of the work of six influential contemporary English novelists (Elizabeth Bowen, L. P. Hartley, Rosamund Lehmann, Christopher Isherwood, Nancy Mitford and C. P. Snow) concluded, 'Not one of our novelists has attempted to portray the industrial aspect of our

[66] Gail Sheehy, *Passages . . . Predictable Crises of Adult Life* (1976), p. 292. Ms. Sheehy feels that the American male 'has been outfitted for a culture in which feelings are demeaned in favor of fact. In which competitiveness is valued over human interconnectedness. In which rules and systems are to be followed and thinking inventively on one's feet is discouraged. He is desensitised. He is rational. And if the technocracy has succeeded in training him as one of its favorite sons, most of the plugs to his intuition have been pulled out.' She feels that 'the market place . . . militates against a kinetic integration of all one's human capacities' and feels that 'modern management techniques' rely on the rational left side of the brain rather than the intuitive right side. But even sinistral lobotomy seems unlikely to defeat entirely the competitive technological culture of North America.

[67] See John Atkins's comments on the different social standing of an academic and a businessman in an Elizabeth Bowen story: 'A Jag is a status symbol to a businessman. It shows he is a bit better than you might think. . . . By the same token it is a differentiation symbol to the artist or the academic – it tells you that its owner is not quite sure of himself.' *Six Novelists Look at Society* (1977), p. 62.

society, though it accounts for at least eighty per cent of the whole. In their picture, industry is always peripheral.'[68] As long as a training in the arts and the humanities remains the dominant background for the educated Englishman, and as long as that training is predominantly Luddite in sympathy and prejudice, then it will be difficult for either business or technology to enjoy the status or understanding they deserve. At the level of decision making and influence it is difficult to see much evidence of any majestic advance on the part of technologists. Taking University Vice-Chancellors and Heads of Oxbridge Colleges as a sample of educational power and influence gives some indication of how modest the advance has been. In 1935, 68 per cent had been trained in the Arts, 19 per cent in Science, 13 per cent in Social Sciences and none at all in Technology. Thirty-two years later the figures were respectively 48 per cent, 41 per cent, 9 per cent, and 3 per cent. And it has to be remembered that many of those scientists would be as Luddite as their colleagues in the humanities. The educational system of England teaches that pure science is superior to applied, just as surely as it teaches that a mandarin career is more worthwhile than a business career.

In a bitter and well publicized controversy in the 1960s, this hostility to science and technology, which characterizes so many in our educational and cultural élite, was vigorously attacked by C. P. Snow and William Cooper. Few in English fiction (or in public life) have done more than they have to try to combat it. They both realized that if the predominant culture fostered by our educational and social values 'not only hates scientists and engineers . . . [but] . . . scorns them too';[69] if the leading civil servants, who run our national industries, are even remotely like Sir Norman Standsfield, KCB, Chairman of the National Power Board, a fictional representative, who, deeply rooted in the mandarin culture of a first in Greats, and a career in Whitehall,

(i) regretted the Industrial Revolution;
(ii) was opposed to the Technological Culture; and
(iii) at the bottom of his heart not only disliked but *scorned* all Scientists and Engineers[70]

[68] J. Atkins, op. cit., p. 250. 'Most people live and work in large industrial towns. No such impression would be gained from reading English fiction.' His six novelists 'have been subjected to the educational pressures characteristic of this country, and the milieu they describe is largely . . . a minority one'.

[69] William Cooper, *Memoirs of a New Man* (1966), pp. 194–5.

[70] Ibid., p. 26.

(and one knows all too well that many of them are), then it is scarcely surprising that they breed the equally undesirable response from the engineer that 'everybody ought to be technical'.[71]

Faced with the stark and unforgiving hostility of D. H. Lawrence-loving, Luddite, English dons, like William Cooper's John Farrow, the technologists retreat into equally hostile and entrenched positions. The fictional *cri de coeur* of the theoretical metallurgist, Professor Sir Jack Carteret (Dr. Gurney Professor of Natural Philosophy at Oxford) is one which is to be heard in many combination rooms and many more university laboratories:

> In the beginning I'd thought it very important that Clarendon's students of physics and engineering should be taught something of the Other Culture. How was I to know they'd be eliminated in favour of men who were not only going to study the Other Culture alone, but were going to be stirred by their teachers to hatred of the scientific culture into the bargain. How was I to know?[72]

The answer, of course, is through a deeper understanding of Britain's social and economic history. The fact that the characteristic response to the historical, as well as the literary, tradition has been so powerfully influenced by the Luddite view, should have served to enlighten Sir Jack as to the likely reaction of those Arts dons who have done so much to promote that view.

William Cooper and C. P. Snow represent that rare breed, the scientifically educated novelist – indeed Snow practised as a professional academic scientist and both spent much of their bureaucratic lives recruiting scientific personnel. Regarded by Leavis as the incarnation of all that is worst in the technological, utilitarian Benthamite school, it is, of course, predictable that they should try to combat the more extreme effects of academic Luddism. But it is revealing to see what values they actively defend from its emotional assaults. Essentially they defend *academic* scientists, and espouse the cause of *bureaucratic* technologists. In their novels science and technology are given their

[71] Ibid., p. 14.

[72] Ibid., p. 270. Clarendon College, a kind of Oxford near-equivalent to Churchill College, Cambridge, is described in the blurb of *Memoirs of a New Man* as 'newly and exclusively founded for students of science and engineering where a small group of Arts fellows, Luddites to a man, are bent on eliminating scientists and engineering'. On my reading of the novel they are bent on achieving what they call 'Parity of Numbers' but the hostility between the two cultures is made manifest throughout.

articulate and passionate spokesmen – the liberal minded Francis Getliffe, or the power-seeking Dr. Thomas Crawford, or the marvellously appealing Professor Albert Woods (the most memorable scientist in modern fiction),[73] the novel-writing engineer Sir Jack Carteret, or Sherriff in *The Search* impatiently waiting for scientists to inherit the earth – but these are all scholars or bureaucrats, or more often, scholar-bureaucrats, fully paid-up members of the mandarin society. Those who apply that technology to wealth-producing industry are largely mute: Lufkin and Matthewson get little more than walk-on parts.

This is not to doubt Snow and Cooper's basic commitment to industrial technology. Snow firmly believes that industrialization is the only hope for the poor. Cooper is in no doubt about the benefits of the Industrial Revolution. But even these two, with their atypical literary sympathy for science and technology, have done little to redress the fictional balance in favour of their industrial or commercial application. Their self-made men are characteristically academics and civil servants – and in this, of course, they correctly identify and reflect the direction in which our meritocratic society channels its talents. There are no major or memorable sympathetic portraits of technological tycoons – either self-made or otherwise. Perhaps the society they are writing about has produced too few for that to be surprising. Probably more significantly, their political sympathies present a further barrier to easy enthusiasm for the entrepreneur in either their own statements or those of their fictional spokesmen. Certainly the ambitious young in search of a business role model would look in vain amongst their characters. Professor Jack Carteret, for example, might rail at those who tried to stymie the march of academic technology or to thwart the scientific mandarins who sought to promote it, but when men speak with 'awe and praise of . . . the last, great, paternalistic, engineering tycoon',[74] his response is immediate and unambiguous:

> Though tycoons might have a great name for giving away their gains, I'd always said it must be through greed that they'd gotten them. As for Free Enterprise, I could always stop the show, especially in the U.S.A., by

[73] William Cooper's creation of Albert Woods, quite apart from Jack Carteret and Bill Taylor, makes it strange that a critic like John Atkins should write, 'It is hard to recall . . . a single novelist beyond Snow who has introduced a scientist into his work', op. cit., p. 252.

[74] Ibid., p. 24.

> remarking that under Free Enterprise the strong were free to get richer and the poor were free to go to the wall. And I meant it too.[75]

The motives are explicitly political, the convictions explicitly socialist. Such sympathies make such men as suspicious of profit as the social nostalgia of their Tory opponents makes *them* so hostile to the technology that has so radically changed the traditional society they admire.

Both political wings in England feed off and exploit aspects of Luddite sympathies. They are both more clearly products of the prevailing cultural attitudes than they seem to realize or admit.[76] Even a lifelong commitment to technology is not incompatible with an instinctive recoil from the self-made tycoons who have made it yield a profit, and in doing so have profited from it themselves.

Even those who recognized an inherent majesty in science and industrial technology, and who would have been in sympathy with the social engineering it could achieve, were stopped in their potentially admiring tracks by the thought of personal profit. J. D. Bernal, for instance, wrote in 1937 that if science and technology 'were applied for human welfare and not for profit' (assumed to be opposites in the orthodoxy of the day), 'society would choose how much work it was worth doing to secure any particular standard of living'.[77] In Bernal's view 'science itself would see to it that none of the work done was unnecessary'.[78] The niggers in his woodpile were the profit-seeking men of business who corrupted and diverted the pure intentions of science.

Society's approving sanction has not, then, been easily earned by the profit-seeking businessmen – not at least from the most influential organs of our society, nor for any considerable length of time – and it is little wonder in the face of such a tide of disapproval that the able and the ambitious have sought their career satisfactions elsewhere. For the problem is not that Britain lacked vertical social mobility. The avenues open to the self-made don or bureaucrat are wide and inviting. The professions have been impressively accessible to talent; and they carry far greater prestige. Business is, and often has been, too tainted to be able to compete.

[75] Ibid., p. 25.
[76] As doubtless are we all!
[77] T. E. B. Howarth, *Cambridge Between the Wars* (1978), p. 191.
[78] J. D. Bernal, quoted in Howarth, op. cit., p. 191.

As a result the Victorian haemorrhage of capital and ability from industry and trade into landownership and politics, has been succeeded by an even more copious flow of talent away from the wealth producing sectors – although in the mid-twentieth century the ability has been transfused more obviously into bureaucracy, the universities and the professions.

There are good and rational reasons for this internal brain drain in Britain – in my view a far more serious drain than the flow of talent overseas. The mandarin world offers greater security, greater prestige, often greater freedom and, more frequently than many imagine, greater financial rewards than the world of industry. But these reasons are buttressed by (indeed they are often the consequence of) the belief that these pursuits are morally better, more worthwhile, socially more valuable, less tainted with the undesirable associations of trade. These assumptions have been little examined in our society, but they are very widely held. Their uncritical acceptance has had important consequences. Professor Hayek has written:

> We cannot blame our young men when they prefer the safe, salaried position to the risk of enterprise after they have heard from their earliest youth the former described as the superior, more unselfish and disinterested occupation. The younger generation of today has grown up in a world in which in school and press the spirit of commercial enterprise has been represented as disreputable and the making of profit as immoral, where to employ a hundred people is represented as exploitation but to command the same number is honourable.[79]

As a result of indifference and ignorance on both sides the gap between British industry and the British intelligentsia has grown too wide. Other countries have proved more willing to close the gap, to encourage the exchange of personnel, to make the best use of applied technology. It is instructive to learn that Professor Gordon Blair of Queen's University, Belfast, whose computer analysis of engine performance allows one to test twenty 'paper engines' in an afternoon which it would take three years to test in practice, works for Yamaha of Japan, not B.S.A. of Britain. It is an instructive example because Britain virtually gave away the world market for motor cycles. One of the most frightening statistics for our economic future is that which tells us that Britain's share of the world market for this product plummeted from 95 per cent to 5 per cent within a decade.

[79] F. A. Hayek, *The Road to Serfdom* (1944).

It underlines the message of Robert Persig in *The Art of Motorcycle Maintenance*. For when asked to identify the differences between the industry in Japan and Britain, Blair picked out their sheer interest in their product and their firm, their fierce loyalty to both, the sheer presence of engineers, the 'real sustained interest in technology'. He spoke of the Japanese delight in new technology. He compared his experience of suggesting a new idea and finding the wherewithall to test it ready that next morning in Japan, with the response in Britain to ideas suggested ten years ago, laconically summed up as 'not too much happened'.[80]

Managerial and marketing decisions killed our motorcycle industry as much as any refusal to accept the best technology, but the lack of interest is an important symptom of entrepreneurial failure. Such attitudes can have important repercussions on the workforce too. If the workforce has been brought up in a culture which is deeply suspicious of technology and the entrepreneur it can breed a damagingly defensive attitude to both.

British industry is notorious for low rates of productivity, for very generous attitudes to overmanning, for a more urgent response to job protection than to job creation on the part of our unions. But it is not enough to parrot these complaints. It is not enough to note that on successive days the *Financial Times* could report that workers at the Honda Motor Company had voluntarily given up four days holiday to keep the three eight-hour shifts at full strength, and that workers at British Leyland had refused on social grounds to work at night at a time when the outstanding orders for the new Rover 3500 had produced a waiting list of nine months. We need to investigate why these 'attitudes and relations distinctive to British society prevent the British economy from working as co-operatively and as vigorously as do some of its neighbours'.[81]

These are not vague, unsubstantiated complaints. They can, and have been, precisely quantified. C. F. Pratten's survey of the productivity in one hundred international manufacturing companies making similar products by similar processes in Britain and other countries suggests how much the difference in performance can be assigned to

[80] Prof. Gordon Blair quoted in 'Being Second is Just No Good at All', the 1978 Trident Science Award for Communication in Science, screened on 18 July 1978.

[81] Sir Henry Phelps-Brown, 'What is the British Predicament?', *The Three Banks Preview* (December 1977), no. 116, pp. 3–29.

the employees themselves.[82] Pratten's survey shows that output per employee hour is exceeded by some 56 per cent in North America, by 35 per cent in Germany, and by 28 per cent in France.[83] The causes of these differences are divided into economic (such as the type of plant, the product mix, the rate of output and the length of production runs) and behavioural (such as strikes, restrictive practices, manning quotas and differences in personal efficiency). The behavioural account for 19 percentage points out of the total 35 difference between Britain and Germany. They are not, of course, a sufficient explanation alone for Britain's lag in industrial efficiency, but they are substantial. They are a real and measurable legacy of the different social attitudes between Britain and our competitors. Our competitors feel sure that these distinctive attitudes account for many of the shortcomings in our industrial relations and our economic performance. Pratten's research suggests that their intuition is not without foundation.

Political convictions play an important part in sustaining and promoting such attitudes, but I am deliberately not dealing specifically, or in detail, with the political traditions hostile to the profit motive and the individual man of enterprise. They deserve to be treated separately elsewhere. My purpose here is to identify that pervasive and instinctive hostility to technology and the self-made businessman which transcends party politics, and which, over the last hundred years or so, has come to reflect a characteristic cultural tradition in this country.

That cultural tradition has been deeply influenced by emotional Luddism. It has contributed to, and been sustained by, an enormously influential literary tradition. When that literary tradition is so potent and so influential we have a special responsibility not to distort it. George Eliot rightly claimed a special status for the artist whose imagined world can shock us into a new moral awareness, because

> Appeals founded on generalizations and statistics require a sympathy ready made, a moral sentiment already in activity; but a picture of human life such as a great artist can give, surprises even the trivial and the selfish into that attention to what is apart from themselves, which may be called the raw material of moral sentiment.[84]

[82] C. F. Pratten, *Labour Productivity Differentials within International Companies* (1976), University of Cambridge, Dept. of Applied Economics. Occasional Papers No. 50.

[83] A merciful veil is drawn over the difference with Japan, but in the car industry it is startlingly large.

[84] George Eliot, quoted in Stephen Gill, op. cit., p. 10.

The historian, however, has responsibilities too. His special rôle is to temper that moral awareness with a knowledge of what actually happened – in this case to ensure that the literary tradition does not produce an antipathy ready made to reject an appreciation of technology and all its works, a moral sentiment wholly inaccessible to the social worth of the businessman. Historical fact has, of course, been used as a weapon in the battle of moral opinion. It has not always been used well. The donnish crack about Dr. Leavis, that the examiners were right in giving him a II.2 in History and a First in English, is an unworthy one, but it would require an excess of piety not to admit that many of the historical judgements which informed his literary and moral views were more consistent with his emotional sympathies than with historical fact.

The Luddite tradition has done more than reject historical fact, it has distorted or ignored much of the evidence provided by literature too. One of the burdens of this introduction is that through the distorting mirror of the Luddite tradition, the fictional Bounderbys, Melmottes, and Undershafts, and the real life Hudsons, Bottomleys and Zaharoffs, have projected, and still do project a far more influential image of the businessman than have the Wedgwoods, Owens and Brunels and their fictional counterparts, the John Halifaxes, John Thorntons and Mr. Ainsleys. These men could sustain a wholly admirable alternative tradition if their positive achievements and personal virtues were given as much prominence and publicity as political polemic and critical propaganda have given to their vulgar, profiteering alter egos.

Instead, while the Smilesian apotheosis of the self-made man has received ridicule and neglect, the Luddite exemplars are continually and effectively projected through our literature and its critical interpreters. Confirmed as factually representative by many historians and upheld as 'morally true' by many critics, the Luddite interpretation of history has, in consequence, been readily absorbed into our educational and cultural tradition. Bounderby is held to be both factually and morally true to type with far too little investigation. For this tradition requires not so much counter-propaganda as an injection of historical accuracy – a recognition of the heroes, an exposure of the villains, an acceptance of the majority who occupy the middle ground, and a critical evaluation of them all.

Of course we need to remember that many self-made businessmen, driven by what Carlyle called 'the terror of "Not succeeding . . . of not making money" ',[85] sacrificed decency to efficiency and humanity to profit. Of course we need to realize that those whom Elizabeth Stone called 'these mushroom princes' 'oftener enacted the tyrannical despot than the considerate master in their domain . . . unless gifted with great natural goodness'.[86] But we must not refuse to accept that such 'great natural goodness' both occurred in fact and was recorded in fiction.

It is a curious, but revealing, irony that our greatest popular novelist, the writer who has done more (with the selective, interpretative help of our critical tradition) to fix in our cultural history the malign character of technology, and the self-made man who exploited it, should also be the author of the most benign exemplar of the benign self-made industrialists. It is a further irony that these benevolent fictional factory owners should be the fictional characters whom we can most definitely and precisely identify with the actual men who inspired them.[87] Dickens tells us several times over 'that the BROTHERS CHEERYBLE live; that their liberal charity, their singleness of heart, their noble nature, and their unbounded benevolence, are no creations of the Author's brain; but are prompting every day (and oftenest by stealth) some munificent and generous deed in that town [Manchester] of which they are the pride and honour'.[88] When one of the Grant brothers died, Dickens acknowledged that 'One of the noble hearts who sat for the Cheeryble brothers is dead'; regretted that he was not in England to go in 'mourning for such a glorious life'; and noted that in his lifetime the self-made calico printer of Manchester had given away 'in charity £600,000, or three million dollars'.[89] However unwelcome such facts are to the Luddite tradition they cannot be dismissed. However tiresome the contemporary evidence that on the way to the Grant factory children chanted 'Hurrah for Grant'; however inconvenient the Smilesian stories of magnanimity and generosity in the face of malice;

[85] Carlyle, *Past and Present* (1843), 1962 edition, p. 140.

[86] *William Langshawe, the Cotton Lord* (1842), I, p. 123.

[87] Research has suggested that Mrs. Trollope's Elgood Sharpton is based on an actual Ellice Needham who persecuted the real-life Robert Blincoe [see W. H. Chaloner, 'Mrs. Trollope and the Factory System', *Victorian Studies*, 4, (1960), p. 164]; and that Disraeli's Joseph Diggs was based on a real-life Banks [see above, p. xxviii], but Dickens himself confirmed that the Cheerybles were directly based on the Grants.

[88] Preface to *Nicholas Nickleby* (1839–39), pp. xvi–xvii.

[89] *The Letters of Charles Dickens*, ed. Walter Dexter (1938), p. 445. Quoted in Ivan Melada, *The Captains of Industry in English Fiction, 1821–1871* (Albuquerque, 1970), pp. 108–9.

however incompatible with the Bounderby image, the description of those who met them that the brothers were 'most exquisite old men'; however incompatible with profiteering the evidence of their massive charity, their willingness to support the unemployed turned off by other millowners; however unsuitable for those portraying an unbridled pursuit of private gain, their unacquisitive sharing attitude to their own profits ('what each wants, that he takes'); and however unacceptable to those whose self-made men must be caricatures of villainy and vulgarity, the fact remains that the Grants lived. They are part of the historical record. Their virtues succeeded when it was very easy to fail. Their profits mounted when bankruptcy was all too common. Their benevolence flourished in perhaps the most difficult years of the whole Industrial Revolution. Their success was entirely self-made. Even hostile contemporary critics were silenced in the face of such (what can only be called) goodness.

Indeed Lord John Manners, whose usual sympathies can be gauged from the two most famous lines he wrote – 'Let wealth and commerce die . . . But leave us still our old Nobility' – talked (after a personal visit of inspection to William Grant's factory) of 'this beautiful history. . . . What a life has that man's been! From the boy wandering penniless by the banks of the uncontaminated Irwell – then without a chimney in its valley – to the princely manufacturing merchant, owning that very valley, and filling the remotest corners of the globe with the products of his industry and wealth, and still more wonderful, retaining all the guilelessness and simpleheartedness of childhood.'[90]

Perhaps the irony that *this* Dickensian portrait of self-made business virtues has for so long gone unsung is partially explained by the other message of the Dickens novel which has provided the *leit-motif* of this introduction. For *Hard Times* not only taught the horrors of the self-made men of industry, not only punctured their pride in their own achievements, not only provided a lasting antidote to any tendency to admire such men. It also mounted a powerful barrage against FACT.

Hard Times was designed as a polemic against the rule of fact. Such was Dickens's revulsion from the new mechanical system of education of Joseph Lancaster, or of his rival Andrew Bell, that he mercilessly satirized what he called the 'utilitarian economists and Commissioners of Fact' and their fascination with facts and statistics. Indeed it was

[90] Quoted in C. Whibley, *Lord John Manners and his Friends* (1925), 1, p. 99.

Gradgrind's rigid systematization and fanatical belief in fact which was Dickens's real target in *Hard Times.* Among the suggested titles were *Fact, Mr. Gradgrind's Facts, Two and Two are Four, A Mere Question of Figures, A Matter of Calculation, Simple Arithmetic* and *The Grindstone.*[91] Facts were presented as remorseless, oppressive and colourless, the enemy of all that was life-enhancing. Poor Mrs. Gradgrind suffered almost as much as the pupils in Gradgrind's academy for 'whenever she showed some symptom of coming to life, [she] was invariably stunned by some weighty piece of fact tumbling on her'.[92] And Dickensian facts could be more crushing than most.

Coketown itself was 'a triumph of fact'.[93] It was 'sacred to facts'.[94] It was the epitome of fact. It was fact incarnate:

> Fact, fact, fact, everywhere in the material aspect of the town; fact, fact, fact, everywhere in the immaterial. The M'Choakcumchild school was all fact, and the school of design was all fact, and the relations between master and man were all fact, and everything was fact between the lying-in hospital and the cemetery, and what you could not state in figures or show to be purchaseable in the cheapest market and saleable in the dearest, was not, and never should be, world without end, Amen.[95]

Most famous of all, of course, was the chorus of factual exhortation directed at the pupils in Gradgrind's model school.

> 'Fact, fact, fact!' said the gentleman. And 'Fact, fact, fact' repeated Thomas Gradgrind.[96]

Who dare say a word in favour of more historical information in the face of that barrage of sarcasm and satire? Little wonder that the critical tradition has been slightly cavalier in its treatment of mere historical information.

So if the historian wishes to raise his horses of instruction above the dismissive comment by Blake, with which this introduction began, then he has a duty to rise above mere factual accuracy. Blake's tigers of wrath are so unforgettably vivid, that the historian must strive to make his instruction as elegant and graceful and literate and lively as his talents allow. If he is content with unvarnished fact, then his

[91] John Butt and Kathleen Tillotson, *Dickens at Work* (1957), pp. 201–5.

[92] Dickens, *Hard Times*, p. 59.

[93] Ibid., p. 65.

[94] Ibid., p. 60.

[95] Ibid.

[96] 'You are to be in all things regulated and governed . . . by fact. We hope to have, before long, a board of fact, composed of commissioners of fact, who will force the people to be a people of fact, and of nothing but fact.' Ibid., p. 52.

instruction has a Dickensian epitaph ready and waiting for it: it is Bitzer's immortal definition of a horse –

> Quadruped. Graminivorous. Forty teeth, namely twenty four grinders, four eye teeth, and twelve incisors. . . . Thus (and much more) Bitzer.[97]

Bitzer after all was so colourless 'he looked as though, if he were cut, he would bleed white'.[98] Too many business historians have been content to look not dissimilar.

If they need a model for their horses of instruction, they should look to Stubbs, not to Bitzer. His horses – the product of painstaking study and intended as much for scholarly instruction as for aesthetic delight – prove that accuracy is no bar to elegance, and that prolonged and detailed research can be made to yield the most graceful results.

But above all Stubbs's horses are completely in touch with reality. Ferocious polemic must not distract us from that reality, and for all that I have been stressing the hostility to technology, the disdain for self-made men of business, and the pervasive wish not to know about either them or their achievement, we should not forget that there is a tradition (albeit a submerged one at present) which honours the man of enterprise.

This introduction has been concerned to identify some of the reasons for that lack of recognition and support in this country. It has not always been so lacking. We should not forget that there have been periods in British history when the inventive technologist who served industry, and the self-made businessman who used that technology, were richly honoured. The periods may have been brief and the admirers limited in number, but they included some of the most effective and productive men our society has ever produced. It is not without significance that they can be most easily found in late eighteenth-century Britain when a mixture of inventive genius and commercial brilliance combined to produce the first Industrial Revolution, to produce rates of economic growth the world had never before experienced, and to initiate the most dramatic rise in living standards the world has ever known.[99]

[97] Ibid., p. 50.

[98] Ibid., p. 50.

[99] Not even those who doubt that living standards rose between say 1814 and 1842 or have grave doubts about what has happened to the quality of life over the last 200 years (and they have very good reasons for their doubts), can deny that in the long run the Industrial Revolution has brought dramatic material benefits to a far larger proportion of society than ever before.

The men who led that great revolution can be characterized by the members of the Lunar Society – to my mind, one of the most admirable, the most deserving and intellectually the most productive, if not the most honoured, group of men who have ever come together in Britain. *They* had no doubts about the gifts, or the value of those gifts to society, of men such as Brindley and Bridgwater, Boulton and Watt, Wedgwood and Bentley, Priestley and Keir, Franklin and Herschel, Arkwright and Wilkinson. In admiring such men, they were, of course, often admiring themselves or their friends, but it is just as well they did for their self-congratulatory optimism about the benefits of industrial technology proved very short lived.

Their admiring attitude, and the irony of their expectations of posterity, can be summed up in a single letter from Erasmus Darwin to Josiah Wedgwood written on 30 September 1772, on hearing from Wedgwood of Brindley's death three days earlier. Darwin was sure that posterity would honour Brindley. He had no doubts about his 'great genius'; he thought he deserved 'a monument in Westminster Abbey'; and he encouraged Wedgwood to write down 'any circumstances you recollect of his life' so that he might 'digest them into an Eulogium'.[100] But most telling of all was his sentence which reads '*These men should not die; this Nature denies, but their Memories are above her Malice.*'[101] Alas, the malice of our society has plagued such men long after they have escaped the malice of Nature.

* * *

Sir Herbert Austin was, in essence, a technologist and a self-made man. His most famous product – the baby Austin – was the result of personal labours which would fit snugly into the Smilesian tradition of perseverance in the face of adversity. Yet his shortcomings in entrepreneurial judgement highlight the problems of the businessman better versed in the technicalities of engineering than in the raising of capital, the judgement of demand and the maintenance of cash flow. Properly

[100] In *The Economy of Vegetation*, III, 329–36, Darwin fulfilled his promise, writing that where

'. . . with strong arm immortal Brindley leads
His long canals . . .
. . . Plenty. Arts and Commerce freight the waves.'

[101] Erasmus Darwin to Josiah Wedgwood, 30 September 1772. (My italics.)

understood he could make a real contribution to our knowledge of modern British industry. His career, as Professor Church so ably demonstrates, reveals so many crucial problems which faced the British car industry in the twentieth century. It reveals the role of imports in fuelling optimism about likely demand, it reveals the importance of the role of the car dealers, it reveals the importance of the role of the First World War in inflating demand, the importance of the role of the banks in controlling the supply of capital, the importance of the role of government and the relative *un*importance of labour problems for Austin.[102]

Austin's career reveals his distinctive managerial goals – to motorize the common man rather than to maximize profits, to lower costs and to raise the quality of production. It reveals how, for all his technical excellence and inventive creativity, his firm could have collapsed without Engelbach to control the system of production and Payton to ensure strict financial control. It reveals how difficult it is to assess rationally the accuracy of business decisions. Does the realization that if his market share was to remain the same, he would have to increase his sales thirteenfold in the post-war years show that his demand projection was wildly extravagant; and reveal that this is where Austin's entrepreneurial weakness lay? Or does the fact that his rival Morris's share of the market increased from 3 per cent to 40 per cent (a thirteenfold increase) in less than five years reveal that it was a misreading of the *type* of car which would sell in those quantities which led to Austin's problems?

It is to such questions that Professor Church addresses himself. How necessary the answers are can be judged from the fact that a recent conference of some forty business historians discussing *Enterprise in Interwar Britain* were wholly unable to agree 'whether Austin should be panned or praised as an entrepreneur of industrial technology'. After reading Professor Church's biography they will possess both the information on which to base their judgement, and Professor Church's comparative assessment of Austin's performance compared with his major rivals.

If Professor Church's research yields little about Austin's private life; and if there are few of those personal details which decorate most biographies, it serves only to confirm how secretive about their lives

[102] The only disruptions were national ones, not labour problems specific to Austin.

so many businessmen have been,[103] and how little urgency our history has attached to preserving what was once known. As long as 'the tigers of wrath' provide our only guide then that secretiveness will increase and that urgency will diminish.

If we listen to our 'horses of instruction' it might lead to a greater realization of a man like Austin's achievements. It might lead to a greater acceptance of Schumacher's posthumous tribute to the man of enterprise:

> To start from nothing and build up a prosperous, prestigious, and internationally respected industrial enterprise is a great achievement in itself. The world is full of studied people who write learnedly, and sometimes even interestingly, on how to be enterprising, efficient, innovative, etc., but most of them, if they tried, could not really run anything, let alone start a new business from scratch. True 'enterprisers' are all too easily taken for granted; they are, in fact, rare and interesting people who deserve our gratitude and respect.[104]

Given Schumacher's attitude, Austin would be part of an honourable and honoured tradition. But then Schumacher was born in Germany. Granted the sceptical ('Was Ford a Fraud?')[105] approach of Galbraith, then Austin would enjoy the concerned critical attention he deserves and has lacked. But then Galbraith is an American.

Gonville and Caius College, Cambridge

[103] Eric Pasold has recently published that rare literary phenomenon, a business autobiography – *Ladybird, Ladybird; A Study of Private Enterprise* (1977) – but then Pasold was a businessman who, although he has flourished in Britain, was born in Czechoslovakia.

[104] E. F. Schumacher, 'Foreword' to S. Hoe, *The Man who Gave his Company Away: A biography of Ernest Bader* (1978), pp. xi–xii.

[105] J. K. Galbraith, *The Liberal Hour* (1960), pp. 141–63.

Preface

IT IS IMPORTANT to declare at the outset that a complete absence of the personal papers of Herbert Austin, and the death of many who knew him, have presented the author with certain limitations. The unsatisfactory chronological balance of the account is also dictated by the lack of documentary sources relating to the period before the First World War, by which time Herbert was already forty-eight with a distinguished and in many respects successful career behind him. Despite these shortcomings we consider that an examination of the history of the man and of the Austin Motor Company is worthwhile because of the importance of both in the development of an industry whose strengths and weaknesses in the 1970s trace their origins to the period between the wars. For good or ill, Herbert Austin is the archetypal figure in the history of the first forty years of the British motor industry's evolution.

The research for this biography was made possible by the co-operation of British Leyland and facilitated considerably by the helpfulness of Mr. Westcott at Longbridge, who retrieved what few company records of the Austin Motor Company remain and on behalf of the Company granted permission to reproduce photographs. I am grateful to him and to those who were kind enough to allow me to interview them: Lord Thomas of Remenham, Mr. T. A. E. Layborn, Mr. J. R. Edwards and Mr. Freddie Henry. The Austin Ex-Apprentices Association was also helpful in contacting those with memories of Austin before 1941. Co-operation was forthcoming from Wolseley Webb Ltd., the flourishing descendant of the Wolseley Sheep Shearing and Machine Tool Company, whose minute books and a small amount of Herbert Austin's business letters were made available to me. My thanks are due especially to Mr. J. Kendrick and to Mr. Branson for their assistance at Wolseley Webb, and to Mr. R. J. Wheatley at Ford, Dagenham, and Mr. Hartley at Standard, Canley, in Coventry. Mr. Edwin Green arranged for access to uncatalogued archives at the Midland Bank and Mr. Eric Kelly directed my attention to the references to Austin in the archives of the Bank of England; the late Mr. D. C. Field, the RAC Motor Historian, was both helpful and hospitable, allowing me to consult the Pollitt Papers lodged with him for safe-keeping; Mrs. Das, Secretary to the Veteran Car Club of Great Britain, made available to me the resources of the VCC Library. I wish to express my thanks also to my colleague, Michael Miller, who generously permitted the use of previously unpublished results from our joint research on the motor industry between the wars, and in addition made available several statistical estimates. Advice and critical reading of the book in typescript by him, by Dr. R. J. Irving, and by Mr. Freddie Henry, have led to some improvements, though none is responsible for the interpretations presented here.

Financial support for research into the motor industry has been forthcoming from a variety of sources, beginning with the University of Birmingham Research Fund, but the SSRC made a small supplementary grant specifically for the preparation of this biography. My thanks are due to these bodies and to Mary Gurteen, who transformed a barely legible and often incomprehensible manuscript into a readable typescript.

ROY CHURCH
University of East Anglia, Norwich, 1978

Part One: The Birth of an Industry: The Pioneering Phase to 1914

CHAPTER ONE

Herbert Austin and Wolseley

A LARGELY RURAL mid-Victorian childhood was the unlikely prelude to the flowering of Herbert Austin's precocious engineering genius. His father, Giles Steven Austin, was a farmer in Buckinghamshire, and Grange Farm at Little Missenden was the birthplace of the Austins' second son, Herbert, on 8 November 1866. Four years later the Austin family removed to Wentworth, in Yorkshire, where Giles was appointed farm bailiff to Earl Fitzwilliam. After attending the local village school, Herbert's education continued at Rotherham Grammar School, five miles from Wentworth, and even at this early age his preferred pastime, encouraged by his parents, was to draw geometrical pictures and patterns. In preparation for a career as an architect he spent two years at Brampton Commercial College, after which he was apprenticed to his paternal uncle, architect to Earl Fitzwilliam. The work of an architect, however, failed to satisfy or to excite, and Herbert's articles were soon cancelled. With the intention of beginning an engineering apprenticeship, lasting five years, his father proceeded to add Herbert's name to a list at the Great Northern Railway Company and await a vacancy.

That apprenticeship was never taken up, for at the age of seventeen he was persuaded by a visiting Australian uncle to return with him to serve an apprenticeship with Messrs. Richard Parks & Co., an engineering firm in Melbourne where his uncle was manager for the Scottish owner, Mephan Ferguson. Two years later, he took his experience of engineering workshop practice to another Melbourne firm, which imported and erected Crossley gas engines and printing presses. After two years there he joined the Langland's Foundry Company, where, in his own words, he received 'a thorough training as a mechanic'. That occurred by day, but at night he attended classes at the Hotham Arts School in Melbourne, where he became a prize-winning student. In his remaining leisure hours Herbert became increasingly absorbed by engineering design, and at the age of twenty-one he submitted designs and estimates for a swing bridge over the Yarra River. Although the award went elsewhere, his own submission received a special commendation, recognition which, Herbert later recalled, strengthened his self-confidence. It is not surprising, therefore, that his next post was as manager of a small engineering firm, a position taken up a few days after his marriage to an Australian, Ellen Dron, in December 1887.

Herbert's new appointment soon proved to be of immense importance to his future career, for it was this connection which brought him into contact with Frederick York Wolseley, a Dublin emigrant turned sheep farmer.[1] Wolseley had pioneered the use of sheep shearing machinery on the sheep station he managed in Victoria, and in 1876 he received a grant for his first patent sheep shearing machine. The next few years brought further improvements to his various inventions which were in practical use on Wolseley's own large sheep station in New South Wales, and in 1887 he established the Wolseley Sheep Shearing Machine Co. Ltd. The Sydney firm was wound up two years later and its head office transferred to London, where a new Company under the same name was duly registered with a nominal capital of £200,000.[2]

By that time Herbert Austin's dealings with the firm had already begun, for the Wolseley Sheep Shearing Machine Co. had placed orders for certain parts with the small engineering company of which he was then manager. Extreme accuracy of workmanship was vital, and Herbert succeeded in meeting the specifications to Wolseley's satisfaction; furthermore, tests enabled him to identify numerous weaknesses in the shears' design and construction. Herbert took out several patents for improvements, and in an agreement reached in 1893 assigned all of his existing patents which related to 'improvements in tools for shearing or clipping hair or wool' to Wolseley's company,

[1] The early history of Herbert Austin is based on an autobiographical article, 'Sir Herbert Austin KBE, His Life Story', *Autocar*, 23 August 1929, pp. 369–72.

[2] St. John C. Nixon, *Wolseley, A Saga of the Motor Industry* (1949), pp. 16–17.

and undertook to sell to it all future patents of this kind. In return, the inventor was allotted forty fully paid-up shares, with a further forty dependent 'on the performance of Herbert Austin'.[3] In the meantime, the WSSMC had encountered supply difficulties following the firm's removal to England, and it was to solve these problems that Herbert was taken on as manager, returning to England in the winter of 1893.

On his arrival, Herbert discovered that many thousands of defective machines had been sold in overseas markets, with a consequent deterioration of Wolseley's reputation. Machine components supplied by a variety of small local engineering firms to the Wolseley workshop in central Birmingham had been inadequately inspected, a critical weakness under the circumstances, for those managing the component firms lacked more than a rudimentary knowledge of the requirements. Herbert decided to try to protect the Company's reputation by buying back all the faulty machinery, most of which proved to be beyond rectification. The episode was costly, and the only way, it seemed to him, to avoid a repetition was to alter the system of production by switching from the assembly of bought-out components to the integrated manufacture of parts in the Company's own works.[4] This is why in 1895 Herbert took the initiative, virtually compelling the directors to acquire the Sydney Works, in Alma Street at Aston, Birmingham.[5] This was to become the centre of operations, based on new plant under his own firm managerial control to ensure standards and punctuality in production. This was also the model he was to adopt when later he manufactured motor cars.

The combined effects of the damage to the Company's standing, already sustained, together with the conservatism of Australian sheep farmers in the face of mechanization and the uncertainty resulting from trading fluctuations, presented Wolseley with a resistance to sales which proved difficult to overcome. Consequently the heavier commitment of capital investment involved in the reformed manufacturing organization led Herbert to cast around for other products to boost turnover and profit. In 1895 the Company began to manufacture

[3] Companies House File 19846, Wolseley Sheep Shearing Machine Co. Ltd., Memorandum of Agreement, 26 January 1897.

[4] Sir Herbert Austin KBE, His Life Story, *Autocar*, 23 August 1929.

[5] The story of how Herbert Austin bid for the property at auction without prior consultation with the Board of Directors is told in Z. E. Lambert and R. J. Wyatt, *Lord Austin – the Man* (1968), pp. 38–9 (hereafter cited as Lambert & Wyatt).

machine tools, principally for cotton machine makers; and parts for bicycles were supplied to the cycle assembly firms of Birmingham and Coventry, then experiencing a tremendous trade boom. Even a few bicycles were built at the Alma Street Works.[6] Indeed, almost any class of engineering work was taken on, including the production of a vertical semi-automatic chucking lathe, which was exhibited in Paris and claimed to be the first of its kind; special machine tools, screw-cutting machinery, milling machines, gas furnaces, high speed steam engines and castings; all appeared in advertisements incorporated in the Company's stationery before the end of the century.

High quality diversified machine tool output and a discerning purchase of selected imported machinery appear to have been the basis upon which the ambitious Herbert Austin established a growing home business to supplement the more volatile export trade in sheep shearing equipment. An article which appeared in the *American Machinist* in December 1897, condemning the conservatism of British engineers, prompted him to launch an intemperate, though characteristic, counter-attack against the American critics.[7] In a letter to the editor, Herbert deplored the 'continued prating about the ignorant conservatism of the Englishman, and the wonderful adaptability of the American . . . enough to make a decent man sick'.[8] Rejecting the idea that specialization in the production of types of machine tool was desirable, he argued that excessive specialization led to a narrowing of experience and restricted opportunities for the individual firm.[9] He also argued that to be set against the advantage of constant operation was the disadvantage of an inferior product, a judgement based on his

[6] Herbert also acted as an agent for bicycles, supplying machines made by the Regal Bicycle Company to at least one Australian importer in the 1890s. Herbert Austin to Howard, 1 October 1895. Wolseley Sheep Shearing Machine Co. Ltd., sundry papers. Hereafter WSSMC papers.

[7] The article was based on a letter written by Joseph Horner and published in *Engineering*.

[8] WSSMC Papers, Herbert Austin to the editor, *American Machinist*, 14 January 1898.

[9] In fact he questioned the extent of specialization in the US. 'There are very few large firms . . . in America that are engaged solely on the manufacture of only one tool. Pratt and Whitney make a large variety of tools. Warner and Swazey make turret lathes and telescopes – not much alike are they? except that they both begin with a t. Messrs. Tangye certainly make machine tools but in an entirely different building and by a separate company. Their other manufactures are kept apart.'

own experience of importing American automatic machinery.[10] These are vital clues to his general approach to production strategy when he branched out into manufacturing only a few years later.

Ever in search of new engineering developments, during the 1890s his interests turned towards the development of internal combustion and its application to wheeled vehicles. Following a joint patent for improvements in the efficiency of steam engines, taken out with the Wolseley Sheep Shearing Machine Co. in 1893, his next patent was for a flat circular furnace for attaching metal tyres to wheels, a joint invention with the Northampton coachbuilder, H. H. Mulliner, registered in 1894. The latter has been interpreted as evidence of Herbert's practical commitment to vehicle manufacture, following his first glimpse of a 'horseless carriage' earlier that year in Paris.[11] Shortly afterwards, Mulliner agreed in principle to join Herbert Austin and Wolseley in the manufacture of 'motor carriages'; but by the summer of 1896 Mulliner had allied himself with the Daimler Syndicate, the first of the specialist motor manufacturers in Britain. Discountenanced though he was by Mulliner's decision, Herbert's desire to follow him into the new trade had been brought one step nearer in the spring of 1896, when the Wolseley directors agreed to invest £2,000 in plant for motor car manufacture under his personal supervision.[12]

Later, he recalled how, at the Paris display, he had examined the very crude vehicles powered by internal combustion, each incorporating complex vertical engines, friction clutches, differential gears and chains. But one particular vehicle, the small three-wheeled Bollée,

[10] 'If the Americans or any other countries have the best facilities for making tools by all means let them make and we will be content to use them, as it usually pays better.' The pithy sentence with which Herbert's letter ended suggests that Professor Floud's comments on the inhibiting effects of American tariffs on the performance of British engineering exports would have made sense to the irascible Birmingham engineer: 'I might point out that several large tool makers here are agents for American tool makers, but where do you find an American house who (sic) represents an English Tool Maker – who is conservative? I do wish you would take down that fence.' WSSMC, Herbert Austin to the editor of *The American Machinist*, 14 January 1898. See also R. C. Floud, 'The Adolescence of American Engineering Competition 1860–1900', *Economic History Review*, XXVII (1974), p. 68.

[11] Lambert & Wyatt, pp. 41–3. Even if that was the first time Herbert Austin had actually seen such a vehicle, a claim disputed by Mr. Freddie Henry, the experiments of Benz and Daimler had been followed with interest by Herbert Austin.

[12] WSSMC Papers, Herbert Austin to Mulliner, 23 May 1896.

made by the Bollée Brothers at Le Mans, was sufficiently impressive to stimulate experiment along similar lines. Herbert's own training as an engineer meant that he was familiar with stationary gas engines using either flame or tube ignition, with belts and shafting to drive machinery; and this was the principle which, in Herbert's estimation, the Bollée Brothers had adopted more simply and more efficiently than other makers.[13] While there is some doubt about the precise year in which Herbert built his first Austin 2 h.p. car (probably in 1895), the discontinuance of its further development from 1896 is explicable, perhaps, by the vulnerability of Austin's first car to legal action under the Bollée patent.[14] The patent had passed into the hands of the British Motor Syndicate Ltd. in 1896, whose flamboyant promoter, Harry J. Lawson, sought to purchase all motor vehicle patents appearing to possess commercial potential so as to be able to extract heavy royalty payments from their use. In order to establish this monopoly on technical innovation no expense was spared in instituting legal proceedings for infringement, a tactic designed to induce caution among would-be inventors.

In attempting to produce a British-made motor vehicle in 1895 Herbert Austin ranks as one of the two British pioneers; the other was the distinguished engineer and scientist, F. W. Lanchester. But whereas Lanchester was experimenting with the manufacture of motor cars proper at this time, Herbert Austin and others followed the lead of de Dion Bouton and Renault, building voiturettes and the other low-powered vehicles.[15] Herbert's second car (another three-wheeled vehicle), was the first true Wolseley known to have been designed and built by Herbert Austin. It was first shown at the National Cycle Exhibition at the Crystal Palace in December 1896.[16] For the next two or three years it was modified in numerous ways, as its creator experimented with one or other mechanism or feature after another. By 1898, the Wolseley Autocar Number 1, as it was called, which completed a 250 mile journey from Birmingham to Rhyl and back, incorporated several Austin patents taken out in conjunction with the

[13] St. John Nixon, *Wolseley*, p. 22.

[14] Lambert & Wyatt, pp. 47–50. I am grateful for enlightenment on this subject by Mr. Freddie Henry.

[15] St. John Nixon, *The Antique Automobile* (1956), p. 70. C. F. Caunter refers to it as 'perhaps more important as the earliest work of Herbert Austin, rather than as a forerunner of the light car'. C. F. Caunter, *The Light Car* (HMSO 1970), p. 5.

[16] Lambert & Wyatt, p. 50.

WSSMC, including tubular frame design, belt transmission and independent rear wheel suspension.[17]

The third Wolseley car of 1899–1900, the Voiturette, demonstrably embodied the results of research on the first two cars, for this, the first of Herbert Austin's four-wheeled vehicles, used a channel section steel frame and incorporated features retained for many years in subsequent Wolseley motor cars. The Voiturette achieved resounding success at the first great public trial organized by the Auto Club of Great Britain in 1900, when over one thousand miles of driving tested the capabilities of the pioneer motor cars.[18] With Herbert Austin himself at the wheel, the Voiturette won the Daily Mail first prize in its class and received a silver medal awarded by the Auto Club de France.[19]

Such achievements established the Wolseley marque, and won recognition for Herbert Austin as a leading innovator. It is hardly surprising that the acclaim which accompanied this victory immediately raised in Herbert Austin's mind the question of commencing the manufacture of motor cars on a business footing, a venture which raised the problem of finance, hitherto provided by Wolseley. Other firms to show an interest in the commercial possibilities included Vickers Sons and Maxim Ltd., the engineering and armaments firm which had decided to enter the motor trade in 1896. The reasons were twofold: one was the Company's considerable experience in metallurgy and mechanics, which the managers thought offered an advantage in developing the trade; the other was the critical association between mechanically propelled vehicles and munitions, which accounted for the bulk of the Company's production.[20] Two years later, Sir Hiram Maxim entered into an agreement with F. R. Simms, an engineer and inventor already prominent in the motor trade through his connections with the Daimler Company, by which Simms undertook to assign to Vickers all of his motor vehicle inventions which might be applicable to military use. Under this agreement he was to design and superintend the construction of a 'motor war car'. When the Wolseley Voiturette amply demonstrated that an all-British car could withstand the rigours of the Thousand Mile Trial of 1900, the arma-

[17] St. John Nixon, *Wolseley*, pp. 28–31.

[18] *Motoring Illustrated*, 12 December 1907.

[19] The 1,000 miles trial of 1900 revealed the weakness of belt drive and it was after this that Herbert Austin redesigned the transmission in order to provide friction clutch and chain drive. St. John Nixon, *The Antique Automobile* (1956), p. 69.

[20] Lambert & Wyatt, pp. 66–7.

ments men were so impressed that Sir Hiram, who had already exchanged letters with Herbert Austin on the subject of aeronautical engineering design, approached him with a view to a closer association.[21]

At the same time that the Vickers and Maxim Company was seeking a foothold in the motor industry, Herbert was attempting to extricate himself from the ailing WSSMC, the directors of which felt unwilling, or unable, to expand the finance necessary to back Herbert's initiative in motor car production. His experimental work was done in the evenings and road tests were carried out at weekends,[22] and the frustration experienced in this period is clearly indicated in a letter written to the directors in 1899, a reply to their request for detailed accounts of works expenditure. In it he criticized their deficiencies and the resulting liquidity constraints which hampered his own managerial efforts: 'I regret I have not the spare time to give you even an approximate statement, that would in any case be very misleading. . . . I am quite conversant with the difficult position the company is in regarding money, but think it would tend to make matters run more smoothly if I were taken a little more into the confidence of the Board instead of being treated as I have been lately, more like one of the mechanics.'[23] His sense of dissatisfaction may well have been aroused by the example of one of the other major pioneers of British motor design, F. W. Lanchester, who in order to supplement his own meagre resources had sought external financial backing for the building of motor cars as early as 1894.[24] Knowing that the financial resources of the WSSMC would be inadequate to support a sizeable investment in motor car production, and despairing of the directors' serious underestimate both of his achievements and his capabilities, Herbert sought financial backing elsewhere.

He began with Captain Frank Kayser, a director of Kayser Ellison &

[21] St. John Nixon, *Wolseley*, pp. 41–3.

[22] 'Sir Herbert Austin KBE, His Life Story', *Autocar*, 6 September 1929.

[23] WSSMC Papers, Herbert Austin to the Board of Directors, 28 January 1899.

[24] That original syndicate had been followed by a second in 1899, when more substantial financial support was provided by the Pughs, the successful bicycle financiers later to become involved in the formation of Rudge Whitworth. A company with a capital of £45,525, of which £25,000 was subscribed, was established to exploit F. W. Lanchester's motor patents, and between 1901 and 1905 it manufactured and sold between three and four thousand motor cars. P. W. Kingsford, *F. W. Lanchester, A Life of An Engineer* (1960), pp. 33–44.

Co. of Sheffield, Wolseley's steel supplier.[25] He was the son of Charles William Kayser, an old friend of Herbert Austin, who had a financial interest in Wolseley and a seat on the Board.[26] To Frank Kayser Herbert complained that he had revived the business by re-organizing and re-equipping the works mainly from reserves; that he had repeatedly paid expenses from his own pocket; and that despite the fact that a good part of the sheep shearing business arose from patents and improvements which he had introduced, the directors had acknowledged it neither in adequate remuneration nor in status. He proceeded to enlarge on his achievement in building up a ramshackle works, the assets of which he claimed had risen from less then £10,000 when he arrived to £40,000. Of a turnover amounting to £25,000, more than £10,000 arose from general engineering for the home trade, which Herbert claimed was due entirely to his own efforts:

> I have worked like a slave ever since I came here . . . and yet today despite having lived a very quiet retired life I couldn't raise £200 outside my household goods. . . . Without wishing to be egotistical, I believe I could do what I have done again; and I ought to be in a position to start better than I did the first time. Do you wonder at my being satisfied? Would you be pleased with the position? After spending years of hard work which has always been successful so far as the works have been concerned? If I had been a drunken waster or an incompetent mechanic then I should expect to be low down but I have got energy still left to make a good bid for something better.[27]

Indeed he had; and two factors explain why the bid was formulated in the winter of 1899–1900. One was the imminent expiry of his contract with the Wolseley Company in February 1900, which by this time he considered unsatisfactory: 'The Company are not in a position, and never will be under the present Board, to take advantage of the many valuable patents they hold and which in the past have been allowed to die out or become obsolete before anything has been done. . . . After February it will be necessary to give me a stake in the Company that will be progressive.'[28] The other factor was the progress made with the third Wolseley car which induced in him a spirit of

[25] St. John Nixon, *Wolseley*, pp. 41, 60.

[26] Companies House File 29846, Wolseley Sheep Shearing Machine Co., Memorandum of Agreement, 26 January 1897. WSSMC Papers, Herbert Austin to Frank Kayser, 19 August 1899.

[27] WSSMC Papers, Herbert Austin to Frank Kayser, 19 August 1899.

[28] Ibid.

optimism. He told Kayser in December 1899: 'Our little motor car is quite a success. Runs splendidly and not a bit of trouble. This is . . . a business we have a good chance in.'[29] The idea he put to Kayser was that the motor and engineering work, for which Herbert would be responsible, might with advantage be separated from the sheep shearing work to form two separate organizations under a parent company. Sheep shearing work for the Wolseley Company would be carried out and charged for at a fixed rate, and all of the home trade, presumably motor and general engineering, completed on its own account. He continued: 'I mention this as being perhaps a good way to fix up matters as I believe I could influence a good amount of capital if a new concern were started.'[30]

Evidently Kayser showed interest, though there is no further mention of the idea of a holding company, and with the intention of securing support from some of Kayser's friends before going to the public for finance, Herbert prepared a draft prospectus together with detailed estimates of the expenditure on plant and equipment required for undertaking general engineering and motor manufacturing independently (Appendix 1). Assuring Kayser that numerous letters of inquiry showed evidence of mounting interest in the Wolseley cars, Herbert concluded: 'I am building great hopes on the success of the undertaking and cannot help being a little enthusiastic.'[31] His plan, therefore, was to try to form a public company with a nominal capital of £30,000. With this in view he sought the assistance of Alfred Hitchen (of Howard & Bullough Ltd., an Accrington firm of engineers), whom he knew to be interested in motor cars, to canvass support among Hitchen's friends; but in the meantime Hitchen had decided to finance his own private venture into the trade.[32]

[29] His car could reach a speed of 1½ miles in eight minutes. WSSMC Papers, Herbert Austin to Frank Kayser, 14 December 1899.

[30] Ibid.

[31] Herbert Austin to Frank Kayser, 29 September 1900. Herbert estimated the minimum initial investment necessary to be £5,000 for machinery, tools, and equipment; £5,000 on manufacture, advertising, etc.; and a weekly outlay on wages, salaries, fees, rates and taxes of £308 17*s.* 0*d.* This assumed a workforce of thirty-two mechanics, forty-three assistants and labourers, together with clerks, storekeepers, foremen, draughtsmen and a manager. He reckoned that in order to break even it would be necessary to turn out one and a half cars at a net selling price of £200 each per week, and the weekly maximum production capacity of the plant he envisaged was between two and three cars.

[32] Hitchen rented part of an old cotton mill and during the next three years produced a total of twenty-four Globe cars. His strategy was to enter the motor

For reasons outlined above, it was round about this time that Sir Hiram Maxim almost certainly approached Herbert with a proposal that Vickers should finance the development and production of Wolseley cars by taking over the machine tool and motor manufacturing side of the existing Wolseley enterprise, retaining him as manager.[33] Not only did this scheme accord with Herbert's own plans, but it also enabled the Wolseley directors to retire profitably from what they considered to be a dispensable experiment in motor engineering. In February 1901 Vickers registered the Wolseley Tool & Motor Car Co. Ltd. with a capital of £40,000, consisting of 10,000 £1 Preference and 30,000 £1 Ordinary Shares.[34]

Herbert's managerial agreement, which extended over five years from 1 March 1901, included a three months' notice clause, an annual salary of £500, and 5 per cent of the Company's net profits. The Wolseley Sheep Shearing Machine Company was debarred from participation in the motor trade, and took up the manufacture of cream separators as a substitute. After an initial transfer period of nine months, Herbert was to be allowed to act as a director or consultant to the old Company, spending such time on its affairs as would not prejudice his full contribution to the management of the new enterprise. This was an opportunity which, despite his differences with the directors in the recent past, he accepted, continuing to serve on the board of the Wolseley Sheep Shearing Machine Company for thirty-two years.[35]

The Wolseley manufacturing operations were located at the Adderley Park Works in Birmingham, acquired by Vickers in 1899

---

trade on a modest scale as an insurance against a serious deterioration in the firm's trade in cotton machinery. Only in that eventuality was it Hitchen's intention to build up a great motor business. When a large expansion in the demand for cotton machinery occurred in 1902 the motor business was closed down. Pollitt Papers, 1, 8/486.

[33] Lambert & Wyatt, pp. 41, 62–8; *Motor Car Journal*, 2 February 1901.

[34] In the following year, as holder or joint holder of some of the patents owned by the vendor company, Herbert entered into an agreement with the two Wolseley Companies for the transfer of the machine tool and motor manufacturing interests and patents to the new Wolseley Tool & Motor Car Company. The purchase price for patents, machinery, stock and uncompleted contracts amounted to £22,500, of which £12,500 was paid in cash and £10,000 by the issue of 5 per cent Second Debentures.

[35] From 1911 until 1933 he was its Chairman. Lambert & Wyatt, pp. 65–9; St. John Nixon, *Wolseley*, pp. 42–4.

and sold to the new Wolseley Company on its formation for £31,545. Herbert Austin and his assistant, Trevor Rapson, formerly of the American machine tool company of Browne & Sharpe, immediately put in hand the construction of a single-cylinder 5 h.p. chassis and a twin cylinder 10 h.p. model, each available with either a 'Forneau' or 'Phaeton' body and a choice between pneumatic or solid tyres;[36] the first catalogue of Wolseley cars issued by the new company in May 1901 also listed a 'racing car' and two delivery vans.[37] It has been estimated that perhaps fifty vehicles were produced in 1901 and around 270 in 1902; 341 in 1903 and 850 in 1904, the peak under Herbert's management. After an initial loss of £5,429 in 1901, profits accrued in 1902 (£5,429 on a turnover of £82,247), and 1903 (£12,512 on a turnover of £132,456). The modest loss in 1904 (£2,579 on a turnover of £137,140) was the first of a series of substantial losses, heralding Herbert Austin's departure from Wolseley and his severance from the Vickers financial lifeline.

In 1903 the Vickers Board had sanctioned the issue of a further £90,000 in shares to expand Wolseley's capital, to which was added a £40,000 personal loan from Douglas Vickers one year later.[38] But soon Vickers's financial investment was also extended to support the manufacture of Siddeley cars,[39] for the directors had already begun to show diminishing confidence in their Wolseley manager. One problem was Herbert's persistence with an engine design which most commentators considered to have become anachronistic, and he remained completely impervious to criticism. The first clear sign that matters were to reach a crisis was the first recorded attendance of J. D. Siddeley at a Vickers Board Meeting in May 1905, when there was discussion of the possibility of purchasing Siddeley's Autocar Company. Whereupon Douglas and Albert Vickers, responsible for capital expenditure and policy, formed themselves into a Committee of Investigation.[40]

Siddeley, formerly a draughtsman in a bicycle factory and afterwards a salesman for a Belfast tyre company, had been selling cars from his

[36] Giving evidence in 1906 Herbert Austin remarked that Wolseley had made a larger percentage of cars with solid tyres than most other companies, but that pneumatic tyres had now become simple, effective, and reasonably priced. *Royal Commission on Motor Cars*, P.P. XLVIII, 1906, Cd. 3081, evidence of H. Austin 6831–2, 6865.

[37] St. John Nixon, *Wolseley*, p. 44; The Pollitt Papers, 1, 8/300.

[38] Lambert & Wyatt, pp. 70–2.

[39] *Automotor Journal*, 18 April 1903.

[40] Lambert & Wyatt, p. 72.

London base since 1902, fixing his own radiators to Peugeot chassis and offering them to the public as Siddeley cars.[41] With its characteristic honeycomb radiator and square bonnet, the commercial success of the Siddeley car since its first appearance at the Crystal Palace Show early in 1903 seemed to augur well for the future prospects of the Siddeley Autocar Company.[42] A significant factor which helped to explain the contrasting prospects of Wolseley and Siddeley was the latter's preference for a newly designed vertical engine incorporated in the Peugeot cars. Convinced of their superiority over horizontal engines, Siddeley approached the Vickers Brothers, whose firm Siddeley hoped could be persuaded to manufacture vertical engined cars of his own design under a licence agreement. Hitherto committed to Herbert Austin's horizontal Wolseleys, by 1905 the Vickers Brothers were well aware that vertical engines had become the accepted trend in design for motor vehicles in Europe, and by agreement with Siddeley a prototype with vertical engine was duly manufactured at the Crayford factory.

Thus, the Company with which Herbert's reputation was identified proceeded to manufacture the vertical engine cars which he had persistently condemned as inferior to his own horizontal Wolseleys.[43] Albert Vickers failed to persuade him to experiment with vertical engines, and it seemed that the acquisition of Siddeley, which occurred in the summer of 1905, offered a prudent insurance against future losses, as did the appointment of J. D. Siddeley as manager. It is not clear exactly what happened next, but some disagreement occurred after which Herbert appears to have left Adderley Park in a huff.[44] Albert Vickers requested Herbert's resignation, which was duly submitted before the end of the year, four months before his contract was due to expire; Herbert also asked the Vickers brothers to buy back his holdings in Wolseley.[45] Siddeley took over the vertical Siddeleys under the Wolseley marque, superseding the horizontal Wolseleys, but profits plummeted for four years following Herbert's departure, total losses amounting to nearly £200,000 in that period.

[41] Kenneth Richardson, *Twentieth Century Coventry* (1972), p. 55.

[42] St. John Nixon, *Wolseley*, pp. 60–1.

[43] Ibid., pp. 61–3; *Motoring Illustrated*, 12 January 1907; *Automotor Journal*, 18 April 1903.

[44] Lambert and Wyatt maintain that the horizontal engine issue was an excuse rather than the reason for the disagreement with Vickers, pp. 87–8.

[45] W. A. Howitt, letter to *Bromsgrove, Droitwich and Redditch Weekly Messenger*, 21 June 1952; Lambert & Wyatt, p. 74.

Under criticism for clinging to out-dated design and blamed by implication for the losses incurred by the car-making company, the circumstances surrounding his departure from Wolseley could hardly have been more prejudicial to the future business career of Herbert Austin, then aged thirty-eight. The prospects for re-establishing his position in the industry appeared less than promising, but they might have been worse. His period with Wolseley had enabled him to experiment, to experience some of the problems of motor car production on a more than modest scale, and to establish contacts within the industry. Indeed, he might have recalled the recent melancholy fate of F. W. Lanchester, whose cash flow problems had forced the Lanchester Motor Company into the Receiver's hands in 1904; who was forced to resign from the position of general manager in 1905 after reconstruction, and who failed to raise sufficient capital even to qualify as a director of his former company.[46] Another leading engineer, R. W. Maudsley, had also seen his own creation, the Standard Motor Company, fall into the hands of an outsider only four years after its formation in 1903, leaving the founder as a salaried managing director without any share in profits.[47] Through the intervention of others outside the firm, and of Barclays Bank, Maudsley was to succeed in retrieving his managerial position at Standard, whereas Lanchester remained on the periphery of motor manufacture.

Herbert Austin's own experience, however, is more similar to that of W. G. Wilson, an inventor and pioneer in the motor trade, whose tiny London car-making firm of Wilson, Pilcher & Co. Ltd., lacking capital and hampered in production, was taken over, with his full agreement, by Armstrong Whitworth in 1904. Wilson had assumed control of Armstrong's motor car venture, the resulting Wilson-Pilcher vehicles being retailed through the Company's London premises. Tensions resembling in essence those which arose between Austin and Vickers led to the termination of Wilson's contract by Armstrong in 1907.[48] Such unstable relationships between inventor,

[46] He eventually resigned in 1914. P. W. Kingsford, *F. W. Lanchester*, pp. 51–4.

[47] The outsider was Charles Friswell, who owned a well-established motor distributing agency and obtained dominance in Standard through an exclusive agreement to sell Standard motor cars. Standard Motor Company Minute Book, 18 January, 8 February, 9 March, 1907; Pollitt Papers, *Red Book of Commerce*, 1911/361.

[48] R. J. Irving, 'New Industries for Old, Some Investment Decisions of Armstrong Whitworth 1900–1914', *Business History*, 17 (1975), 166–7.

offering ideas and technical expertise, and industrialists, providing capital, connections, and other resources, are typical of the early phase of motor manufacture. They reflected the uncertainty produced by a rapidly changing technology and the search for marketable models.

CHAPTER TWO

The Foundation of the Austin Motor Company

CONVINCED THAT HIS OWN FUNDAMENTAL ERROR was to have managed a business without owning it, Herbert had formed his own company within months of his departure from Vickers. By September 1905, before he had actually resigned from Wolseley, he had already chosen a disused printing works at Longbridge, near Birmingham, as the site where he would begin to manufacture motor cars on his own account. The works were of relatively modern construction, capable of employing about 800 men, and equipped with engines, generators, boilers, piping etc. for power, lighting, and heating purposes, and sprinklers with water supply. With little alteration required he reckoned that production could begin only three weeks after taking possession.[1]

The asking price for land, buildings and fixtures was £10,000. For the initial weekly production target of two chassis, each valued at £400, investment in plant and equipment was estimated to cost £7,900, which was expected to sustain output at that level for a year (Appendix 2). To weekly purchases of about £250 and a similar sum for wages was added £2,000 a year for salaries, £1,000 for advertising, £500 for exhibitions and trials, £350 for catalogues and stationery, £1,000 for insurances and other sundry items, legal charges and rates. Against an anticipated total current expenditure of £36,850 for the year was set the sale of 100 chassis to bring a revenue of £45,000.[2] But the lag between production and sales posed a considerable financial

[1] Austin Motor Company Papers (hereafter AMC papers). Estimate of expenditure in connection with the establishment of a works for manufacture of motor vehicles at Longbridge near Birmingham, 6 September 1905.

[2] Presumably the figure of £45,000 includes a 12½ per cent mark-up on the cost, or 'value', of the chassis referred to above.

problem. His calculations assumed that the works would be rented and that the owner would agree to take four quarterly instalments to pay for fixtures and plant. This meant that the initial outlay required over the four months, before the first Austin car could be offered for sale, would be about £11,000.[3] Scribbled estimates reveal hypothetical methods of financing his new venture, which required supplementation in addition to the £4,000 raised by the Wolseley debentures when sold back to Vickers, plus whatever personal savings he had.[4]

It has not been possible to establish which of these options was agreed when the Austin Motor Co. Ltd. was formed in December 1905 with a nominal capital of £50,000 in £1 shares; but it seems likely that whereas most, if not all, of the £5,629 ordinary share capital subscribed belonged to Herbert himself, much of the remaining initial financial support, consisting of £3,000 in debentures, £8,500 loaned on mortgage, and a simple loan of £2,850 was provided by Kayser.[5] About a year later, the two directors, Herbert Austin and Frank Kayser, were joined by Harvey du Cros, Junior, managing director of the Swift Cycle Company and a director of Components Ltd.[6] from whom the Company received further financial support. In 1906 paid-up capital increased to £28,648, doubling in 1907. The initial expenditure consisted of £7,750 for purchase of the works, £6,521 spent on plant, fixtures and tools, £2,272 for building, and £317 on preliminary expenses: a total of £16,861.[7] Frank Kayser's personal guarantee, supported by preference shares in Kayser Ellison & Co., enabled the

[3] AMC Papers, 'Estimates of Expenditure'.

[4] 'If K. or other lends 5,000 pay him 6% interest = £300
10,000 pay him 6% interest = £600
and give him one-fifth share on net profit for three years
15,000 £900
and give him one-quarter share or so for three years.
Loan to be for five years or at my option to pay off altogether in three years.'

[5] In his autobiographical article in *Autocar*, 6 September 1929, the starting capital was put at £15,000, but what was probably the Certified Report of the Company's first meeting shows the total to have been £19,979. AMC Papers, December 1905.

[6] Harvey du Cros (Senior) was Chairman of the Dunlop Pneumatic Tyre Co. Ltd., of the Patent Tyre Co. Ltd., of the Coupé Company and Motor Cab Company of Great Britain and of the Société des Cycles Clement and Gladiator Ltd. He held a directorship, too, in the Clipper Tyre Co. Ltd. *Directory of Directors*, 1905; 'Sir Herbert Austin', *Autocar*, 6 September 1929, p. 453.

[7] AMC Papers, Certified Report, 28 February 1908.

Company to secure working capital from the Midland Bank in the form of an initial overdraft of £5,000; this was extended to £10,000 in 1907, when profits fell from £5,308 on the first year of trading to only £1,393 on a vastly increased turnover of £84,930[8] (Table 1). This was a critical year when the Bank's support was of vital importance to Austin.

After solving the problem of finding initial capital, the growth of the firm depended upon three principal sources of finance. Of these the largest contribution came from suppliers and from customers' deposits, the confidence of both groups reflecting Herbert's reputation and the success of the first motor car produced by the new Company. The second most important source was the Midland Bank, well satisfied with the Company's profit record which, after the first two years of disappointment, improved steadily until 1913. Profits retained in the business provided the third element in Company finance; although high as the percentage figures were in comparison with other sources, the Bank's contribution exceeded reinvested profits by a considerable margin in most years (Table 2) and not until 1913 did the Company's bank balance move into the black. One source of financial weakness after 1908 was the relatively high proportion of net profits distributed in the form of dividends, Kayser and du Cros undoubtedly being the major shareholders and the major beneficiaries (Table 2). The finely balanced liquidity ratios, showing current assets barely covering current liabilities in this period,[9] are evidence of a recurrent problem in finding working capital to finance rapid growth. Turnover nearly doubled between 1908 and 1910, and more than doubled again in the following three years to reach £425,641. Nonetheless, thanks to banking support and an extended overdraft to £30,000, by 1911 the debentures and loans had been paid off and a small reserve had been established.[10]

Expanding trade required much larger and longer term capital than the overdraft. In 1913 a chance remark by Herbert to the chief director

[8] Midland Bank Archives (hereafter MBA) 509 Midland Diary, 2, 22 May 1907; Midland Diary, 3, 8 June 1911. AMC Papers.

[9] Not until 1913 did the ratio of current assets to current liabilities exceed 1.2.

[10] 'The opinion is strongly held that the permanent character of the motor trade is more established than ever and it looks like being a continuous and prospering industry. The Lanchester Company tells us that they have more orders on their books now than at any previous period of their history, while the Austin Motor Company has no less than £300,000 of orders on hand for the coming season.' MBA, 509, Midland Diary, 3, 23 November 1911.

Table 1: Sales Turnover and Profits of Austin Motor Co. Ltd., 1906–1918

Year	Net trading profit* (a) £	Sales turnover (b) £	Net tangible assets† (c) £	(a) as % of (b)	(a) as % of (c)
1906‡	5,308	14,772	31,279	35.9	16.9
1907	1,393	84,930	57,525	1.6	2.4
1908	14,915 (11 months)	119,744	79,350	(13.6) §	(20.5)
1909	18,439	169,821	98,903	10.9	18.6
1910	26,111	209,048	99,889	12.5	26.0
1911	34,062	276,196	155,065	12.3	21.9
1912	50,533	354,209	190,695	14.3	26.5
1913	31,399	425,641	289,605	7.4	10.8
1914‖	30,302	633,186	471,596	0.5	6.4
1915¶	63,909	890,083	534,872	7.2	11.9
1916	227,177	2,208,187	977,323	10.3	23.2
1917	262,642	3,765,029	1,638,925	6.9	16.0
1918	358,272	9,535,680**	1,837,853	1.4	19.5

* After taxes, maintenance and depreciation, fees and debenture interest. Profit figures before these deductions are not available.

† Defined as fixed and current assets less liabilities.

‡ October year.

§ Percentages in brackets refer to twelve-month estimates.

‖ The figures for 1914–16 refer to the Austin Motor Co. (1914) Ltd.

¶ From 1915 Austin's profits were subject to Excess Profits Duty, payable after 1918.

** This figure includes £5,546,680, for shell production at the Ministry factories, known as the North and West Works, and £2,591,376 for aeroplanes.

of Krupps, from whom he purchased pressed steel underframes, that his own Company was 'rather cramped for want of capital' led to an immediate offer from Krupps of £100,000, secured by debenture for five years. Herbert approached his own bank manager for a reaction; this proved to be the offer of an advance of £100,000 over a fixed term against debentures and £20,000 more against guarantees at current interest rates. An agreement was prevented by the Bank's insistence that should Austin default in repayment of any of the annual instalments, then the balance of the advance was to become due immediately. Herbert also wished the Bank to treat both current and loan accounts as one for the purpose of calculating interest payments, but this the Bank declined to do.[11] Whether Krupp's offer was accepted

[11] When the bank's terms were refused and a public issue mentioned, the Midland's Chairman's comment was 'let them do it; I am not going to be jigged about by them'. MBA, 509, Midland Diary, 23 January, 20 February, 30 December 1913.

Table 2: Capital Structure and Finance

Year	(a) Capital employed: Ordinary paid-up capital	(a) Capital employed: Debentures, mortgages and loans	(b) Net profit after maintenance, depreciation, interest and tax	(c) Retained in the Company for development	(d) (c) as % of (a)	(e) Net profit as % of ordinary and preference shares, plus debentures, mortgages and loans	(f) Dividends on ordinary shares, %
	£	£	£	£			
1906	28,648	13,500	5,308	5,308	100	12.6	—
1907	56,648	13,500	1,393	1,393	100	2.0	—
1908	56,648	13,500	14,915 (11 months)	7,238	48.5	(22.6)	15
1909	64,400	8,500	18,439	53	0.3	25.9	36
1910	80,000	—	26,111	20,194	77.3	32.6	—
1911	80,000	—	34,062	16,194	49.8	36.4	25
1912	90,000	—	50,533	35,953	71.1	41.9	10
1913	90,000	103,000	31,399	15,940	50.8	12.1	17.5

Figure in brackets indicates twelve-month estimate.

we do not know, but in 1913 the debenture mortgage and loan liability rose from zero to £103,000 (Table 2).[12]

Viewed as an investment, the Company yielded high returns on funds after the difficulties of the first two years (Table 2), a financial success behind which lay a somewhat less impressive trading efficiency, as indicated by the rate of profit on turnover and on assets employed (Tables 1 and 3). Meanwhile, the work force expanded steadily. Series of production and employment figures are not available and we must rely on random observations from diverse sources. In 1929 Sir Herbert recalled that 147 cars were built in 1907 and that 400 workers were involved.[13] By 1910 production had risen to 576, to more than 1,000 in 1912, with about 1,500 workmen, and to 1,500 units in 1913, when the total workforce had risen to 2,300.[14]

* * *

Much of the initial finance had been required to purchase the factory, a derelict printing works at Longbridge near Rubery, which at that time was a truly rural village close to the Lickey Hills, seven miles to the south-west of Birmingham. Situated between the Bristol Road and the branch line of the Midland Railway, which was adjacent to the factory, the Longbridge location offered direct communication with the Black Country and immediate access to the major arterial Bristol Road. While communication was doubtless the most important factor influencing his decision, other advantages were the ample space for expansion on two and a half acres of land remote from the expanding City, and the unpolluted atmosphere considered to be necessary to achieve high quality paint and varnish finishes. Despite criticism for locating his business so distant from the City, Herbert Austin remained convinced of the wisdom of such a choice.[15]

Early in November 1905 he moved into the uninviting buildings with his staff, and selected a room for his personal office, whence he ruled Longbridge until 1940 shortly before he died.[16] Before the new

[12] AMC Papers.

[13] 'Sir Herbert Austin KBE', *Autocar*, 23 August 1929; J. S. Critchley, *British Motor Vehicles* (1912), p. 56; *Garage and Motor Agent*, 7 February 1914.

[14] Car production fell to 983 in 1914. 'Sir Herbert Austin KBE, His Life Story', *Autocar*, 6 September 1929.

[15] 'Sir Herbert Austin KBE, His Life Story', *Autocar*, 6 September 1929.

[16] Lambert & Wyatt, p. 170; W. A. Howitt, letter to *Bromsgrove, Droitwich and Redditch Weekly Messenger*, 21 June 1952.

Table 3: Profits and Assets Employed 1906–1913

Year	(a) Net tangible assets	(b) Net tangible assets plus loans	(c) Net profit after maintenance, depreciation, tax and debenture interest	(d) c/a	(d) c/b
	£	£	£	%	%
1906	31,279	47,684	5,308	16.9	11.1
1907	57,525	76,753	1,393	2.4	1.8
1908	79,350	107,843 (11 mths)	14,915 (11 mths)	(20.5)	(15.1)
1909	98,903	121,117	18,915	18.6	15.2
1910	99,889	125,312	26,111	26.0	20.8
1911	155,065	182,266	34,062	21.9	18.7
1912	190,695	219,323	50,533	26.5	23.0
1913	289,605	392,605	31,399	10.8	8.0

It has not been possible to show cash flow defined as profits before tax and depreciation, as these are not identifiable in the financial data to be found among the AMC Papers. Debenture interest is also unrecorded, but when a 5 per cent allowance is made on debentures, mortgages and loans and added to the profit figures the result, when expressing estimated net profits plus debenture interest expressed as a percentage of net tangible assets, is to increase the rate of return by barely 1 per cent in most years.

Column b has been included, as has the ratio $\frac{c}{b}$ in recognition that capital employed is sometimes defined as net tangible assets less current liabilities but including loans.

firm could begin to think of manufacture, it was necessary to design the Company's first 'Austin' motor car and to test its public appeal; consequently it was in the study of Herbert Austin's Erdington home in the autumn of 1905 that he, together with A. J. Hancock and A. V. Davidge, set to work to prepare drawings for display at the Crystal Palace Motor Exhibition in November 1905.[17] It is a testimony to Herbert Austin's reputation that even on the basis of these drawings the new Company obtained several orders. The single model was a four-cylinder car of approximately 20 h.p. (18/24) of medium size, incorporating the vertical engine which he had spurned during his time at Wolseley, and with petrol tank at the rear.[18] The 'clean layout' of

[17] Among his original management team, recruited from Wolseley, were A. J. Hancock (design), A. V. Davidge (advertising), A. W. Jones (office staff, later to become company secretary), and W. A. Howitt, Herbert's personal assistant, who was to remain at Longbridge until 1941. *Austin Advocate*, XV, September 1926, XVI, January 1927; 'Sir Herbert Austin KBE, His Life Story', *Autocar*, 6 September 1929; A. J. W. Hancock, 'Lord Austin – Engineering Genius', *Motor*, 6 July 1955.

[18] 'Sir Herbert Austin KBE, His Life Story', *Autocar*, 30 August 1929, p. 400.

this model, according to one motor historian, 'started a new trend in the general design of motor cars as a whole . . . the life and reliability of these early models undoubtedly established a foundation upon which the dependability of Austin-made cars was built'.[19] When the first Austin car was completed, journalists and others attended an inaugural lunch at the Longbridge Works in April 1906,[20] and in November the chassis of two Austin Longbridge Limousines, priced at £800, were displayed at the Olympia Exhibition.[21] By the end of 1906 the fifty or so workers had produced twelve cars, and in the first full year of trading output reached 120.[22]

It was not long before Austin was producing three types of chassis, the original 18/24 h.p., a 40 h.p., and a 60 h.p. model, but to these could be fitted more than a dozen different Austin-built bodies, whose quality also drew praise from observers.[23] Austin was one of the leaders in switching from the open landaulet to the closed limousine body, and through the columns of the motor trade press Herbert urged other British manufacturers to follow his example.[24] He feared that British manufacturers would continue to lag behind their French competitors, both in design and economy, unless chassis builders and body makers

[19] Lambert & Wyatt, p. 92.

[20] *Automotor Journal*, 28 April 1906; *Times*, 28 June 1926.

[21] The *Autocar* commended the car to its readers. After praising the soundness of design throughout, the notice continued: 'It is an engineer's job in the best sense of the word, and the accessibility of those parts which should be readily available and easily opened to examination is very much above average.' *Autocar*, 7 September 1907.

[22] 'Sir Herbert Austin KBE, His Life Story', *Autocar*, 6 September 1929; *Times Engineering Supplement*, 2 October 1912; *Motor Trader*, 4 February 1914; *Times*, 10 February 1914; *Times*, 28 June 1926. Sir Herbert later recalled that in 1906 the Board had considered additional expenditure to enable production to rise to three chassis per week but deferred the matter.

[23] *Austin Advocate*, I, December 1911.

[24] *Autocar*, 5 January 1907. In a letter to *Autocar* in 1907 Herbert Austin compared the merits of the limousine and the landaulet, listing the features possessed by the limousine which made it a more comfortable and convenient touring carriage. These included the ability of 'a gentleman' to drive his own limousine, greater all-round visibility, the possibility of installing hat racks and receptacles for books and papers, the greater convenience of carrying light bulky packages, and the easier control over ventilation: 'It should be possible for a lady to raise or lower any portion from the inside while travelling without undue exertion, so that if the weather changes, or the current of air is too strong for any quarter, the windows may be instantly raised or lowered, so that sufficient ventilation is obtained without discomfort.'

co-operated in the design and construction of motor vehicles. Such was the message he delivered in a lecture before the Institute of British Carriage Manufacturers in 1911. Outlining the problems of body design and construction for the motor car, and offering detailed suggestions as to possible solutions for the various problems produced by the practical needs of motorized transport, he referred to his own early experience in carriage and body building with Wolseley, and thereafter at Longbridge. The chief difficulty had been persuading those responsible for carriage building to appreciate the necessity for accuracy in their measurements and construction in order to ensure a proper fit when the bodywork was mounted on the chassis. Yet the reluctance of clients to pay for the chassis before the body was completed (often several months later) rendered separate carriage building necessary, and this required absolutely accurate measurements both in chassis and body manufacture.[25]

Lack of co-operation from the carriage builders in this respect explained why, like some other large motor chassis builders, Austin's car bodies were produced in the same factory, and in 1912 Longbridge possessed one of the largest body building departments in Britain.[26] The result was that both the methods applied, and the materials used, were increasingly those more familiar to the engineer than to the carriage builder. The trend towards reduced weight, partly by the substitution of metal panels and mouldings for wood; standardization of design, made possible by the production of various parts by machinery; and the development of a vehicle's ability to withstand high speed and rough usage, all illustrate the increasing importance of the engineer, not only in chassis manufacture but in body building, too.[27] It was utterly characteristic that on the occasion of his election to the Presidency of the Institute of British Coachbuilders in 1913 Herbert Austin should have launched an attack on their conservatism, comparing them unfavourably with their French counterparts, and blaming them for having too long ignored the requirements and advice of the chassis manufacturers. He urged them to adopt greater standardization of frames and to assist chassis makers further by building

[25] *Motor Trader*, 11 February 1914.

[26] *Times Engineering Supplement*, 2 October 1912.

[27] Herbert Austin, 'The Carriage Body as Fitted to a Motor Chassis', *Autocar*, 9 September 1911; Sir Herbert Austin's 'Foreword' in Herbert J. Butler, *Motor Bodywork, The Design and Construction of Private, Commercial and Passenger Types* (1924).

for stock.[28] The combination of body with chassis production at Longbridge formed the basis of integrated manufacture by which he achieved a high degree of control over the quality of output, which the expensive Experimental Department at Longbridge also helped to secure. Rejecting any claim to produce the fastest or the quietest motor cars, Herbert regarded reliability as his highest priority,[29] though the 'carriage work' illustrated in Austin advertisements before 1914 tends to belie Herbert's claim to be progressive in this respect.

Achieving a reputation for reliability required demonstration and publicity, but Herbert seems to have been sceptical of pushful sales methods and claimed that his Company's advertising expenditure, principally in the trade press, formed a lower proportion of turnover than expenditure by competitors.[30] While managing Wolseley he had criticized the practice of allowing discounts over and above the normal trade discount to agents touting for commission on sales,[31] and later he became a persistent advocate of orderly dealing in the motor trade.[32] He was, however, one of the first motor manufacturers to establish showrooms outside the place of manufacture, beginning (curiously) with Norwich in 1910, followed in 1911 by Manchester, and by London's West End in 1912, where Austin owners could take advantage of a repair service or hire a car, or use the Club Rooms.[33] The introduction in 1911 of the *Austin Advocate*, 'as a weapon in the advertising armoury', was another innovating development, with Austin the first British car manufacturer to publish such a journal.[34]

[28] He conceded that some carriage builders were 'allying themselves' with chassis makers and offered to interpret his election as President as a sign that the old antagonism between chassis builders and carriage builders was at last passing away. *Autocar*, 1 February 1913.

[29] *Austin Advocate*, I, November 1911.

[30] *Austin Advocate*, I, July 1912.

[31] *Autocar*, 21 November 1903.

[32] Sir Miles Thomas, *Out on a Wing* (1964), pp. xx.

[33] *Autocar*, 11 October 1913; Companies House File 133747, Austin Motor Company leasehold agreements; *The Coming of Age of the Austin Motor Company 1905–1925* (AMC Publication, Birmingham 1926), p. 14. Armstrong Whitworth cars built in Newcastle were sold from premises in London from 1904, and a few years later arrangements were made to establish selling agencies in all major provincial towns. R. J. Irving, 'New Industries for Old; Some Investment Decisions of Armstrong Whitworth 1900–1914', *Business History*, 17 (1975), 166–7.

[34] It was described as 'a house organ without that insistent trade atmosphere – interesting, instructive, humorous, Austin owners have a right to it'. *Austin*

As for racing and exhibition, the two other main forms of advertising in the early history of the trade, Herbert had much to say. Clearly, in the pioneering phase of motor car development organized road trials provided both manufacturers and public with useful information, which the trade press expanded upon by ample coverage afforded to them. The sharp increase in Napier motor sales after S. F. Edge had driven a tuned production model to victory in the Gordon Bennett Trophy race in 1902[35] pointed to the benefits to be derived from competitive racing at that time by attracting enormous publicity for the car's qualities under testing conditions.[36] Herbert had driven the first Wolseley car in the 1,000 miles trial of 1900, drove as mechanic in one of the two 30 h.p. Wolseleys entered for the Gordon Bennett competition in 1902, and did so again in 1903. In neither race were the Wolseleys successful, but modifications were made as a result of the weaknesses identified in the course of the competitions, including the introduction of force feed lubrication.[37]

So long as he thought racing was capable of influencing car design and construction, he approved.[38] Nonetheless, the costs involved in international racing were, in Herbert's view, excessive, and the financial weakness of Wolseley at the time is doubtless relevant to the view he had expressed from an industry standpoint after the Gordon Bennett race in 1903. 'To achieve the Gordon Bennett cup next year we shall have to build a car which will be quite useless for anything but a speed contest, and we ought to do as little of this as possible if we are to husband our resources.'[39] For the individual company, however, successful exposure was critical in educating public opinion, and even during the first year of the new Company's existence Austin motor cars entered the 1906 three-day Scottish Reliability Trial and the Irish

---

Advocate, I, November 1911, II, November 1912; *Austin Magazine and Advocate*, I (new series), October 1927.

[35] Charles Wilson and William Reader, *Men and Machines: A History of D. Napier & Sons, Engineers, Ltd., 1808–1958* (1958).

[36] While he was with Wolseley, Herbert never lost an opportunity of entering the lists of competitive trials and races 'with a view to proving that simplicity and reliability were . . . valuable features in a car'. Furthermore, he always attended personally, superintending the arrangements.

[37] Lambert & Wyatt, p. 80. The investment in the racing Wolseleys was £2,000, the sum voted to Herbert for their construction.

[38] H. O. Duncan, *The World on Wheels* (Paris, 1926), p. 862.

[39] *Autocar*, 21 November 1903.

Reliability Trial where an Austin won the 100 Guineas Dunlop Challenge Cup. In 1908 Austin entered his cars for the first of a series of international competitions, and for the next four years a near standard-built 40 h.p. Austin Touring Car performed successfully, securing immensely valuable publicity.[40] It was in the same year that he also built the famous 100 h.p. Sports Car, which received publicity when Jack Johnson, the boxing champion, became a purchaser.[41] The construction and racing of high-power sports cars were enthusiastically encouraged by the *Autocar*, where it was argued that international success was vital if British manufacturers were to overcome the continental idea that British cars were inferior to those of European manufacture.[42]

Whereas Herbert was critical of international racing, grudging the costs incurred, nonetheless he accepted the case for British participation, advocating a more systematic organization and policy by the trade as a whole. His condemnation of the annual motor show at Olympia, however, was unqualified. He dismissed it as a waste of time, effort, and resources. In a letter to the *Autocar* in 1912, he argued that the Exhibition was no longer necessary to attract buyers as it was no longer common practice for most firms building cars to book their orders for the year ahead or for agents to place contracts for a whole year.[43] He argued that since neither agents nor private buyers now waited for the Exhibition before placing orders, it was not in the interests of manufacturers to reveal improvements and arrange sales only at the annual show. Austin's policy was to disregard the motor 'season' and not to await the Olympia Show before bringing out 'some startling novelty to the gaze of a marvelling world'.[44] Apart from the resulting spurious annual innovation which he thought the Show encouraged, Herbert was critical because of the damaging effect he alleged resulted from the

[40] Lambert & Wyatt, pp. 97–8. Herbert Austin also took the water speed record between 1910 and 1913 with *Irene*, *Irene II* and *Maple Leaf IV*, each incorporating a V.12 all aluminium, overhead camshaft unit. By communication from Mr. Freddie Henry, 6 April 1978.

[41] I am grateful to Mr. Freddie Henry for this information.

[42] *Austin Advocate*, I, November 1911; *Autocar*, 6 September 1929.

[43] That had been true when the Exhibition was inaugurated, and it had also been customary for the names of members of the public who purchased cars to appear on printed lists. By this arrangement customers had sought to derive reflected glory if the particular car of their choice had won some major event during the year. *Autocar*, 26 October 1912.

[44] *Austin Advocate*, I, November 1911.

organizers' exhibition policy. For he complained of the lack of discrimination in favour of British manufacturers, the preferred locations being allocated by ballot and so risking the display of inferior motor cars in favoured positions.[45]

By 1913, Herbert Austin's search for excellence and public appeal had led to a reduction in the number of basic models from six to three, though each was available with long or short wheel-base and a variety of body designs.[46] That year also saw the introduction of Austin commercial vehicles, light delivery vans, and a two to three ton lorry.[47] Missing from this range is any evidence of his previous experiments with really small 'light' cars. By 1909 Herbert had become influenced by a current trend towards the production of miniature replicas of four-cylinder motor cars, a reaction against the technical shortcomings of the cyclecar and a positive response to the apparent desire on the part of consumers, demonstrated later by the interest which the cyclecar boom of 1911–12 generated, to purchase a vehicle for less than £250. Peugeot had pioneered the miniature car on the Continent, and in Britain the 6 h.p. Rover of 1906, a single-cylinder model but with the appearance of a proper motor car, was the forerunner of four-cylinder vehicles designed for the small car market.[48] Herbert's experiments along these lines began in 1909 with a single-cylinder 7 h.p. car to be produced jointly with Swift, one of the du Cros companies,[49] followed by a four-cylinder Austin Ten, resembling

[45] He feared that these stands might be filled with 'any rubbish that may be imported or made in this country, and while our Press fill their columns about the cheap car, and incidentally encourage the public to think that we are backward or getting shameful profits, is it to be wondered at that the serious and conscientious manufacturer may sometimes "throw up the sponge" and forsake his ideals to the certain future detriment of the good name of an English automobile? If the Exhibition cannot be the means of encouragement to merit, and education and influence to the buying public, where is it likely to be obtained? Do the exhibitions at the Royal Academy draw lots for position? Is a motor designer any worse than a man who paints a picture or less deserving of encouragement to excel?' *Autocar*, 26 October 1912.

[46] Details are to be found in the annual issues of the *Autocar Buyers' Guide*.

[47] *Austin Advocate*, II, March 1913.

[48] *Cyclecar*, 10 September 1913; E. J. Appleby, 'The Small Car, An Outline History of the Modern Bijou Automobile', *Autocar*, 9 May 1930.

[49] In 1909 the *Autocar* reported plans for the joint production of a single-cylinder 7 h.p. car by Austin and Swift. This venture was described as 'a carefully considered effort to make a good miniature car for two persons embodying all the essential features of a larger vehicle and which shall [*sic*] have all its working

closely in miniature the successful Austin Twenty.[50] The Ten, which appeared on the market in November 1910, consisted of a four-cylinder engine, with the RAC rating of 10.1 h.p. and a chassis price of £290, roughly half the price of the Company's best selling model, the 18/24 h.p. four-cylinder Austin Twenty. But the initially under-powered Ten failed to secure a niche in the market for low to medium-priced motor cars, an enlarged engine generating 14.3 h.p. introduced in 1912 pushing it out of the newly emerging market for light cars.[51]

Model diversification is indicative of Herbert Austin's fertility as a designer, yet ran counter to the economical production of high quality cars on a repetition basis, which he claimed was his intention.[51a] Indeed, in 1912 a commentator pointed out that despite 'the large and comprehensive use of more or less automatic means of output' at Longbridge, the amount of hand-finishing still carried out showed that there was scope for further automatic tooling.[52] As a result of errors in jigs and machinery, cars required to be fitted manually at the assembly stage, which made it all the more difficult to supply accurate spare parts. The same observer also noted that the plant at Longbridge was remarkable more for the extraordinary variety and range of machine tools, than for the size of groupings. In the latter respect Austin's practice was not dissimilar from that characteristic of other up-to-date motor erecting shops. Components were manufactured in numerous small shops, then assembled in the chassis erection shop by groups consisting of three or four skilled mechanics competent to fit any part. A similar system brought component parts to the body department, which was quite separate from the chassis department, though before the body was finally mounted on to the chassis a test body was fitted to ensure that the final match was perfect.[53]

Such strictures are justified when applied to the years before 1912, from which time Austin car production increased from 576 to 1,500

parts up to their mark. It is not and does not profess to be cheap in the accepted sense of the term, but it is good throughout and cheap for quality.' There was no explanation as to how the joint venture was to be organized, and there is no evidence that co-operation did occur. *Autocar*, 23 October 1909.

[50] *Autocar*, 15 October 1910; *Austin Advocate*, I, December 1911.

[51] See below, pp. 37–8.

[51a] *Austin Advocate*, I, November 1911.

[52] *Automobile Engineering*, July 1912, pp. 212–7.

[53] *Motor Trader*, 4 February 1914.

within three years,[54] the investment associated with this expansion transforming the Longbridge factory, and eliciting considerable praise from the *Motor Trader* correspondent in 1914, who commented on Austin's plant and machinery of the most modern kind.[55] Herbert's personal experience with, and interest in, machine tools was undoubtedly an important contributory factor,[56] as was his difficulty in securing labour.[57] Investment in modernization also became easier (though not easy) as Austin's bank manager, characteristically cautious in industrial affairs, came to acknowledge the motor industry's 'permanent character' and extended credit accordingly.[58]

While the exceptionally heavy use of special purpose machine tools reduced the proportion of skilled to semi- and unskilled workers, which helps to account for the lesser specialization among Austin's workforce as compared with those of Wolseley and Sunbeam,[59] the introduction of such machinery was not always accomplished without friction. In the spring of 1913 the installation of a new and complex American duplicate drill into the erection shop caused a 'labour revolt' at Longbridge, and although the machine remained it was still operating at only half its full capacity in the spring of 1914.[60]

With a payroll at Longbridge on the eve of the First World War in excess of 2,000, Herbert paid increasing attention to communications within the firm and to relations with labour in particular.[61] An article in the *Motor Trader* in 1914 described the Austin Motor Company as a 'democratic body', in which Herbert Austin held weekly conferences with his departmental heads, including those in charge of the depots 'and others likely to have views useful to management'. But his recruitment policy, which required some practical knowledge of the mechanics of motor manufacture as qualification for appointment,

[54] *Austin Through the Years* (AMC publication, Birmingham, 1949).

[55] It included 455 machine tools, mostly British, valued at more than £50,000, and six of a new type of fully automatic turret lathe (Cincinnati) capable of the heaviest repetition work. *Motor Trader*, 4 February 1914.

[56] His patent machinery was of such quality as to enlist Armstrong Whitworth among Austin patent licensees. In 1920 the Austin Motor Company paid Sir Herbert £25,000 after independent valuation, for the transfer of a list of patent inventions to the firm. AMB, 2 January, 20 December 1920.

[57] S. B. Saul, pp. 38–9.

[58] MBA, 509, Midland Diary No. 3, 8 June 1911.

[59] S. B. Saul, 'The Motor Industry in Britain to 1914', *Business History*, V (1962).

[60] *Motor Trader*, 11 February 1914.

[61] 'Sir Herbert Austin', *Autocar*, 6 September 1929, p. 453.

even for administrative and sales staff,[62] may well have limited the range of views ventilated at those weekly conferences. It is difficult to believe that Herbert's managerial organization was not dominated by his own personality and by his firmly held belief in the identity of interests between himself and his workpeople.

This is clear from a speech he delivered at the second works subscription dinner in 1913, an event organized by both staff and manual workers, and attended by about one-fifth of the entire workforce. On that occasion he affirmed that the welfare of the workforce depended first and foremost on capital and labour; that capital should not be defined in terms of a class (presumably to the benefit of a class) but as an abstract means of conducting trade (presumably to the benefit of all); that the rising aspiration of workers with all grades demanding 'an opportunity to live on a higher plane of civilization with more intellectual and personal comforts' was very reasonable, but must be earned. 'We must be prepared to work harder and scheme more. We must prevent waste of materials and effort, must take advantage of every possible improvement in regard to organization, equipment and conditions of employment, working harmoniously together inter-departmentally, and individually, all of which goes a long way towards the reduction of useless labour.' With such resounding banalities Herbert sought to stimulate effort and secure the co-operation of his workers. The maintenance of quality of output was the remaining factor which he emphasized as a vital condition for their common success.[63] Both the workforce and management were put to the test a year later, for the demands of war, which intensified pressures for even more rapid expansion, were met by changes in production methods and physical capital which were to have critical and long-lasting effects on the Company's future.

The domestic market was undergoing rapid development when hostilities commenced. According to the SMMT estimates the total production of motor vehicles probably increased threefold between 1909 and 1913, to about 34,000. Of this total, D. G. Rhys suggests that slightly more than two-thirds were private cars.[64] In 1913, 13,000

[62] *Motor Trader*, 4 February 1914.

[63] *Austin Advocate*, II, March 1913, II, April 1913.

[64] D. G. Rhys, *The British Motor Industry* (1972), p. 9. He compares the 25,000 private cars produced in Britain with 45,000 produced by French manufacturers.

vehicles were imported and only 9,000 exported,[65] figures which reveal a serious lack of competitiveness on the part of British manufacturers. Small-scale and fragmented in structure, the industry produced a staggering variety of models for what was still a tiny market. Like a 'cottage industry',[66] most firms built vehicles in almost total disregard of standardization, perpetuating a restricted market for the standardized components which within a few years were to revolutionize the trade through the growth of large-scale suppliers. But while the size of the market was admittedly limited, Saul's study has identified motor manufacturers' attitudes to it as the key weakness – in particular their inertia when confronted with American production methods and competition, and the inhibiting influence of traditional ways of engineering.[67]

Austin's commercial policy exemplified the tendency for British makers towards a proliferation of models, which hindered standardization and specialization in component manufacture, though by the First World War the Company manufactured three basic chassis, the Ten, rated at 14.3 h.p., the Twenty, rated at 22.4 h.p. and the Thirty, rated at 30.5 h.p. These were available with numerous bodies or 'coachwork', including commercial truck and bus bodies. From 1912 Austin had also entered the market for stationary and marine engines.[68] Among British producers, William Morris was the first to perceive the relevance of model concentration combined with American production methods, based on the assembly of standardized parts, to the fulfilment of the growth possibilities of the British industry – and to act upon this perception. Armstrong Whitworth's directors had turned down a

[65] Apparently these figures exclude Model T parts imported by Ford for assembly at Trafford Park since 1911, and if, as seems reasonable, Ford car sales are counted as imports, the total figure for imports in 1913 increases by 7,310, bringing total imports to *c.* 20,300, compared with *c.* 9,000 exported. The Ford figures are from Mira Wilkins and Frank Ernest Hill, *American Business Abroad: Ford on Six Continents* (Detroit, 1966), p. 51.

[66] The description belongs to W. Plowden, *The Motor Car and Politics* (1971), p. 304.

[67] S. B. Saul, 'The British Motor Industry', pp. 42–3. Apart from such items as wheels, tyres, and even pressed steel underframes from Krupps, Austin manufactured most of the components at Longbridge, electrical equipment and machine tools, too. Many of the machine tools Herbert designed personally. *Times Engineering Supplement*, 2 October 1912; *Motor Trader*, 4 February 1914; MBA, 509, Midland Diary No. 3, 23 January 1913.

[68] Lambert & Wyatt, pp. 98–102; Fletcher & Son, *Motor Car Index 1916–1929* (Norwich, 1930).

proposal put forward by C. R. F. Engelbach, the production engineer with executive responsibility for vehicle manufacture, for the mass production of motor cars at an annual rate of 6,000.[69] Thus, before the war only William Morris was to pursue effectively the commercial potential of a British car aimed at driving the Model T from British roads. In 1913 the Morris Oxfords proved an immediate success.[70]

Nonetheless, Austin motor cars sold well enough both at home and overseas[71] to justify business expansion, even if the method of achieving it was later considered by Herbert to have been the biggest mistake in his career. That was the conversion of his firm into a public company with a nominal capital of £650,000. He reflected on this fifteen years later: 'Had it remained a private concern, its development would have been more personal and less spectacular.'[72] The private Austin Company was sold in February to the new Austin Motor Co. (1914) Ltd. for £399,993, including building assets valued at £56,957, and plant and machinery at £110,342. The nominal capital of the public company consisted of 250,000 7 per cent cumulative preference shares and 400,000 ordinary shares. Each of the new directors took 250 £1 preference shares plus a single ordinary share. Allotment of 186,663 ordinary shares each were made to Herbert Austin and to Harvey du Cros, Junior, and a further 26,667 to Major Frank Kayser, as vendors of the old Company.[73] With an annual salary of £3,500 plus 2½ per cent of the company's net profit after deducting the amount required to pay the 5 per cent dividend on the preference shares,[74] Herbert Austin was to be Chairman and Managing Director for five years.

[69] R. J. Irving, 'New Industries for Old: Some Investment Decisions at Armstrong Whitworth 1900–1914', *Business History*, 17 (1975), 150, 171 fn 4. Engelbach became manager of the Coventry Ordnance Works during the war and was appointed to the Board of Austin in 1921. See below, p. 64.

[70] P. W. S. Andrews and Elizabeth Brunner, *The Life of Lord Nuffield* (Oxford, 1955), pp. 68–70.

[71] About 40 per cent of production was sold overseas on the eve of the First World War. *Motor Trader*, 4 February 1914.

[72] 'Sir Herbert Austin KBE, His Life Story', *Autocar*, 6 September 1929, p. 453.

[73] Hyam Marks, a director of three other firms, including Kynoch Ltd., took 250 preference and one ordinary shares, as did a man named Ball. A. W. Jones was appointed Company Secretary and shortly afterwards John Hannay, originally employed by Alfred Herbert, Daimler, then B.S.A., on tool equipment and experimental work for motor production, was recruited from the works manager's job at David Brown's. He became Austin's Production Manager. *Austin Advocate*, XV, September 1926, XII, November 1924.

[74] Companies House File 133747. Austin Motor Co. (1914) Ltd., Prospectus.

Within months of the new Company's formation, orders for munitions and military vehicles for both the British and Russian Governments made further expansion of productive capacity imperative. Early in 1915 Austin received instructions from the War Office to lay down and equip large workshops for the forging and machining of shells, as a result of which the North and West Works were built adjacent to the Longbridge factory in 1916 and 1917. Large shops were also erected for the manufacture of aeroplanes, aeroplane engines, armoured cars, lorries and electric lighting sets in the South Works, and an airfield was laid out alongside.

Power stations were built to ensure continuous supply for the efficient utilization of the huge new plant and equipment at Longbridge. After negotiation with the Midland and Great Western Railway companies, several miles of sidings were built adjoining the works in order to accommodate the unprecedented volume of goods traffic and the several thousand workers who, within a very short period, were to be added to the Longbridge payroll.[75] When the war began, Austin employed between 2,000 and 3,000 workers; in the last year of hostilities the workforce exceeded 20,000.[76]

* * *

In the pre-war years Sir Herbert had demonstrated competence as a manager and distinction as an inventor. In designing and building the Austin motor cars and in the design and construction of machine tools for their production, by 1914 he had succeeded in establishing the Austin Motor Company as one of the leading British firms of car manufacturers.[77] By that time the Company's turnover had risen from £85,000 in its first full year of trading in 1906, to £209,000 in 1910, and £425,000 in 1913 (Table 1). The firm showed a healthy balance on profit and loss account and a sizeable reserve, and the public flotation

[75] *Times*, 29 January, 3 February 1919.

[76] The immediate pre-war figure reported in 1914 was 2,300. *Motor Trader*, 4 February 1914; this included 1,900 production workers. The 1918 figures were reported by Herbert Austin, *Times*, 29 January 1919.

[77] The Company probably ranked fifth in terms of output in 1913 after Wolseley (3,000), Humber (2,500), Sunbeam (1,700), and Rover (1,600). Only five other firms produced a thousand or more motor vehicles in 1913. The estimates are from Table 3 in S. B. Saul, p. 45. Ford's output in 1913, consisting mainly of American parts assembled in Manchester, was 6,139. P. L. D. Terry, 'The Ford in England', *Ford Times*, II, March 1914.

in 1914 was aimed at securing finance for a major expansion of output based mainly on a newly designed Austin Twenty, a symptom of optimism justified by the firm's recent growth and its prospects for the future.

Undoubtedly, in comparison with American firms Austin's sales and production methods were much inferior; yet in the British context, does Herbert Austin deserve the unfavourable comparisons which Saul makes with other motor car producers in Britain before 1914? Describing Austin as having been behind the times in 1914, Saul remarked that Herbert's approach to the technical and business problems of motor manufacture 'was not particularly inspired', speculating whether his company's success may 'have depended upon finance rather than upon entrepreneurial and managerial capability'.[78]

Austin has been criticized for following the common practice of laying down a chassis only on receipt of an order and a substantial cash deposit,[79] but this was a partial solution to the Company's need for finance, cheaper than borrowing more than could be avoided from the bank, and in any case was only possible because customers wanted to buy Austin cars. The availability of customer deposits was a reassuring indication to the bank manager that the Company's prospects were sound, and this in turn helps to explain the continued support from that source to supplement re-invested profits necessary for growth. Even so, the narrow liquidity ratios which characterized Austin's financial dealings before 1914, current assets covering current liabilities only in 1906 and 1912, reveal the supply of working capital to have been barely adequate to meet the Company's needs,[80] and suggest that it is a mistaken view to suppose that easy finance played a part in Herbert's hard-earned success before 1914, as his complaints of lack of capital also indicate.[81] With production based on orders, which doubled between 1910 and 1912, and increased by 50 per cent in 1913, even the rapid rise in profits accompanying expansion was insufficient to allow major investment, improvement, and enlargement of capacity. That became possible only after Company reorganization and the public issue in 1914.

Wolseley has been described by 1914 as having been 'advanced' in

[78] S. B. Saul, pp. 34, 39. 40.

[79] S. B. Saul, p. 39.

[80] The ratio of current assets to current liabilities were as follows 1906 – 1.0; 1907 – 0.9; 1908 – 0.8; 1909 – 0.8; 1910 – 0.9; 1911 – 0.9; 1912 – 1.0, 1913 – 0.9.

[81] See above, p. 19.

its policy, of recent introduction, of building for stock, just as its methods of production, although behind those to be found at Sunbeam, were also reckoned to have been in advance of those at Longbridge.[82] It is possible that Austin, too, built for stock by 1913,[83] while productivity at Longbridge was probably not very different from that of competitors. But Saul's own figures of output and employment at the three firms indicate a crude labour productivity of between 1.5 and 1.8 at Sunbeam, 1.3 at Wolseley, and 1.5 at Austin.[84] Moreover, whereas Austin's pre-war record was a profitable one, Wolseley's was a financial disaster. Sunbeam's profit performance was almost certainly better than that of Austin beginning in 1911[85] but due as much, we suggest, to the production of the high quality 12/16 h.p. light car designed by the Company's joint managing director, Louis Coatalen, in 1909, as to immenseley superior manufacturing methods. Sunbeam's trial and racing victories ensured maximum publicity for the touring car of this model.[86]

Saul's more detailed adverse criticism of Austin's productivity and financial record in comparison with his contemporaries is unfounded; though in his approach to the market, with a weakness in the early years for proliferation of designs, Herbert was certainly open to censure. Even if we exclude the vision and organizational innovations of Ford and Morris, Herbert's perception of market changes was

[82] S. B. Saul, pp. 39–40.

[83] His acknowledgement of the wisdom of building for stock is suggested by his address to the carriage builders in 1913 when he urged them to adopt this policy. See above, p. 24.

[84] S. B. Saul, Table 3. Even as crude indications of productivity these figures are suspect, for the employment figures may not be comparable. Of the 2,300 Austin employees recorded in 1914, 400 were not employed at Longbridge but were to be found at depots and repair works elsewhere. *Motor Trader*, 4 February 1914.

[85] Sunbeam's 'net profits' as published by *The Economist*, 10 November 1915, may not be strictly comparable to those of Austin, Table 2, and there is no information on turnover or assets. The figures do, however, exceed the Austin figures by more than 20 per cent in each year and were three times as great in 1913.

[86] *History and Development of the Sunbeam Car* (1924), pp. 28–34. Sunbeam was established on the basis of capital from a tinplate firm in 1905, and grew through subsequent ordinary share issues supported by existing shareholders and the capitalization of reserves. Thus in the boom after 1910 Sunbeam's issued capital rose from £60,000 to £100,000, and to £150,000 in 1912. *Motor Trader*, 10 November 1915.

inferior to some of his contemporaries and constrained his immediate post-war policy. At the 1910 Motor Show the Austin Ten, rated at 10.1 h.p. by the RAC, was one of a few light cars which aimed at economical motoring in a four-seater, four-cylinder motor car by avoiding the disadvantages of unreliability and discomfort.[87] The Humber 11.3 h.p. model was slightly cheaper, £285 compared with £290 for the Austin Ten; the Rover Twelve, rated at 13.9 h.p., cost £315 and the Singer Fifteen, rated at 15.8 h.p., cost £430.[88] Although the cheapest version of the Ten claimed to seat four people, achieved by the provision of a dickey seat for two, the engine proved insufficiently powerful to carry the more customary carriage-built body for four, with the result that the 1912/13 chassis incorporated an engine with slightly larger bore to generate 14.3 h.p. and was classified in Fletcher's Motor Index as the Austin 12/14 at £325.[89] This compared with the four-seater Humber at £310, the four-seater Singer at £375 and the Rover four-seater at £315. However, the Rover's engine capacity was a good deal larger, and could seat four comfortably.[90] So successful was the Rover Twelve from its introduction in November 1911 that two years later Owen Clegg decided to concentrate production solely on that model, a policy which continued until munitions production absorbed Rover's manufacturing capacity.

Priced for the 1914 season at £350, including electric lighting sets and accessories (compared with £330 excluding sets and equipment for the Austin Ten), the Rover's commercial appeal meant that by the outbreak of war the Rover Twelve was probably the most successful British light four-seater car. Four hundred had been produced in 1911, rising to 1,300 in 1912, and to 1,800 in 1913,[91] which compared with between 100 and 300 Austin Tens in 1912 and 495 in 1913.[92] By that time the Singer Fourteen and the Standard Fifteen competed in the four-seater category, priced at £375 and £385 respectively. Each of the firms producing these models offered either two-seater versions on

[87] *Cyclecar*, 10 September 1913.

[88] *Autocar*, 28 October 1911.

[89] *Autocar*, 2 November 1912; Fletcher & Son, *The Motor Car Index 1916–1924* (Norwich, 1925).

[90] *Autocar*, 2 November 1912.

[91] George Oliver, *The Rover* (1971), p. 61. These figures exceeded Austin's total car production; Fletcher & Son, *The Motor Car Index 1916–1924* (Norwich, 1925).

[92] I am grateful to Major R. J. Wyatt for these production figures.

the standard chassis, with the exception of Austin; or like Singer, Standard, and Hillman, sold specially designed motor cars.[93]

These were the cars which appealed to what in 1913 the *Times* correspondent reported as a potentially large and rapidly expanding section of the motoring community, a section of society to whom £250 represented the maximum possible outlay for a vehicle.[94] But here also, so far as the production of low cost light cars is concerned, Herbert Austin showed little interest, relying upon the professional man, the commercial traveller, or the couple in search of stylish motoring for pleasure, to purchase the Ten for a considerably higher price than they could buy a Singer, Hillman, Standard Nine or Ten, or by the 1913 Motor Show a Morris Oxford.[95]

R. J. Overy stressed the ability of Morris, unique in the British motor industry, to produce 'what the rest of the industry could not: more than one car per man per year',[96] but we should not read too much into crude comparisons between productivity of Austin and Morris Motors. In 1907 Austin produced about one car for every three workers employed; by 1913 this had risen to two units. Although superficially it appears that Morris's labour productivity was 50 per cent above the level achieved at Longbridge, we should bear in mind that the Morris labour force merely assembled components produced elsewhere. Comparisons between Austin and Morris productivities related to value added, if the figures were available, would reveal a very different result. More instructive is the crude comparison of labour productivity between Austin and the two British motor manu-

[93] Fletcher & Son, *The Motor Car Index 1916–1924* (Norwich, 1925).

[94] *Times*, 12 November 1913.

[95] At the November 1913 Motor Show the comparisons were as follows, as listed in the *Autocar Buyers Guide*, 2 November 1913:

Model	*RAC rated h.p.*	*Bore and stroke*	*Engine capacity in c.c.'s*	*Seating capacity*	*Price £*
Austin Ten	14.3	76 × 89	1,616	4	330
Rover Twelve	13.9	75 × 130	2,298	4	350
Singer Fourteen	14.0	78 × 125	2,384	4	375
Singer Ten	9.7	63 × 88	1,096	2	185
Standard Nine	9.5	69 × 90	1,087	2	195
Hillman Nine	9.0	60 × 120	1,360	2	200
Morris Ten Oxford		60 × 90	1,018	2	200
Ford Twenty	22.4	95 × 102	2,892	5/6	125

[96] R. J. Overy, *William Morris, Viscount Nuffield* (1976), p. 11.

facturing firms which Saul considers to have led the industry, Sunbeam and Wolseley.[97]

In addition to Morris, Singer, Standard, and Hillman offered cars at less than £200 for the 1914 season, and in the £201 to £250 range Humber, Riley and Swift were the most notable British producers. Austin's cheapest car, the Ten, barely qualified for the £301 to £350 class, for, unlike Rover, lighting equipment and accessories were excluded from the price.[98] When price lists were announced a year later the price of the Austin Ten was £390, compared with £350 for the Rover and £375 for the Singer Fourteen,[99] a deterioration in price competitiveness which suggests that economical motoring was not uppermost in Austin's approach to the market. Such a possibility receives support from the evidence provided by Austin advertisements, which rarely focused upon a single model, and hardly ever made a special feature of the Ten, described from its introduction as a 'superior class of 10 h.p. car',[100] except to illustrate the car's upmarket appeal, complete with elaborate coachwork embodying such items as an emergency fifth seat, speaking tube, lady companion's glass screen, spring roller canopy, etc., priced at between £400 and £500.[101] The emphasis was upon comfort and quality, rather than upon economy and performance, and whereas before the production of the Ten the high-powered Austin cars had entered races and trials,[102] with some success, the Ten secured no publicity from such activity. This contrasted with the enormous success of the Singer cars at the Brooklands trials between 1912 and 1914, which in addition to claims of modest price and low running costs became a major feature in advertising these popular light cars. Rover exploited the *Motor Trader*'s choice of the Rover Twelve as 'car of the season' in 1913, while Standard's advertisements often stressed low petrol consumption.[103]

C. F. Caunter described the Austin Ten as having 'represented a form that was then passing rather than . . . a new one that was in process of evolution'.[104] Such was not the case with Singer cars, and

[97] See above, p. 36.
[98] *Autocar*, 8 November 1913.
[99] *Autocar*, 14 November 1914.
[100] *Autocar*, 30 December 1911.
[101] For example, *Autocar*, 3 October 1914.
[102] Lambert & Wyatt, pp. 97–9.
[103] *Autocar*, 18 January, 31 May, 1913, 18, 25 April 1914.
[104] C. F. Caunter, *The Light Car, A Technical History* (1970), p. 53.

Singer, selected both by the *Cyclecar* and the *Motor* as the leading manufacturer of light inexpensive cars at under £250 before 1914, was reported to have dominated that section of the market[105] and formed the basis for the Company's continued success after the war.[106] In a much more spectacular fashion, the Morris Oxford, already in production in 1914, provided a springboard as soon as the war ended, the Oxford, and subsequently the Cowley, appealing to the growing middle-income market spotlighted by the *Times* correspondent. The ability of Perry to increase the sale of Ford cars assembled at Trafford Park from 3,081 in 1912 to 6,139 in 1913, a figure which doubled again in 1914, is indicative of an attractive price (from £135) overcoming resistance to what the trade press considered to be an unattractive, if sturdy, motor car,[107] offering to British manufacturers a clue to the future.

It was the concept of such a 'popular' car that from 1912 a handful of British car manufacturers sought to translate into forms which took account of the different characteristics of the home market, and by 1914 a breakthrough seemed imminent, though requiring heavy investment to commence volume production on an appreciable scale. To this extent the backwardness of the British motor industry has been exaggerated. Myopia was not the prevailing weakness among the leading light car firms after 1912, though only William Morris had made the imaginative leap from car manufacture in the orthodox engineering tradition practised by British firms to the assembly of component parts. This was the *coup d'entreprise* which not only induced simple, but attractive, design, but also set him free from many of the problems associated with the financing of motor production. This advantage was important before 1914, by which time the rapidly increasing sale of Ford cars exposed the opportunities for a people's car. With that lesson learned, the freedom from financial difficulties after the war was for Morris a critical asset.

Herbert's design and promotion of the Austin Ten, designated by 1914 the 12/14, suggests that he had not learned the lesson from the Ford's success before 1914, as does the omission of a car smaller than the Austin Twenty in his post-war strategy. But in view of the Company's profitability before 1914, making and selling mainly relatively

[105] *Cyclecar*, 10 September 1913; *Motor*, 17 September 1919.

[106] *Midland Daily Telegraph*, 9 October 1931.

[107] P. L. D. Perry, 'The Ford in England', *Ford Times*, March 1914, June 1914.

high-powered vehicles, there was no pressing financial economic incentive to extend the range to include smaller cars to compete with Ford. In this respect Herbert's approach to the market before 1914 is comprehensible in the short term, even though it ignored the long term implications of designing a popular car suited to the tastes of the home market. A handful of British manufacturers were tackling this problem between 1912 and 1914, though Austin, more representative of the industry and more important because of its potential for development in motor car design and production, was a laggard in this respect. The intervening war ensured that this deficiency in policy was to prove even more unfortunate when peacetime production resumed in the most difficult financial circumstances, and when the popular market resumed an even more rapid growth.

Part Two: The Impact of War: Receivership and Reconstruction

CHAPTER THREE

War Production and Post-War Policy

THE EVENTS OF 1914–18 marked an important turning point in the history of Austin, for the immediate effect of the post-war economic convulsions precipitated a crisis at Longbridge which Herbert proved able to surmount only by agreeing to participate in a drastic reorganization and re-orientation of Company policy. The solutions which in the longer term successfully resolved the financial crisis threatening the firm's existence in 1920–21 left a legacy of a reformed managerial structure and a greater commercial orientation, though it also brought a heavy burden of fixed debt which seriously impeded the progress of the Company.

By creating the unsettled economic conditions between 1919 and 1922 the war must bear a heavy responsibility for the difficulties facing Longbridge at that time, but there are other, if less important, factors which explain why Austin should have experienced a greater trauma than many other firms faced with the task of adapting from war production to peacetime manufacture. One was Sir Herbert's misguided post-war planning; the other was his attempt to float off the inherited difficulties by the mere infusion of risk capital and the adoption of a series of expedients which thrust the Company into the arms of the Official Receiver. This brought upon the unwilling Austin a managerial upheaval instigated by his principal creditors,[1] the effect of which was to restrict the scope for initiative even of the Company's

[1] Notably the Midland Bank and Eagle Star and British Dominion Insurance Companies.

founder and largest shareholder, and which culminated in capital reduction. Following his son's death this scourging, as he saw it, by the City, a mortification of the entrepreneurial spirit, explains why these years held the bitterest memories for Herbert, experience for which driving hard work could provide an antidote, partial consolation, and fulfilment. The details of this *via dolorosa* are tortuous but important, not only because resurrection was the sequel, but also because of the long-lasting effects of these developments upon the subsequent history of the Austin Motor Company.

Between August 1914 and November 1918 the Longbridge plant produced over 8 million shells, 650 guns, more than 2,000 aeroplanes, nearly 500 armoured cars, and vast quantities of other equipment, including generating sets, pumping equipment, aeroplane engines, ambulances and lorries. Output for 1918 was valued at more than £9 million compared with £600,000 in 1914. The finance required for this rapid expansion of munitions work was provided by the Ministry of Munitions, and the North and West Works, which were built on Austin's land for Ministry work, became the subject of an agreement giving the Company option to purchase them, together with the associated power plant, when the war ended. As for the 123 acres of farmland acquired by the Company for the site of the Longbridge Estate residential development in June 1917, these were financed by a Ministry mortgage which included provision for the cost of building. Within months of the purchase, an estate consisting of 252 dwellings had been laid out on 'garden suburb lines', linked by tarmacadam footpaths and roads.[2] By 1918 amenities included a block of old farm buildings converted into a village hall and clubrooms, a steam laundry specially built by the Company, and a temporary Church of England Mission room.[3]

Such measures, however, could only contribute marginally to a solution of the problem of securing an adequate labour supply, and arrangements were made to build and operate a fleet of 35 buses to bring workers from various centres in the West Midlands. The purchase of a house at Bromsgrove, and its conversion into a hostel, was another measure designed to accommodate migrant labour on a

[2] Fifty dwellings were semi-detached brick houses while the remainder were prefabricated wooden bungalows, imported from the United States due to shortages of raw materials. Companies House File 133747, Austin Motor Co. (1914) Ltd., Deed of Mortgage; *Times*, 29 January 1919.

[3] *Austin Advocate*, VII, October 1918; *Times*, 16 July 1918, 3 February 1919.

temporary basis,[4] for men were attracted from a wide area. Indeed, several hundred were recruited in Cornwall, in contravention of the Defence of the Realm regulation which prohibited employers from canvassing or advertising outside a radius of ten miles from the factory.[5] According to the report of a Ministry representative, early in 1917 a man named Cahill, acting on behalf of Austin, 'had made a sort of Royal progress through the South-West of England'; on his visits to the West Country he had carried posters bearing the Royal Arms and appealing for workers.[6]

In addition to employing more people Herbert Austin sought to utilize labour more intensively, persuading unskilled workers, among whom an increasing number were women, to perform tasks which hitherto had been the preserve of skilled workers. He seems to have been forced into this expedient as a result of advice taken from the Ministry of Munitions. For the suspension of night shift and Sunday work from December 1915 led to an exodus of labour from Longbridge to join other firms which continued to offer weekend work and double pay. In fact, he soon found unskilled workers both adaptable and helpful in keeping costs down.[7] For this reason, in 1916 he called on the unions to repudiate those 'who preached restriction of output as the only means of regulating work and preventing non-employment'. Looking already to the future after the war, he argued that the elimination of restrictive trade union practices could be much more effective in improving Britain's international competitive position than fiscal policy: 'Now would be appropriate for employers' federations and unions to get together and discuss encouragement of the better instincts among workers generally and the conditions under which it would be practicable after we have beaten the enemy, in a military and naval sense, to pull together and beat them in manufacturing and commerce. A return to the old narrow-minded ways, small and uniform wages, restricted and misdirected efforts, seems impossible. Both sides would have to make changes, but the possibilities for all are enormous; if we can commence operations in a well-organized way

[4] PRO T.161/52 S 3776/1, Memorandum by Sir Reginald Brades, 1920; *Times*, 16 July 1918, 29 January 1919.

[5] This measure was designed to assist the efficient operation of the labour exchange system.

[6] *Times*, 3 July 1917.

[7] *Times*, 14 April 1916.

immediately, after the war, the losses (due to the costs of war) will be wiped out quickly.'[8]

Such exhortations did not, however, prevent a strike of 10,000 Longbridge workers in January 1918 over an alleged case of victimization. This followed agitation for a guarantee of higher weekly wages in lieu of bonus, during which Arthur Peacock, chairman of the Works Committee and a munitions volunteer, was informed by the Ministry of Munitions that he was to be transferred to Lincoln. Although local Ministry representatives denied the charge of victimization, the outcome was a stoppage lasting four days before a return to work was secured as the basis for Peacock's reinstatement pending an enquiry.[9] Unfortunately there is no trace of this enquiry, but the circumstantial evidence is not ambiguous.

Herbert Austin's attitude to the activities of organized labour cannot be described as sympathetic. His criticism of the striking coal miners in 1919 was enlarged into a more general condemnation of labour for hampering British industry's ability to compete: 'Let us get back to work again and make better terms afterwards. The country has been spoonfed by government for four and a half years and some people are waiting to be spoonfed for the remainder of the time.'[10] In sharp contrast was his enthusiasm for the encouragement and care of apprentices, with whose aspirations he identified entirely. In part, of course, this is explicable by the more readily perceptible coincidence of his own interests in individual betterment and business performance, but he also held strong views on industrial training, some of which he had presented in an inaugural speech as the first President of the Automobile and Cycle Engineers' Institute in 1904.[11] He claimed that

[8] Ibid.

[9] *Times*, 18 January, 22 January 1918.

[10] *Times*, 21 January 1919.

[11] On that occasion he had criticized the prevailing system of education in technical schools, which he claimed produced too many young pupils 'fit for nothing else but lecturers or assistants in similar colleges' to those from which they graduated. He dismissed as totally inadequate the inducements offered to the artisan to improve his knowledge of the technical side of his trade. Conceding that the aims of the schools might be excellent, he accused them of failing to produce practical men, in large part due, he thought, to the complete separation of commercial from the engineering aspects of business, and to too often ignoring the cost implications of alternative technical processes. The Institute was formerly known as the Cycle Engineers' Institute, which had been established in Birmingham in January 1898.

the young men from technical schools were often none the better for their technical training when they came into the employ of a practical engineering firm, a deficiency which he attributed to the fact that they were taught by men who lacked manufacturing experience.[12]

Apprenticeships at Longbridge took the same form as in other engineering shops at this time, but in 1917 Herbert formed the Austin Technical Society. Its aim was to promote the study of engineering and other branches of applied science, and to stimulate interest in, and knowledge of, commercial techniques. All employees, male and female, were eligible for membership, and grouped into one of three sections, according to an individual's technical abilities. Through classes and meetings held regularly to discuss papers delivered by various speakers in a new purpose-built lecture hall, members were encouraged to pursue their interests with the management committee's assistance and advice. A lending and reference library of engineering literature, including books and periodicals, was opened, while a cinema was available for the showing of instructive as well as other films.[13]

Although the Company did not charge apprenticeship premiums, wages were withheld during the three months' probationary period, after boys joined the firm at the age of fourteen. Thereafter, all apprentices received time off for special technical instruction, of which one-half was free in that no deductions occurred. Although all boys began as shop apprentices, those who were selected to become works apprentices (boys with a 'good education') were given experience throughout the works, including the research laboratories and the drawing office. One difference between apprenticeships at Longbridge and most other large engineering firms was that each boy below the age of eighteen could opt for instruction in workshop mathematics; another was the free provision of classes in mechanical drawing. Students who became works apprentices also received pay for attending any of the classes offered by the Company and were almost self-supporting as a result.[14] A major step forward occurred in 1919 with the establishment, in a disused convent adjacent to the works, of a Company engineering college where student apprentices in residence received theoretical instruction, practical instruction taking place in the plant. In referring to this development the *Motor Trader* corre-

[12] *Autocar*, 29 October 1904.

[13] *Motor Trader*, 16 May 1917; *Austin Advocate*, VI, May 1917.

[14] *Austin Advocate*, VII, January 1918.

spondent stressed the relevance of a skilled labour shortage, rather than philanthropy, in explaining Austin's motives.[15] Herbert Austin also established a scholarship to enable successful candidates to continue their studies at the University of Birmingham,[16] which in 1937 was to award him an honorary degree, adding to the KBE conferred for contributions to the war effort in 1917.

Careful attention to ensuring the continued quality and supply of Austin's labour force in the long term was accompanied by preparation of the Company's commercial strategy for the return to peace. But the plan which was announced in November 1918 was to prove as ill-founded as Sir Herbert's prediction, in April 1918, that the war would continue for a further two years.[17] His intention was to concentrate production on an improved version of a 20 h.p. car modelled on the new 'Sports Twenty', which had been advertised in August 1914 but whose manufacture had been prevented by munitions contracts.[18] When the war came to an end, the firm was exceptionally vulnerable because it was at its most extended. Carl R. F. Engelbach, later to become one of the ruling triumvirate at Longbridge, recalled that when the war ended in November 1918 'the firm was left with a plant of an entirely useless character for its future needs, and with a geographical disposition of its buildings that was very difficult to work economically',[19] a remark the truth of which is shown by the works plan (p. 48). Beneficial effects felt by other munitions producers[20] were also experienced at Longbridge, where in some ways war had increased the Company's post-war potential; these included the adoption of large-scale repetition production, the addition of research and metallurgical laboratories, the construction of special hardening and heat treatment plants, and the installation of a huge sheet metal press shop for panels and frames. Compressed air sprays had been introduced for

[15] *Motor Trader*, 5 February 1919; *Autocar*, 24 May 1919. The demand for places on this scheme was so great that the house at Bromsgrove used to accommodate wartime labour became an overflow dormitory for senior apprentices at 'Nazareth House'.

[16] Lambert & Wyatt, p. 112.

[17] *Austin Advocate*, VI, November 1916, VII, April 1918.

[18] Lambert & Wyatt, p. 103.

[19] C. R. F. Engelbach, 'Some Notes on Reorganizing a Works to Increase Production', *PIAE*, XXIII (1927–8), p. 32.

[20] A. A. Remington, 'Some Probable Effects of the War on the Automobile Industry', *PIAE*, XIII, 1918–19, p. 7.

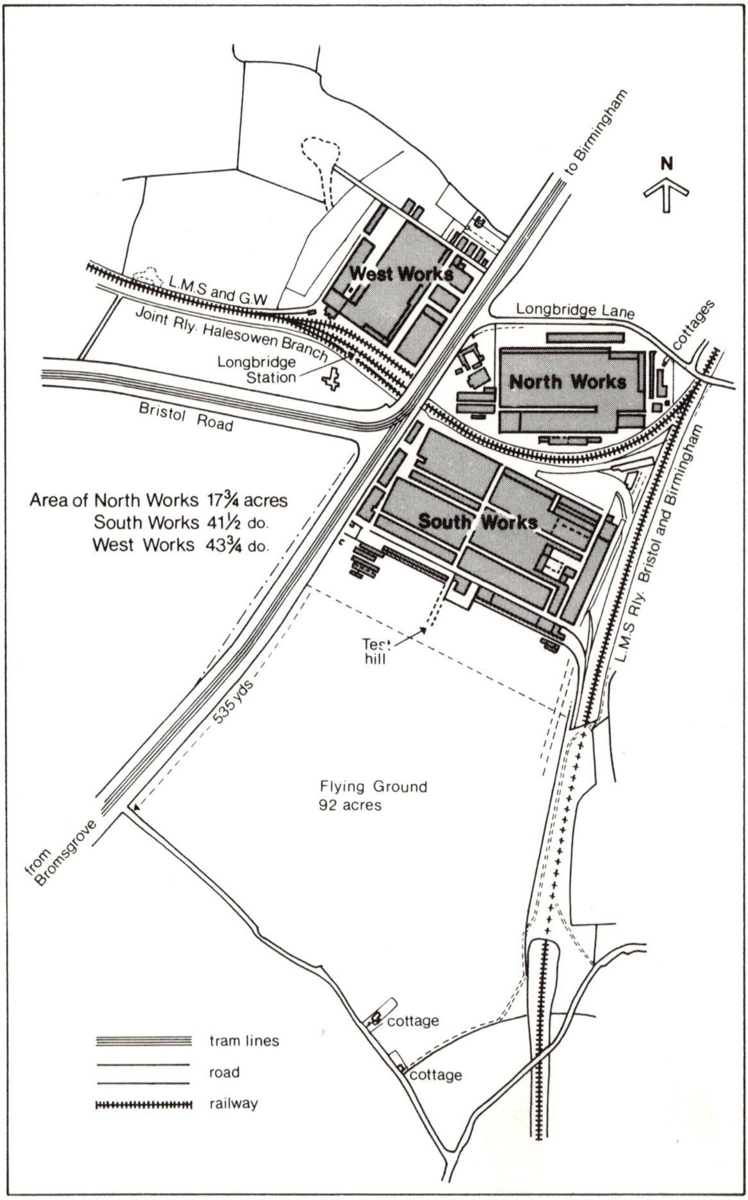

Plan of Longbridge, *circa* 1920

rapid car painting, and the Company became the only car manufacturer in the Midlands with an annual production capacity of 5,000 tons of steel.[21] Nevertheless, given the unsuitable disposition of the works, and the unsuitable layout and character of plant and equipment installed for war purposes, a major capital expenditure programme was vital before car production could proceed efficiently on a substantial scale.

Compared with the problems of reconversion facing Austin, which was one of the major shell manufacturers after October 1914, Morris Motors was in an advantageous position. Without any engineering capacity to offer, the Cowley Works had been equipped to assemble munitions parts supplied by other factories. When the war ended, therefore, Cowley's flexibility enabled a rapid resumption of private car production, which had continued, albeit at low levels, during the war; indeed, speed in returning to normalcy is acknowledged to have been of vital importance to the success of Morris.[22] In January 1919 Austin announced that orders to the value of £4 million for delivery over a period of three years had been received for the new models (the 20 h.p. motor car and 30 cwt. lorries), for tractors and electric house-lighting sets.[23] Sir Herbert decided to expand tractor production at the same time, a venture initiated in 1917 in response to the national drive to increase domestic food production.[24] His aim was to double the weekly output of one hundred 20 h.p. motor cars achieved in the autumn of 1919, to raise tractor output to one hundred per week, to produce sixty 30 cwt. lorries, and to manufacture 500 lighting sets. Such an optimistic outlook, imperative if the enlarged capacity and workforce was to be employed, warranted immediate reorganization and re-equipment.[25]

[21] *Austin Advocate*, VIII, June 1919; Lambert & Wyatt, p. 107.

[22] R. J. Overy, *William Morris, Viscount Nuffield* (1976), p. 12.

[23] 'Sir Herbert Austin KBE, His Life Story', *Autocar*, 6 September 1929, p. 453.

[24] *Motor Trader*, 4 February 1914; *Austin Advocate*, VI, February 1917; *Times*, 20 July, 22 November 1919; AMB, 21 January 1920.

[25] At first Sir Herbert had imported tractors from Europe, and the first batch of Austin-made tractors left the factory in July 1919, winning competitions in Britain and France. These successes, and the prospect of mechanization of food production especially in Europe prompted Sir Herbert to form a company at Liancourt in France where he bought a factory for Austin motor tractor production. This was the beginning of the 6 million franc Automobiles Anglaises Austin Société Anonyme of which Sir Herbert was President. The Board of Directors included the Chairman of a French firm of agricultural engineers.

The war years brought a huge rise in turnover and increasing profits, though these were subject to Excess Profits Duty against which only small reserves were made before 1919 (Table 4). A sharp drop in turnover by nearly 40 per cent, and the allocation of £425,000 to add to the £50,000 reserve to meet the tax liability in 1920, led to a sharp fall in assets at the same time that stocks remained at high levels. A public issue in 1919 eased the cash position and the rates of current assets to current liabilities rose from 0.8 to 1.1. Pressure intensified, however. A significant drain on the Company's limited resources was due to expenditure incurred not in the reinstatement of the pre-war plant, which was small, but in the rearrangement of the plant acquired during and immediately after the war. An analysis of fixed assets, including the reconstruction of the North and West Works, shows such expenditure to have amounted to £289,624, much of it spent in 1919 and 1920 when turnover, two-thirds of which arose from the sale of the Twenty, did not justify such substantial investment.[26]

Excess Profits Duty took up most of the reserves set aside in 1919, and the repayment of £650,000 to the bank in 1920 combined with an increase in stocks necessary for peacetime production offset the rise in turnover which occurred in that year. In 1921 the balance sheet revealed a deficit of more than £1.5 million, the financial position deteriorating as turnover fell during the depression of 1920–21. Austin's deficit for the two years 1920 and 1921 amounted to £381,922 after meeting depreciation charges, while the current ratio plunged to 0.5, evidence of the critical shortage of working capital. Lack of finance was the major single factor which prevented the Company from re-establishing its position in the industry during the post-war period. There are, however, question marks surrounding Sir Herbert's immediate post-war single model strategy, which he had announced two years before the Armistice.

An annual output of 10,000 cars, 6,000 lorries and 5,000 tractors (each incorporating 20 h.p. engines)[27] was a target which in the post-war euphoria did not seem to be excessively optimistic in order to meet a boom confidently and widely predicted. Because other companies were equally optimistic during the immediate post-war boom which collapsed towards the end of 1920, there followed a period altogether as unsettling to the trade as the war which preceded it – not least

[26] AMC Papers, Notes on the history of the Company in the last war (n.d.).

[27] Austin also announced a light two-seater aeroplane, 'the whippet', at £275, first flown in 1918.

Table 4: Capital Structure, Profits and Dividends, 1914–1921

Year	(a) Paid-up total capital: (i) Ordinary and preferred capital £	(a) Paid-up total capital: (ii) Debentures, mortgages and loans £	(b) Net profit after maintenance and depreciation, taxes (excluding EPD) and debenture interest £	(c) Ordinary dividends (and bonus), %	(d) Reserve fund	(e) Due to bank
1914	649,982	—	30,302 (14 months)	2	—	—
1915	649,982	92,305	63,909	6	1,750	84,128
1916	650,000	343,451	227,177	10	6,500	—
1917	650,000	1,087,874	262,642	10	6,500	132,902
1918	650,000	984,650	358,272 (13 months)	15	50,000	324,554
1919	1,650,000	315,451	237,866*	—	50,000	836,595
1920	3,327,097	332,080	} −381,922	—	—	187,087
1921	3,327,107	758,619	}	—	—	—

* Profits 1916–19 subject to EPD.

The figures for 1914–16 refer to the Austin Motor Co. (1914) Ltd., thereafter to the Austin Motor Co. Ltd.

because the post-war optimism was to some extent necessary if the swollen manufacturing capacity of car and other engineering firms was to be absorbed. There were, however, some real grounds for expecting demand to grow after the war. The number of cars on British roads had dwindled, the effect in part of restrictions on petrol licences, and of an increase by more than twofold in the price of petrol between 1914 and 1918. The imposition of the $33\frac{1}{3}$ per cent *ad valorem* McKenna Import Duties, which came into force in 1915, was a further deterrent to the car user and to the potential purchaser of new cars, and led to a drop in consumers' expenditure;[28] likewise the introduction of additional restrictions on the sale or importation of motor vehicles, except under licence, in 1916 and 1917. Together these developments account for the fall in new car sales in Britain to perhaps only 12,000 by 1918.

The home market recovered rapidly with the return to peace, as pent-up demand, rendered more effective by the existence of forced savings and servicemen's gratuities, was generated not only by the need for replacements but also by the growth in new owner demand. Whereas before the war the purchase of a motor car was associated with conspicuous consumption or the occasional sportive jaunt, greater familiarity with motorized transport resulting from its widespread use during the war, together with the removal of petrol restrictions, produced a climate of expectancy and optimism among would-be consumers and potential suppliers alike, a climate whose temperature can be gauged by the crusading motto, coined by the British Motor League, of 'Motoring for the Million'.[29]

Further impetus for this movement derived from several sources, among which financial promoters, trade journalists, and the example of genuine progress towards a wide car ownership in the United States were important. But the aspirations nurtured by all of these various groups were quickly dispelled, in part due to the galvanic effect of their sanguine predictions upon potential producers of motor vehicles. Pre-war manufacturers with enlarged productive capacities and inflated expectations, erstwhile general engineers, garage proprietors, and of course those equipped with enthusiasm for motoring but lacking any other qualifications for building vehicles, rushed to announce plans for the first post-war season.[30] Financial correspondents were quick to warn

[28] A. R. Prest, *Consumers' Expenditure in the United Kingdom 1900–1919*, p. 142.
[29] W. Plowden, *The Motor Car and Politics* (1971), p. 116.
[30] R. J. Wyatt, 'The Year 1919', *Old Motor*, July 1963.

their readers of the nature of the boom in motor companies. *The Economist* referred to promoters who advertised engineering companies as car manufacturers, and reaped 'a rich harvest' from investors seduced either by the promise of 40 per cent profits, or by attractive photographs of cars never to be produced.[31]

At the other extreme, but almost certainly equally unproductive, was the Manchester CWS, which in April 1919 had announced to the motoring world its intention to produce motor cars on a large scale for sale to shareholders.[32] Indeed, the frequent reference to mass production in the trade press and in particular in the prospectuses of those firms receiving the most publicity, provides a further reason for the inflated expectations at that time, for mass production was the speculators' rallying cry. No fewer than ten companies each announced hopes of producing between three and six thousand cars a year from 1919,[33] while the ambitions of the £6 million Harper Bean Company, with its plans for ultra-modern production methods at the £1 million National Projectile Factory at Dudley, ran to 10,000 cars in the 1920–21 programme, exceeding by three times the rate of output achieved in 1920.[34] Even the long established Wolseley Motor Company claimed to have the capacity to produce 20,000 cars a year in 1919.[35] The opportunities perceived, however, proved illusory, for rapid reconversion to peacetime production was seriously hampered by shortages of raw materials, strikes of coal miners in the winter of 1918–19 and again in the spring of 1921, and a more damaging cause was the iron moulders' stoppage, lasting eighteen weeks in the winter of 1919–20.

Not surprisingly, the difficulties of British manufacturers were exploited by the American producers, who accounted almost entirely for the flood of imports which increased from 5,000 cars in 1919 to 29,000 in 1920. This was despite the 33⅓ per cent import duty, and reflects not only the inability of British manufacturers to supply the demand but also the improvement in the price of American cars relative to their British competitors, as costs soared in the face of rapidly rising demand.[36] Within eight months of the cessation of

[31] *Economist*, 7 February 1920; *Investors' Monthly Manual*, February 1920.

[32] *Motor*, 15 April 1919.

[33] R. J. Wyatt, 'The Year 1919', *Old Motor*, July 1963.

[34] *Motor Trader*, 26 March 1919; *Autocar*, 17 April 1920.

[35] *Motor Trader*, 26 March 1919.

[36] Various estimates suggest that home market sales more than doubled in 1920 compared with 1919 and fell to about half that level in 1921. If Model T Fords

hostilities the new 20 h.p. Austin motor car, with a centrally controlled gearbox to facilitate entry and a streamlined body and integral boot, began to leave the factory. The chassis was available with three bodies: open tourer, coupé, and landaulette, and rose within months from an initial price of £395 to £550 in 1920, the cheapest complete car rising to £695.[37] The price which purchasers were prepared to pay was relative to the type of vehicles available, and for those wishing to possess a high-powered car with a shorter delivery date the Americans were supplying, and customers were buying, the 21.9 h.p. Chevrolet at £450 and the 18 h.p. Overland at £495. It is not surprising that sales of the Austin Twenty remained disappointing, particularly when the extraordinary boom conditions of 1919 began to peter out the following year.

In September 1920 Sir Herbert denied publicly that the motor industry faced a 'dark outlook', maintaining that the drop in sales was limited to highly priced cars, and that despite the temporary recession a car moderately priced to maintain and run was better able to hold its own.[38] For Austin, however, this was a serious problem, the post-war strategy having concentrated on the production of a single, relatively highly priced, 20 h.p. model, of which by July 1920, 3,000 had been delivered to customers.[39] The Twenty not only put Austin in direct competition with American cars but found difficulty in selling in a market which even then was beginning to turn away from high-powered vehicles.[40] For when the hectic buyers' market of 1919 collapsed under the weight of rising prices, its character also began to alter in such a way as to favour the lower horsepower cars, notably the Morris Oxford, the four-seater luxury model of its maker's range. The Finance Act, which from January 1921 raised the horsepower tax to £1 per h.p. on all passenger cars, was another factor adding to the relative disadvantage of the higher horsepowered cars in the post-war

---

are excluded both for import and production figures, the share of imports in total home sales in 1919 was 38.5 per cent, and for 1920, 50.7 per cent. If Fords are counted in production figures the percentages become 17.4 per cent in 1919 and 40 per cent in 1920.

[37] Fletcher & Son, *Motor Index 1916–1924* (Norwich, 1925); Lambert & Wyatt, pp. 116–17; AMB, 9 March, 13 April 1920.

[38] *Birmingham Post*, Letter from Herbert Austin, 16 September 1920.

[39] AMC Papers, Statement to Shareholders, 26 July 1920. In the same period the Company had sold 1,000 tractors.

[40] *Motor Trader*, 26 July 1922, p. 95.

market. It was at the nadir of the post-war depression in 1921 that the Oxford's price was cut dramatically from £590 to £415. The two-seater Cowley fell from £465 to £299.[41] Meanwhile, the loss of Austin's sales momentum adversely affected the Company's cash flow and forced Sir Herbert to the banks and to the public.

The speculative activities, which were responsible for many of the extremes characteristic of the new issue boom immediately after the war, reduced the chances of even the most solidly based firms in need of assistance receiving sympathetic treatment from the financial institutions to which they turned. Like so many other companies, Austin had suffered from the simultaneous unprecedented rush to the City, followed by a corresponding failure to obtain finance adequate to cope successfully with the various post-war strains of material shortages, of strikes, of re-entry into overseas markets now dominated by American cars.[42]

Recognizing the urgency of establishing large-scale production if a substantially higher share of the market was to be secured compared with pre-war, Sir Herbert tried to solve the capital shortage by a public issue in 1919, when the Beecham Trust, Myers & Co., and Bentleys of Huddersfield were eventually persuaded to underwrite 6 per cent preference shares to the value of £1 million in the Austin Motor Company. The Midland Bank, to whom the Company was heavily indebted, had agreed to appear on the prospectus as principal bankers only after Sir Herbert agreed to some 'rearrangements for the management of the company'. This involved the substitution of Sidney Van dem Burgh and Harold Anderson[43] for two retiring directors, one of whom was Colonel Frank Kayser.[44] The Midland Bank was asked for assistance also in purchasing the North and West Works by accepting a mortgage in return for cash and providing an advance of up to £500,000 on current account. The Midland Manager advised against creating any form of debentures, which he thought would be unfair to preference holders taking up the new issue and would also damage the

[41] R. J. Overy, *William Morris, Viscount Nuffield* (1976), p. 37, Table 5.

[42] *Times*, 25 February, 28 May 1920.

[43] Harold Anderson was a director of Portland Cement, Sidney Van dem Burgh held directorships in the British Dominion Trust Company, British Investors Associated, Industrial Mutual Trust, Boston Tanneries Ltd., John Mackintosh & Sons Ltd., and San Paulo Manufacturing & Finance Co., *Directory of Directors* (1922).

[44] MBA (509), Midland Diary 5, 7 January 1919.

Company's credit standing. It was for this reason that the Bank urged Austin to avoid a debenture issue in reaching a settlement with the Government on the North and West Works. But Austin appears to have had little alternative, and the Company and the Treasury duly reached a provisional agreement involving a mortgage of the works as security, with payments by annual instalments beginning in December 1921.[45] To the mortgage value of £24,000 (the boom price of the North and West Works) was added the £75,000 mortgage on the housing estate, which had been advanced to the Company by the Government in connection with the Austin Housing Scheme three years before.[46] Having purchased the North and West Works, much of the existing plant was scrapped, and the works reorganized, so far as it was possible, to adapt to the needs of vehicle production for the re-establishment of Austin cars in the post-war market.[47]

[45] MBA (509), Midland Diary 5, 7 February 1919.

[46] PRO T.16152 53776/1, Memorandum by Sir Reginald Brade, 1923; Companies House File 133747, Austin Motor Company, Mortgage Deed.

[47] The first Austin car leaving Longbridge for sale to the public was on 22 July 1919. In the succeeding twelve months 543 cars were produced. C. R. F. Engelbach, 'Some Notes on Reorganizing', p. 498.

CHAPTER FOUR

Financial Constraints and Managerial Reform

WITHIN A COMPANY CONTEXT of minimal liquidity the task of expanding production proved a daunting one, and negotiations with the Bank and the Treasury between 1919 and 1923 brought few concessions. This was despite the admission by a senior official at the Ministry of Munitions that to Austin, more than to any other firm, was to be attributed the saving in the price of shell during the war. 'They helped to break the ring of armament firms which was keeping up the price of shell and on a turnover of £8 million are said to have made only a profit of £80,000.'[1] Profits on other contracts with Austin were described as having been either negligible or involving considerable losses, and a Treasury memorandum referred to the Birmingham firm as 'particularly virtuous contractors'. Such profits as were made were considerably diminished by Excess Profits Duty, for unlike other armament firms Austin was not run as a National Projectile Factory, and therefore not eligible for exemption from E.P.D.[2] But sympathy within the Ministry of Munitions could not alter Austen Chamberlain's view, erroneous though it was (see Table 2), that the Company was in difficulties before the war, that the war had served the Company well, and that its difficulties were in no way due to Government action.[3]

A further drain on the Company's resources arose from the Housing

[1] PRO T.161/52 S 3776/J. Memorandum, Sir George Barstow to Chancellor of the Exchequer, 4 September 1922. The Company had been granted £25,000 by the Ministry at the time of final settlement in acknowledgement of the under-profitability of Austin's shell contracts.

[2] The yield on the munitions contracts was at most 1 per cent.

[3] PRO T.161/52 S 3776/1, 17 May and 25 May 1920.

Scheme, for the effects of inflationary conditions under which it occurred imposed serious financial burdens after the war. Whereas the Government had contributed to the project by way of a £75,000 loan on mortgage, the debt had been reduced subsequently, not on the basis of the value of the scheme at the time of construction, but on the basis of the difference only in the cost of erecting the dwelling houses. Furthermore, rental revenue from the estate yielded no more than £2,500 annually towards interest charges and no provision could be made for repayment of capital. One effect was that accumulated losses on the estate reached £200,000 by 1923.[4] The four-month moulders' strike during the winter of 1919–20 imposed an added strain on the Company's finances. Not only were some 3,000 cars lost to production, but Sir Herbert's necessity for retaining his labour force meant the accumulation of massive stocks of materials and work in progress in order to keep them employed.[5]

The Company's marked absence of cash had already attracted comment in *The Times* in January 1920,[6] and current ratios hovered around unity, falling to 0.5 in 1921. With a deficit on the balance sheet exceeding £1.5 million, Sir Herbert sought to meet it by repeating the issue of 1919. Against the Midland Bank's advice, Sir Herbert succeeded in persuading other shareholders to approve an increase in the Company's capital to £5 million by creating £3.35 million new ordinary shares.[7] Of that additional sum, £1.25 million was reserved, as Sir Herbert explained to shareholders, 'for the purposes of a negotiation which your directors have in hand, with a very large and influential company, which, if successful, will secure for the Austin Motor Company an alliance the benefit of which it is impossible to estimate'.[8] This allusion was to discussions about to begin with General Motors, in which James White, for the Beecham Trust, played the broker's role. Indeed, amalgamation assumed an increasingly

[4] PRO T.161/52 S 3776/1, Memo by Sir Reginald Brade, 1920; Memo by Sir George Barstow to Sir W. Joynson-Hicks, 6 July 1923.

[5] PRO T.161/52 S 3776/1, Memorandum by Sir Reginald Brade, 1920.

[6] *Times*, 26 January 1920; *Autocar*, 22 May 1920.

[7] Reluctant to return to the Stock Exchange within a year of the first post-war public issue, in December 1919 Ash had discussed other alternatives with the bank manager, including an issue of £1 million short term notes, following B.S.A.'s example, or acceptance of an offer made to Austin by Dunlop of £500,000 cash advance in return for an exclusive tyre contract. MBA (509), Midland Diary, 12 December 1919.

[8] AMB, 21 January 1920; *Times*, 26 January, 4 June 1920.

attractive prospect for the British company when after a month more than 80 per cent of the stock issued in January still remained in the hands of the Beecham Trust.[9] It was the failure of this issue which heralded the eventual financial crisis leading to receivership.

The fresh capital issue was the reason given by the bank for its refusal of increased overdraft facilities, a step which Sir Herbert had feared would also seriously affect the Company's general credit standing.[10] By the spring, Ash reported to the Bank that the dealings with General Motors had 'entirely gone off', and that Austin was now wooing Explosive Trades Ltd. for a £1 million debenture through direct negotiations with Arthur Chamberlain.[11] What was not mentioned was an overture which Sir Herbert had already made privately to Sir Harry McGowan, the leading financier who was associated with the Nobel Industries Group, controlling companies in and on the fringes of the motor industry, and with a seat on the Board of General Motors.[12] To him Sir Herbert had dispatched a telegram offering £1.85 million ordinary shares at par in the event of General Motors turning Austin down.[13] It is clear that although Sir Herbert was quite prepared to merge with any suitor commanding abundant financial resources, his Board of Directors was not, having resolved formally in January 1919 that every effort should be made to avoid an American company securing a controlling interest.[14] Not surprisingly, when his co-directors learned of the Chairman's offer to McGowan they persuaded Sir Herbert to try to get his telegram rescinded.[15]

In the event, none of these approaches proved fruitful. Yet at a time when the Company was incurring losses, ordinary shareholders were pressing for a capitalization of £200,000 of undivided profits and the issue of one ordinary share for every two held, a scheme which in profit terms could only be justified by a substantial rise in earnings.[16] Profits depended upon enlarged output, and at the time when the capitalization proposals were being discussed, Ash explained to shareholders that in order to double production, which was Austin's plan,

[9] *Times*, 25 February 1920.

[10] AMB, 5 February 1920.

[11] AMB, 11 May 1920; MBA (509), Midland Diary, 17 May 1920.

[12] W. J. Reader, *Imperial Chemical Industries, A History*, Vol. II, *The First Quarter Century 1926–1952* (1975), pp. 13–15.

[13] AMB, 17 February 1920.

[14] AMB, 7 January 1920.

[15] AMB, 17 February 1920.

[16] *Times*, 28 May 1920.

investment in plant alone was estimated to cost £200,000. The total requirements were presented to the bank by Harvey du Cros and Sidney Van dem Bergh, namely £350,000 for ordinary trading and £150,000 to meet any further loan contingencies.[17] In May 1920 the Company issued £1.5 million 10 per cent preference shares, but this proved to be another failure. Only £67,000 was subscribed, less than £1,000 coming from the public, with the remainder from the Beecham Trust, £30,000 from the underwriters, and £10,000 from the Harvey Consolidated Estate, which was one of the du Cros companies and, in fact, defaulted on payment.[18] Personal guarantees provided by Sir Herbert, Harvey du Cros and Randle Ash in order to secure further capital involved them in a financial loss of £11,500, the deficit registered by the trust company, which unsuccessfully negotiated the issue. Not until 1923 was this taken over as a corporate responsibility.[19]

The capital structure of the Company had altered fundamentally in 1919, when to the 400,000 ordinary shares and 150,000 preference shares were added 1,000,000 of the latter, and a further 1,500,000 preference shares in 1920 (Table 4). The higher gearing resulted from the additional preference shares of course imposed a greater annual dividend commitment to shareholders, which was in excess of a quarter of a million pounds in 1920. That figure fell short of net profits made in 1919 by only £10,366.[20] Following the issue failure in 1920, the Midland Bank offered a £350,000 debenture which the Austin directors turned down on the grounds that Austin's suppliers of raw materials could not be expected to countenance greater protection being extended to the Midland Bank than to the suppliers themselves. Their contribution to Austin's survival had been, and would continue to be, critical.[21] But the bank's position hardened, the manager proceeding to condemn not only Austin's failure to pay off the overdraft out of the recent capital issue, but also its failure to clear that overdraft, as had been agreed, by the end of April 1920. Sir Herbert was told that under the circumstances the bank would prefer his Company to borrow elsewhere.

[17] MBA (509), Midland Diary, 17 May 1920.
[18] AMB, 17 February 1920.
[19] AMC Papers, AGM, 18 December 1923.
[20] The profit of £237,866 recorded for 1919 was before the 1916–19 liability for Excess Profits Duty had been met.
[21] MBA (509), Midland Diary, 17 May 1920.

In order to expand production Sir Herbert decided upon an offer to clear the Company's indebtedness within six weeks by the extremely risky step of deferring payment to creditors, mainly the principal suppliers, by one month to two, and by the issuance of short term notes at 7 per cent.[22] There was general recognition that an Austin issue of *any* kind was risky. The Company's financial difficulties, and in particular the failure of the 10 per cent Preferred Ordinary issue, were the subject of considerable adverse comment in the City. They were accompanied, too, by a continual fall in the Stock Market quotation so serious as to prompt a public statement from Sir Herbert in July 1920, when he entertained some of the Company's larger shareholders at Longbridge. On that occasion he urged Austin shareholders to 'get the names of anyone spreading . . . untrue reports (about the Company)', promising to 'do our best to make an example of them'. After justifying the Company's policy and practices during the reconstruction period, especially in respect of stockholding and continuous working during the eighteen weeks moulders' strike, he drew attention to the fact that the bulk of the ordinary capital was owned by the directors and their friends. With rather more than half of the total ordinary share issue in the hands of Sir Herbert, he stressed that he had never sold a share and had no intention of so doing.[23]

The September coal strike caused a postponement of the short term note issue, and as stocks rose suddenly the Company's overdraft, which it had been agreed should be reduced to £100,000 by weekly payments of £10,000, now rose to levels quite unacceptable to the bank. With the bank now insisting on immediate repayments of the overdraft as a necessary condition for continued credit facilities, in desperation Sir Herbert offered a debenture as security in order to keep production going.[24] The offer was refused, and in search of relief Sir Herbert turned to the Government with the twin aims of eliminating the £200,000 overdraft on the Estate Account and reaching a settlement relating to the mortgages held by the Treasury. Austin's dilemma was explained to the Treasury: 'The undertaking must stop if capital be not forthcoming and immediately. Neither the bank nor the suppliers can any longer finance the Company. The bank has called in the over-

[22] AMB, 24 August 1920, 22 September 1920.

[23] AMC Papers, statement made by the chairman of the Austin Motor Co. Ltd., 26 July 1920.

[24] MBA (509), Midland Diary, 2 October 1920.

draft[25] and the creditors are in danger of themselves failing for want of discharge by the Company of its liabilities to them.' But the Treasury rejected a proposal that it should accept £315,000 of the proposed £1 million five year 7 per cent note issue in lieu of the mortgages. The Chancellor of the Exchequer added a note to the Treasury memorandum presenting the case for refusal, rejecting the claim for special treatment: 'I believe the Company to have been in difficulties before the war and that the war saved them. I do not believe for one moment that their troubles are due to government action.'[26]

Spurned by the Midland, Sir Herbert's next step was to try to persuade Lloyds Bank to extend a £150,000 overdraft in return for debentures. But again he was warned of the dire consequences such an arrangement would have on the Company's major creditors, and the matter dropped.[27] Rejected by the banks, Austin's directors could see no alternative but to issue a first mortgage debenture of £150,000, which the Eagle Star and British Dominion Insurance Company was persuaded to take up in exchange for a loan to that amount in January 1921, with an agreement that the bank should claim no more than £25,000 of that loan.[28] Once this was settled satisfactorily the Midland Bank undertook to accept a second mortgage debenture as security for a temporary overdraft of £250,000, though it was agreed that the proceeds of the initial loan should be paid to the bank to clear off the existing overdraft.[29] In fact, these arrangements led to the Austin issue of First Mortgage Notes and Second Debentures to the value of £400,000 issued in January 1921.[30]

As the ultimate financial crisis approached in February, temporary financial assistance was secured by an issue of short-dated notes for £150,000.[31] The directors decided that after paying wages in the third

[25] Which then exceeded £0.8 million. Trade creditors' claims rose to nearly £1.5 million in 1920.

[26] PRO T.161/52 S 3776/1, Memorandum, George Barstow to Chancellor of the Exchequer, 4 September 1920.

[27] AMB, 23 November, 14 December, 23 December 1920.

[28] AMB, 23 December 1920.

[29] AMB, 23 December 1920; Companies House File 133747, Austin Motor Co. Ltd.

[30] In order to raise larger longer-term finance, in February the Company proposed issuing a £1 million 10 per cent First Mortgage Debenture, of which one-half to be offered to the public. But when the scheme was put to Lloyds Bank in an effort to enlist its support and persuade Lloyds to take over the Austin account from the Midland, Lloyds refused. AMB, 22 February 1921.

[31] AMC Papers, letter to shareholders from Sir Herbert Austin, 6 March 1923.

week of April all subsequent incoming cash payments should be used to pay accounts coming under their personal guarantee, meanwhile requesting 'friendly' creditors, the Midland Bank and the Eagle Star, to file a petition for the appointment of a receiver and manager. Before the month had ended, the Company had passed into the hands of the Receiver, who installed Sir Arthur Whinney as Manager of the Austin Motor Company.[32] Representatives from the banks, Eagle Insurance, and principal trade suppliers formed the Creditors' Committee. Under the Receiver it became clear that a further public issue would be doomed to failure, and that only by securing the confidence and support of creditors and existing shareholders could the Company expect to obtain adequate finance necessary to continue production.

Both confidence and working capital were forthcoming after a change in the composition of Austin's Board of Directors, together with a personal loan from Sir John Leigh, Chairman and Managing Director of the Triumph Motor Cycle Company, of £200,000 on 10 per cent debentures.[33] The long term solution to Austin's financial problem was the issue of a £1.5 million debenture of three different kinds to be repaid over five years, the basis of the scheme unanimously accepted by the creditors in January 1922.[34]

32 *Times*, 27 April 1921; *Motor Trader*, 9 November 1921; AMB, 25, 31 January 1921; 19, 26 April 1921.

33 Later Lord Leigh, he was also Chairman of Leigh Mills Co. Ltd. *Directory of Directors; Motor Trader*, 9 November 1921. Directors remaining on the Board were Sir Herbert, as Chairman and Managing Director; Harvey du Cros as Deputy Chairman, and Randle Ash. The additions were: Sir Reginald Brade, GCB, director of the Victory Insurance Company; Sir Arthur Henry Hardinge, KCB, formerly British Ambassador to Spain; Alfred T. Davies, MP, since the war a director of Salmon Cars (England) Ltd., and T. D. Neal, FCA, a chartered accountant of Agar, Bates & Co. Companies House File, 133747, Austin Motor Co. Ltd., *Times*, 25 March 1922. Du Cros was also a director of Amalgamated Cotton Mills Trust Ltd., Alex Mosser Ltd., and Chairman of W. & G. du Cros Ltd. Ash was Managing Director of R. G. Ash & Co. Ltd., a firm of distributors. *Directory of Directors* (1922). Alfred T. Davies was also Chairman and Joint Managing Director of the Glynbendy Tin Plate Works, and a director of Old Silkstone Collieries, Regent Carlton Company, South Wales Fuel Company and Wenex Flax Factories Ltd. *Directory of Directors* (1922); *Times*, 25 March 1922; *Who's Who in the Motor Trade* (1934), p. 44; *Birmingham Gazette*, 8 February 1938; Companies House File, 133747. T. D. Neal was also a director of C. Akrill & Co., and T. Perry & Son. *Directory of Directors* (1922).

34 It consisted of an issue of £200,000 8 per cent first mortgage debentures tax free up to 8 per cent, to be a first charge on the freehold and leasehold properties of the Company together with all buildings, plant and machinery. This excluded

Capital reconstruction formed only a part of the reform called for by the Creditors' Committee. The appointment of Carl R. F. Engelbach, OBE, to the post of Works Director with a seat on the Board was a Committee decision, taken on the advice of the Midland Bank, as was its wish that he should assume sole charge of production, the works drawing office, the purchase and stores department, works maintenance, and also assume supervision of the plant and all works staff. Engelbach was formerly Works and General Manager of Armstrong Whitworth's car making enterprise, a professional engineer particularly concerned with organization and who during the war had been in charge of the Howitzer Department at the Coventry Ordnance Works. The Committee also proposed that whereas the ultimate control of the works should be in the hands of the Board of Directors, a Board of Management should act for them, with the Chairman as Technical and Sales Director (but not Managing Director), Sir Reginald Brade as Secretarial Director, and Carl Engelbach as Works Director. It was the last appointment, and in particular the terms of reference attaching to it, which aroused Sir Herbert's suspicions. As a rearguard action he discussed the matter with Engelbach before informing the Creditors' Committee of his view. In a letter to the Creditors' Committee Sir Herbert refers to Engelbach's declared willingness to act as 'Lieutenant, . . . an arrangement in which I agreed to give him all the loyal and friendly assistance to enable him to effectively take up the position of Works Manager with a seat on the Board. In doing this I am suppressing my own desires and judgement, but if the position is left at this I think it may work itself out satisfactorily. I . . . cannot accept the limitation of the effective management of the Company's affairs to any three of its directors. As the new Board will presumably

---

the Longbridge Estate, which was to be sold. The proceeds of that issue were to enable the £150,000 10 per cent first mortgage notes of the British Dominions Insurance Company to be paid off and meet other claims. The second debentures were increased from £250,000 to £285,000, carrying interest at $\frac{1}{2}$ per cent above bank rate with a minimum of 5 per cent and payable at seven days' notice, these to be held by the London Joint City and Midland Bank as security for bank overdraft. A third mortgage debenture for £248,000 replaced the Government security for the £240,000 advance on the North and West works. Repayment of the third debenture was by eight annual instalments, the first due on 31 December 1924. The fourth debenture stock was also created to meet the claims of unsecured creditors, bearing no market rates of interest until 30 June 1923, thereafter holders receiving 6 per cent. *Motor Trader*, 18 January 1922.

be fully capable of controlling the Company's affairs in an effective manner, matters such as these must be left to their discretion to determine from time to time. The outline of Mr. Engelbach's duties can, I am confident, be left to the decision of the Board, after he has had a chance to get a grip on the work. But they cannot include design, cost or purchase. The design I shall be responsible for; cost the secretarial director; and purchase under the commercial director'.[35]

The Creditors' Committee held a second meeting, at which the members accepted Sir Herbert's principal modifications to their own proposal. Engelbach's duties were clearly specified; his responsibility for control of the production office, including buyers and the storekeeper; the inspection staff,[36] the works engineer and his staff; the various production shop superintendents and repairs staff; and the jig drawing office and staff. Engelbach was to be on trial for six months at an annual salary of £2,000 tax free, plus 2 per cent on net profits.[37] Sir Herbert was temporarily to relinquish the title of Managing Director.

Despite shareholders' opposition to changes which appeared to deprive Sir Herbert of effective management, Sir Herbert's support for the general shape of reconstruction, and his acknowledgement that the appointment of a Works Director was necessary 'in the Company's interest', proved sufficient to silence further opposition. Nevertheless, Sir Herbert and his co-directors continued to insist that the creation of a Works Director was acceptable to them subject only to the acceptance by the creditors at large (as distinct from the Creditors' Committee and Sir Reginald Brade in particular) of the reconstruction scheme. Sir Reginald Brade objected strongly to this view and promptly resigned from executive management and from the Board.[38] His successor as secretarial director was a nominee of the Midland Bank, Ernest L. Payton, who was duly appointed with the support of the Creditors'

[35] AMB, 22 November 1921. 'That bloody interloper' was a description alleged to have been used by Sir Herbert to describe Engelbach. H. W. Holbeche recalls that when Engelbach arrived at Longbridge he insisted on moving out of the modest, somewhat remote office allotted to him, into more imposing quarters at the front of the building facing Sir Herbert's own office. By communication, 5 November 1977.

[36] Except final inspection, which was to be the responsibility of the sales department.

[37] Sir Herbert objected to the percentage clause. AMB, 22 November 1921; 6 December 1921.

[38] AMB, 25 January, 3 February 1922; AGM, 14 March 1923.

Committee. Later to become Deputy Chairman (in 1928) and Chairman and Joint Managing Director (on the death of Lord Austin in 1941), Payton was a financier involved in property development and insurance, bringing much needed expertise to the Company as financial director.[39]

The conditions for continued support from the creditors included the payment of 5 per cent interest on unpaid balances of creditors' claims after the end of the first year, and the issue of debentures to creditors, which were to become enforceable in the event of a minimum of £25,000 in any three months not being paid to the trustees.[40] The reconstruction scheme came into operation in March 1922, the directors resuming full control of the Company in April;[41] but Sir Herbert continued to make it clear that so far as he was concerned the creditors, rather than the Creditors' Committee, were the external arbiters of the Company's activities.[42] Moreover, in the negotiations over the new scheme he drew attention to his confidence in the Company's future yet again by retaining his shareholding, which at that time exceeded more than 50 per cent of the 300,000 ordinary shares.[43]

With the receivership ended, renewed efforts were made to eliminate indebtedness to the Government. The terms on which the Company had secured the initial finance to purchase the North and West Works when the war ended had involved the issue of a First Mortgage Debenture for £240,000 with a charge over the entire Longbridge Works.[44] The Government's security was the original sale price, instead of the current value, repayable in eight annual instalments. Such an arrangement seemed particularly irksome to the Austin directors in 1923, for even the Treasury acknowledged privately that the North and West Works had been sold to the Company at boom prices in the exceptional circumstances of there being no other possible purchaser, and that in 1923 one of the works was idle and the other only in marginal use.[45] To clear that indebtedness, and the debt of

[39] *Directory of Directors*, Obituary, AMC Papers.

[40] AMB, 31 May 1921.

[41] *Times*, 19 September 1923.

[42] The distinction, in effect, was between business suppliers and financial institutions.

[43] AMC Papers, Circular to shareholders, 14 February 1922.

[44] Companies House File 133747, Austin Motor Co. Ltd., Mortgage Deeds.

[45] The tortuous details of these negotiations beginning in 1919 are to be found in a memorandum by Sir George Barstow to Sir W. Joynson-Hicks, 6 July 1923, PRO T.161/522, S 3776/1.

£37,500 on the Housing Estate thirty-year mortgage, the Company offered a cash settlement of £115,000. The Treasury asked for £200,000.

Payton was asked to provide satisfactory reasons why it would not be in the public interest to allow matters to take their course and enforce, if necessary by liquidation, the Company's obligation to the Government. He drew attention to the size of Austin's payroll, which then consisted of 5,000 workers, and to the risk of defection by suppliers if the Company returned to the hands of the Receiver caused by renewed uncertainty. Payton predicted that in the event of liquidation the poor layout of the works would necessitate dismemberment, and consequently complicate and delay realization of assets which at that time were large enough to cope with a turnover two and one-half times current production levels. As a compromise, Sir George Barstow suggested that in liquidation of its debts to the Government the Company might offer £100,000 cash and a further £100,000 payable by annual instalments of £10,000, though unsecured and without interest. Joynson-Hicks approved the offer, but initially only on condition that the Company undertook to employ 5,000 men for two years and that instalment payments should carry interest.[46] Payton drew attention to the impracticability of guaranteeing employment levels, but on behalf of the Board agreed to 10 per cent interest payments on the £100,000, repayable at the rate of £10,000 per annum. The Company was to issue a debenture for this sum to rank prior to the Fourth Debenture then in existence.[47] At this point in the negotiations the Midland Bank reminded Austin's finance director of the temporary nature of the loan extended to the Company during reorganization, and decided to restrict the Company's credit by £85,000 to £200,000 from the moment such a debenture was created, or on 1 January 1924, whichever occurred sooner. 'At the present time', Payton wrote to Sir George Barstow, 'the attitude of banks towards industry seems very unfair.'[48]

Not surprisingly, Sir Herbert looked back on the immediate post-war period as one in which sheer survival seemed at times highly

[46] PRO T.161/52, Memorandum, Sir George Barstow to Sir W. Joynson-Hicks, 6 July 1923.

[47] PRO T.161/52, E. L. Payton to Sir George Barstow, 13 July 1923; Sir George Barstow to PRO T.161/52, A. Ashton Smith to E. L. Payton, 7 September 1923; E. L. Payton, 16 July 1923.

[48] E. L. Payton to Sir George Barstow, 10 September 1923.

problematical.[49] This was true not only with respect to the solvency of the Austin Motor Company, for his private affairs were also adversely affected by the post-war slump. His investments turned sour, including the French and Belgian tractor companies, making it impossible to liquidate assets amounting to £200,000 to relieve pressures at Longbridge, while as guarantor to several firms on his own account his debts on their behalf had risen sharply in the depression.[50] Yet, amazingly, this was the time when his inventive genius created two motor cars, the effects of which in the medium term were critical in transforming the ailing Longbridge giant into a highly profitable enterprise which, within ten years, was to challenge Morris Motors for dominance in car manufacture. For the year 1921 brought abandonment of aircraft and lighting set manufacture at Longbridge[51] and the beginnings of commercial production of the Austin Twelve, followed in 1922 by the first appearance of the famous Austin Seven.

Not only in terms of product development did 1921 mark a turning point, for the financial and managerial reconstruction were also critical in Austin's revival; Engelbach and Payton were key appointments, and the latter's firm control of financial policy, when the Receiver withdrew, was as vital to the Company's future as Engelbach's reorganization of production and Sir Herbert's two new motor cars. With both Sir Reginald Brade and the Receiver removed from Longbridge in April 1923, Sir Herbert agreed to allow the distribution of the Company balance sheets for 1920 and 1921, wherein he was referred to as other than Managing Director;[52] but only on the understanding that it was without prejudice to his position. Again, Sir Herbert was assured that his co-directors meant no personal criticism, that his position must be such as would comply with the terms of the arrangement between him and the Creditors' Committee, and that the latter's interpretation of the agreement must be sustained in return for their

[49] Sir Herbert Austin, 'The Importance of Purpose', *Pall Mall Magazine*, V, 1929, pp. 12–15.

[50] Lambert & Wyatt, p. 118.

[51] Thereafter, lighting sets were built at Rugby by a separate Austin company, Austinlite, until it was acquired by Chance Bros. in 1932. Although Austin announced the discontinuance of tractor production in 1921, according to Freddie Henry tractors were still being produced in the mid-1920s, and a new design and prototype built for Liancourt in 1929.

[52] Sir Herbert reserved all rights normally exercised by a managing director to himself as outlined in his agreement with the Company, the issue over which Sir Reginald Brade had resigned. AMB, 25 April 1923.

continued support. Later, the arrangement whereby a Committee of Management became part of the Articles of Association, gave Sir Herbert the chairmanship 'in general supervision of the Company's affairs', with Payton as Deputy Chairman, controlling finance, and Engelbach in charge of the works.[53]

The financial crisis which threatened the firm's survival brought about important and far-reaching changes in the scope and strategy of production. In 1922 and 1923, however, there was little opportunity for manoeuvre, for even though financial and managerial reconstruction had been achieved in part, working capital continued to be in short supply. Engelbach later recalled that 'alterations, however much they tended to economy, had to be sacrificed to the cash position. New machines, however desirable as additions to plant, couldn't be purchased. . . .'[54] As output contracted, the workforce fell to between two and three thousand and round about 2,500 cars were built.[55] It is true that by the summer of 1923 the Company had paid off the First Mortgage Notes and issued in their place a First Debenture issue of £200,000; that the amount due to the Company's bankers had been secured to them by the issue of a Second Debenture for £285,000; that the government mortgage of £248,000 had been exchanged for Third Debentures; and that a Fourth Debenture of £106,650 had been issued to sundry remaining creditors. But the bank was already demanding a reduction of its debenture by £50,000, over and above the £35,000 already repaid, a demand which the Company condemned as a breach of faith between the bank and the Fourth Debenture holders.

The Board pleaded for time.[56] 'We have space and much equipment', Sir Herbert wrote in 1923, 'but we need *additional working capital*, or at any rate a moratorium for a reasonable period of the cash payments to be made to the Fourth Debenture trustees'.[57] By that time finance was required not merely for survival but for the implementation of a new commercial strategy, proposed by Sir Herbert with the support of Payton, following the success of the Austin Twelve introduced in 1921 and the promise shown by the Austin Seven.[58] The

[53] Companies House File 133747, Austin Motor Company, July 1927, Special resolution. E. L. Payton replaced Harvey du Cros as Deputy Chairman.

[54] C. R. F. Engelbach, 'Some Notes on Reorganizing', p. 498.

[55] *Autocar*, 6 September 1929; *Times*, 8 March 1930.

[56] AMB, 14 March, 18 July 1923.

[57] AMB, 1923 Memorandum, H. Austin and E. L. Payton.

[58] See below, p. 83.

conviction that a major investment in plant and equipment was necessary received confirmation during Sir Herbert's visit to the United States in 1922, where (despite the effects of the horsepower tax) he became apprehensive of an imminent American invasion of British motor car markets in a big way.[59]

* * *

The purpose of his American visit had been to investigate production methods in order to discover 'the means by which U.S. manufacturers were able to deliver a car from their works for about the same price that our Company had to pay for materials and accessories for building a similar sized car'. He spoke to Durant and to Henry Ford, and remarked on the intensified effort to be found at the Ford factories, where conveyors created 'an atmosphere of push and go which couldn't be obtained by the mere piecework wage system'. He recalled a similar atmosphere which had only existed at Longbridge during the war in the manufacture of shells. What is interesting about his comments is that while he attached considerable importance to 'atmosphere' in relation to productivity, the same lesson had not been learned from munitions production in his own works several years before.[60] He concluded that because the Americans could produce the equivalent of cheaper versions of 20 or 12 h.p. cars at prices with which the Company could not compete, it would be unwise to try to redesign them for a lower quality market. 'On the other hand the manufacture by us of a low-priced utility car would not only meet a large part of the requirements so far as prospective competition is concerned, here and in foreign markets, it would also help decrease the cost of our present models and provide a substantial means of early repayment of our Fourth Debentures.' Urging immediate consideration by the Board, he added: '. . . if we don't build a car, other interests will do so we feel certain.'

The low priced 'utility car' which he had in mind was that which later became known as the Austin Seven. The Austin Twelve had originated in requests made by Austin agents since 1918 for an alterna-

[59] AMB, 1923 Memorandum, H. Austin and E. L. Payton.

[60] He considered the key to such an atmosphere was the avoidance of excess material between operations. 'Each operation is being pushed forward by the one behind and drawn forward by the car in front.' An inscribed photograph of Henry Ford was a feature in Sir Herbert's otherwise austere office at Longbridge.

tive car, smaller than the Twenty, which could meet the demand, demonstrated before the war and which the Ten had not met, for more modest and lower cost motoring.[61] But not until June 1921, following the introduction of a new tax scale in January which penalized high powered cars, was a decision taken to manufacture a dozen 10 h.p. cars for testing prior to production in quantity. The estimated cost of this initial experiment was £10,000, a sum well spent in view of the warm reception given to the new car by Austin agents on their visit to Longbridge in August 1921, and which was soon to be transformed into the Austin Twelve.[62] When the decision to begin commercial production of 100 cars was taken by the Board in September, by common consent the question of going into larger production was to depend on future circumstances, in view of the considerable expenditure necessary for jigs and fixtures.

At the same time that agents' views were canvassed on the new prototype Austin in August, Sir Herbert had also received an enthusiastic response to his suggestion for introducing a 6 h.p. car, and that occasioned the first reference to this model in the Board Minutes. But just as the development of the Twelve was necessarily cautious due to lack of finance, so the future of the 6 h.p. car, the low priced 'cyclecar' as it was referred to in the Minutes, was hampered even before it took shape on the drawing board. Sir Herbert had proposed that the agents should finance its development by putting down deposits amounting to £25,000, paid by instalments over a period of several months, beginning when production commenced. For their part the agents asked for some form of security, but that could only be given to them after the various interests under the scheme of reconstruction had been brought into line. The alternative was to manufacture the Twelve in large quantities in order to offset the swing against large cars predicted by the agents in 1918, since reinforced by the higher taxation imposed in 1921 and affecting the Austin Twenty. The 6 h.p. (subsequently the Austin Seven) experiment was not approved, though it was agreed that Sir Herbert's scheme should be reconsidered later, pending arrangements of the Company's finances.[63]

[61] Sir Herbert not only stressed the Twelve's economy features, including savings on garaging costs, but also the greater appeal to the owner-driver in general and women drivers in particular. *Austin Advocate*, XI, March 1922.

[62] The new car was still referred to as the Ten in the summer of 1921. *Austin Advocate*, X, July and August 1921.

[63] AMB, 6 April, 23 May, 20 June, 13 July, 13 August, 9 September 1921.

But Sir Herbert refused to be deterred, either by financial stringency or by discouragement and ridicule from his co-directors and friends.[64] So began Sir Herbert's bid to realize his declared ambition to motorize the masses.[65]

[64] He also claimed that distributing agents had also been sceptical, but the evidence suggests the contrary. Ford Archives, Dearborn Detroit, ACC 285, Box 444, Sir Herbert to Henry Ford, 10 November 1926; *Motor Trader*, 26 July 1922.

[65] 'Sir Herbert Austin KBE, His Life Story', *Autocar*, 13 September 1929, p. 369.

Part Three: Invention and Innovation

CHAPTER FIVE

Commercial Policy: The Models

THE NADIR IN THE COMPANY'S HISTORY was reached in 1921, when rumours of impending collapse and closure before the Receiver stepped in caused Austin cars to be excluded from the Olympia Exhibition.[1] The Company's commercial policy seemed to exemplify the basic weakness of the industry, which, with the exception of William Morris, had largely ignored such exhortations as that made by Sir Auckland Geddes, President of the Board of Trade, who in 1920 had urged British manufacturers to cultivate mass production of moderate priced cars. *The Autocar* carried similar advice, advocating the design and production of utility cars like the Americans, lowering production costs by standardizing components. Again and again, attention was drawn to the Model T Ford which held a unique position in the British market as the only car neither too small, nor too fast, nor too expensive.[2] While he remained somewhat sceptical of the wisdom of American style mass production methods, nonetheless the error in committing the Company to specialization in the Austin Twenty became evident even to Sir Herbert. In the course of 1921, three years after his agents had pressed for a smaller Austin car,[3] he designed a small version of the Austin Twenty.

Small by Austin's standards, the Twelve represented Sir Herbert's bid for a share of the rapidly growing market for medium sized cars

[1] The convention adhered to by the show organizers was to prohibit exhibitors in the hands of a Receiver.

[2] *Autocar*, 13 March 1920; 22 January, 19 March, 26 November 1921.

[3] AMB, 6 April 1921.

Figure 1. Price Competition in the Market for Popular Cars 1921–27 (model years)

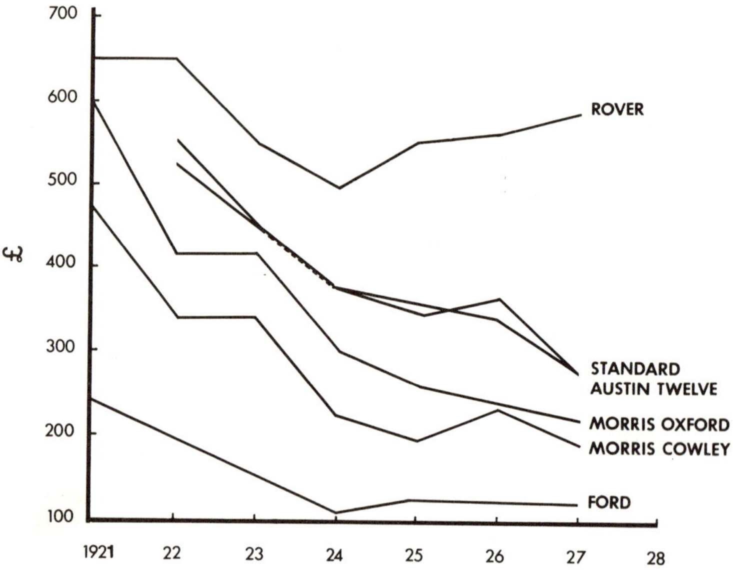

The prices used in preparing this chart are those for basic models of four-cylinder, four-seater cars quoted in the *Motor Car Index 1916–1927* (Fletcher & Son Ltd., Norwich, 1927). Prices for Rover refer to the 12 h.p. model 1921–23, the 14 h.p. model 1924–26 and the 10.25 in 1927; Standard prices refer to the 13.8 and 13.9 h.p. models; Singer prices refer to the 10 h.p. model 1921–24, thereafter the 10.26 h.p. model.

between 12 and 15 h.p.,[4] a market in which Rover was a leader towards the top end of the price range, with Ford and Morris at the bottom (Fig. 1). The Austin Twelve quickly established a reputation for appearance, comfort, and reliability, features which explain why, despite the failure of Austin to substantially reduce price differentials, the Twelve managed to survive competition and sell well (Fig. 2). Rover's competitor, priced at £750 in 1922, was outdated and lost favour with buyers.[5] From its launching in 1921, however, it was clear that at a price of £695 the Austin Twelve would find it difficult to seduce purchasers of the Oxford at £565, and even more so buyers of

[4] *Economist*, CX (1930), p. 581.

[5] George Oliver, *The Rover* (1971), p. 68.

Figure 2. Austin Motor Company Sales 1922–39

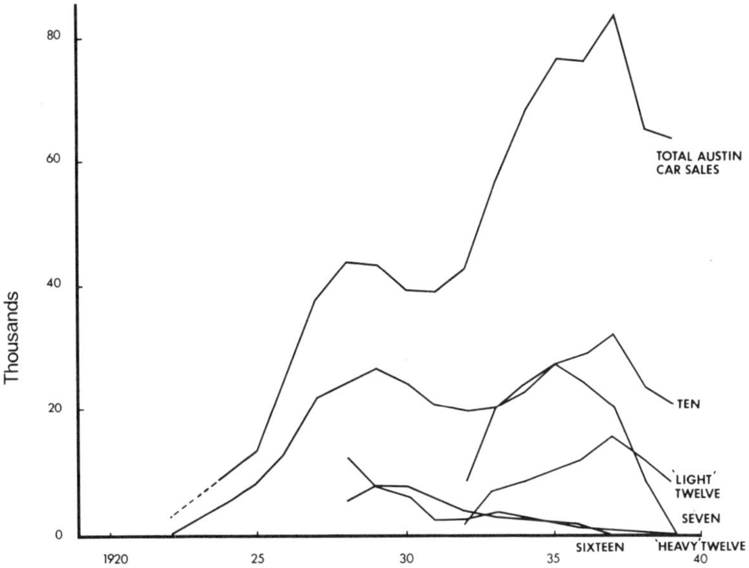

Source: Information supplied by the British Leyland

the Cowley at £425.[6] Furthermore, price differentials widened in subsequent years until 1926 (Fig. 1).

Thus, while Austin had produced an effective competitor for Rover, Ford and Morris proceeded to dominate the cheap end of the burgeoning market for cars of medium horsepower, size, and price. Sir Herbert acknowledged this even in 1921, when he decided to evolve a vehicle smaller than the Twelve, a miniature car which would be cheap to buy, economical to run, yet sufficiently robust, reliable, and weatherproof, to compete with cyclecars and motor cycles and sidecars.[7] Receiving no encouragement from his new colleagues, who probably regarded him with as much suspicion as he accorded to them, he decided to take the initiative independently and to develop his ideas for the production of a prototype in isolation from Longbridge, at his

[6] R. J. Overy, Table 5, p. 37.

[7] *Autocar*, 19 November 1921; Maurice Sampson, 'Yesterday and Today', *Autocar Austin Supplement*, 19 May 1939.

house at Lickey Grange. The first practical step was to arrange for an assistant, to be paid from Sir Herbert's own pocket, and to convert the billiard room into an office and workshop. The assistant he chose was Stanley Edge, a draughtsman at Longbridge, aged only seventeen, trained at the Austin Technical College and with whose enthusiasm for motor engineering and design Sir Herbert was already acquainted.[8] For eight months, beginning in the autumn of 1921, sometimes all day and well into the night, the two men grappled with the problems of designing a utility car which would break down the cost-price barrier which hitherto had hindered the development of a mass market.

Before the war the 1912 four-cylinder 850 c.c. Peugeot had combined the economy of the cyclecar with some of the comfort and versatility of larger motor car designs,[9] and although Sir Herbert had already designed a single-cylinder 7 h.p. model in 1910[10] it did not go into commercial production.[11] When the war ended, the ultra light, or baby, cars made by British manufacturers consisted of cycle-type cars of less than 1,000 c.c., fitted with noisy and often rough running two-cylinder engines. The 827 c.c. Jowett and the air-cooled Rover Eight of 995 c.c. represented the best of the popular twin-cylinder cars of the time; indeed it was the Rover, with its horizontally opposed two-cylinder engine, reminiscent of the early Wolseleys, which Sir Herbert had initially chosen as a model for his new prototype.[12] In the course of design development, however, preference was given to a water-cooled four-cylinder engine of small dimensions, along lines already developed successfully on the Continent.

Stanley Edge has claimed responsibility for persuading Sir Herbert to alter his original designs in this way,[13] and maintains that it was achieved by presenting Sir Herbert with a list, compiled from the pages of *The Motor Trader*, of small four-cylinder British and Continental cars. Of the twenty-six small cars listed, only one of the British 4 h.p. cars fell below 1,000 c.c., whereas several of the French companies,

[8] Stanley Edge, interviewed by Jonathan Wood, 'The Birth of the Austin Seven', *Thoroughbred and Classic Cars*, June 1977, p. 29.

[9] C. F. Caunter, *The Light Car, A Technical History* (1970), p. 49.

[10] C. F. Caunter, p. 52; 'Jubilee of the Austin Seven', *Austin Magazine*, May 1935, pp. 747–54.

[11] See above, pp. 28–9.

[12] S. H. Edge, 'Sir Herbert Austin, KBE, MP, During years 1920–25', *Magazine of the Austin Seven Club Association*, publication no. 73, p. 4.

[13] Stanley Edge interviewed by Jonathan Wood, 'The Birth of the Austin Seven', *Thoroughbred and Classic Cars*, July 1977, pp. 16–17.

and not only Citroën and Peugeot, produced small 4 h.p. cars with a capacity of less than a litre. The pre-war Peugeot Twelve had been discontinued, replaced in 1920 by the Quadrillette with a tinier engine than its predecessor – only 690 c.c. Although Edge did not see a Quadrillette, that was the model on which his own designs were based, once his employer had agreed to adopt a four-cylinder engine for the revised Seven prototype. When the design was completed, Edge, together with a works superintendent, a foreman, four mechanics, and an apprentice, spent six weeks in secrecy in a corner of Longbridge.

In order to build the first three Sevens, cylinder blocks, heads and crankcases were bought in from the Midland Motor Cylinder Company, radiators from Serck, carburettors from Zenith, magnetos from Watford, aluminium parts from Stirling Metals and springs from Richard Berry. The wire wheels were supplied by a local builder accustomed to making them for the motor cycle trade. Typical of the method of construction of other components at Longbridge itself were the crankshafts and connecting rods, which were machined from solid while the Seven team waited.[14] In the spring of 1922 the prototype emerged from the Longbridge Experimental Department Workshop.[15] Perhaps because his co-directors were sufficiently sceptical of the commercial prospects for the baby car, they agreed to a payment of a two-guinea royalty on every Seven sold by the Company, but this proved to be an arrangement which at least one of his co-directors, and the Creditors' Committee as a whole, strongly resented.[16] Another sceptic was William Rootes, whose Austin agency in Maidstone was important in the South-East.[17]

Sir Herbert had announced the Company's intention to build the Seven early in 1922, but the official launching occurred at Claridges on 21 July 1922, when Sir Herbert spoke to the press about the prototype on view in the Company's Oxford Street showroom. He described the market he was aiming at as consisting of 'the man who, at present, can

[14] Stanley Edge, interviewed by Jonathan Wood, 'The Birth of the Austin Seven', *Thoroughbred and Classic Cars*, July 1977, pp. 17–18.

[15] R. J. Wyatt, *The Motor for the Million: The Austin Seven 1922–1939* (1968), pp. 19–20.

[16] AMB, 28 January 1925; *Times*, 5 January 1927.

[17] Stanley Edge recalled Rootes's initial reaction to the Seven's early design, declaring in Sir Herbert's presence: 'My dear Sir, the public will just not stand for this', to which Sir Herbert replied: 'My dear Sir, I am educating the public.' S. H. Edge, 'Sir Herbert Austin, KBE, MP, During years 1920–25', *Magazine of the Austin Seven Club Association*, publication no. 73, p. 11.

only afford a motor cycle and sidecar, and yet has the ambition to become a motorist'. The new car was also designed to appeal to existing motorists who, owing to taxation and the high cost of motoring, might be encouraged to buy a cheaper car which offered reasonable comfort and reliability and was economical to run.[18] The most expensive motor cycle combination, a 1,000 c.c. B.S.A., could cost £200, complete with accessories,[19] whereas the Seven was launched on the market at only £25 more than that; moreover, with only a 2.125 inch bore engine it was reckoned to achieve a fuel consumption of fifty miles to the gallon and a top speed of 52 m.p.h. Despite these characteristics normally associated with motor cycle combinations, and despite its size, the Seven also *looked* like a motor car, closely resembling the popular Austin Twelve model.

Economy of operation was an important selling point, for the small engine offered relatively cheaper motoring, a benefit enlarged by the tax on motors of £1 per RAC horsepower rating. The effect of the tax, which was based upon the number bore of the cylinders and took no account of the stroke, was to penalize the large, long bore engines, whose owners became liable to heavier tax than owners of motor cars with engines of short bore; thus the luxury car (and the Ford) became more expensive compared with the smaller cars which became relatively more attractive on economy grounds. This is clearly consistent with Sir Herbert's decision to develop the baby car. Indeed, it is still sometimes suggested that the 1921 tax forced British designers to produce long stroke engines with high piston speeds, and that 'this distortion of technical design policy to avoid abnormal taxation costs continued to have detrimental technical and sales effects upon British cars until the horsepower tax was repealed . . .'.[20] The emergence of the British baby cars proper, beginning with the Austin Seven in 1922, might be construed as circumstantial evidence to support such an interpretation. But a comparison of small car developments does not suggest that the general thesis possesses validity.[21]

Already in 1920 correspondents for *Automotive Industries* had described an emerging tendency towards smaller-engined cars in Britain and on the Continent, and at least one attributed this trend in

[18] R. J. Wyatt, p. 21.
[19] *The Motor Cycle Buyers Guide* (1922).
[20] C. F. Caunter, p. 73.
[21] For corroboration see also the bore and stroke characteristics compiled by W. C. Bersey and W. F. Foucard, *A List of Motor Cars 1908–1914* (1914).

design to the influence of racing, beginning well before the First World War. He remarked on the stress in Britain, right from the beginning, on the practice of racing standard touring models, and the emphasis in tests placed upon reliability, economy of operation, consistent performance and fuel economy. In 1908 the elimination of fuel restriction had been followed by a requirement that engine bore should not exceed four inches for a four-cylinder engine, and that chassis weight (including driver) should be less than 1,800 lb. By taxing on the basis of bore dimensions and ignoring stroke length the motor tax introduced in 1910 reinforced this trend in Britain.[22]

In a careful review of the 'rating question', as he called it, A. E. Berriman argued that an examination of a table listing the technical specifications of cars available in 1924 showed a wide variety of strokes to be in common use in every class, and that while there was an undoubted concentration on low stroke/bore ratios used by a large number of different manufacturers and for a variety of models, the influence behind this was a consideration of manufacturing convenience and cost.[23] That the small bore, long stroke, high r.p.m. engine was identified typically by Americans as the *European* model also suggests that the high horsepower tax of 1921, the formula for which was unique to the British market, had little initial effect on the design of the popular motor cars made by British, as compared with Continental, manufacturers.[24] Small popular cars of the characteristically European type nevertheless did receive a degree of protection in the British market as a result of the horsepower tax,[25] the effect of which was to reinforce the technical bias towards high efficiency engines.[26] The construction of motor cars with shorter stroke and larger bore, characteristic of the American automobile, was discouraged by the tax, which meant that the standard British models,

[22] *Automotive Industries*, 15 January 1920.

[23] A. E. Berriman, 'A Review of the Rating Question', *PIAE*, XIX, 1925, p. 100.

[24] R. Carl Hicks and G. D. Babcock, 'Report of the Automobile Situation in the World and Europe', typescript report addressed to the President of the Dodge Motor Corporation (1927), p. 3, at Detroit Public Library.

[25] C. E. Haynes, *Motor Vehicle Taxation in Foreign Countries*, Trade Information Bulletin 463, US Department of Commerce (1927), pp. 32–3; E. G. E. Beaumont, 'The Influence of Law on Design', *PIAE*, XXXII, 1937–38, p. 69.

[26] Sir Herbert was critical, however, of the implications of this bias, for he was convinced that the horsepower tax 'cost the British nation in terms of lost export trade'. Sir Herbert Austin, 'The Future Trend of Automobile Design', *PIAE*, XXV, 1930–31, p. 8.

suited in terms of size to the American market, were technically ill-equipped to compete with the typically large engined but low performance American cars.

None of the evidence relating to the initial conception, design, and manufacture of the baby Austin suggests that either the behaviour of Sir Herbert or the decisions of his co-directors were directly influenced by the horsepower tax. In answer to a reporter in search of confirmation of such a possible relationship, Sir Herbert replied that the reason why he had adopted a 2.125 inch bore engine with a 3 inch stroke was the same as his reason for opting for the small size engine: 'It is all that is necessary with so small a car'[27] – a technical, rather than a fiscal, explanation. While a causal connection cannot be established between the horsepower tax and the initial development of the Austin Seven, neither is there much evidence that the ratio of bore to stroke of the average British car was very different from the general trend of European design. An important effect of the legislation, however, was to create more room for British cars in the home market by imposing heavy taxation on American cars, which, designed as they were for contrasting motoring conditions, typically possessed large bore, short stroke, high horsepowered engines, compared with British cars. American cars were very competitively priced in the 1920s but more expensive to run and to tax than those made in Britain, and these characteristics of British models, in a market whose growth depended upon new owner sales to less wealthy sectors of society, offered important incidental protective advantages to British manufacturers. It was no coincidence that even the Model T, the American people's car, which from 1921 became subject to a tax in the UK amounting to £23, experienced a rapid diminution in sales thereafter, despite its manufacture in Britain to avoid that tariff.

The high power-to-weight ratio contributed much to the Austin Seven's lively road performance which so impressed observers at the road tests and hill trials in July 1922, and popular interest was enormous when the Seven was exhibited for the first time at the Olympia Motor Show in November. Sir Herbert's daughter thought the commercial turning-point occurred when a Cambridge undergraduate purchased one, conferring upon the Seven a degree of social acceptability[28] which would thereafter offset the risk, perhaps, that an owner of such a small

[27] R. J. Wyatt, p. 22, quoting from the *Light Car and Cyclecar*.

[28] Lambert & Wyatt, p. 127. There is a parallel in the way that Issigonis achieved a similar breadth of social appeal when he designed the Mini.

inexpensive car should be identified with the motor cycling and sidecar set. Throughout the 1920s the social acceptability of the Seven, an attribute which the cyclecar had never possessed, was necessary for its commercial success, for the market for motor cars continued to be restricted to middle income groups. Sir Herbert considered the Cambridge seal of approval to have been of inestimable publicity value at a time when even the purchase of raw materials was barely within the Company's financial capacity.

As for Sir Herbert's explicit threat to the market for motor cycle combinations, it is not absolutely clear whether the impact upon it of the Seven was immediate, but it seems unlikely. The first census of mechanically-propelled road vehicles appeared in 1926, when 201,042 motor cycles with trailers or sidecars were recorded, rising to 205,450 in 1927. From that time, however, numbers fell by about 3,000 in 1928, by 7,000 in 1929, by 15,000 in 1930 and by 10,000 in 1931. The decline continued, though at a lower rate, for the remainder of the decade, falling to 106,200 in 1938.[29]

When we examine the level and trend of the prices of motor cycle combinations and compare them with prices of the Austin Seven, the explanation for the Seven's failure to achieve that which Sir Herbert had intended can be seen at once. It is true that the most expensive motor cycle combination could cost only £25 less than the most basic Austin Seven in 1922 (generously described as a three-seater, but including only a dickey seat for the second passenger), but few combinations of more than 1,000 c.c. were sold. By far the most popular were those between 350 and 700 c.c., with those machines of approximately 500 c.c. the most common choice. The prices of these were considerably lower than the B.S.A. 1,000 c.c. model and throughout the 1920s were substantially below those of the Austin Seven (Table 5). The prices of motor cycle combinations fell more rapidly than did car prices in this period, from an approximate ratio of two-thirds down to one-half. For this reason, and given a barely perceptible rise in real incomes until the end of the 1920s, the market for the most basic motorized transport for the family continued to be met by the motor cycle combination, and the Austin Seven found its initial market elsewhere. The decline of the motor cycle combination coincided, for

[29] Curiously, the tiny tricar market does not seem to have been badly affected by the Seven; indeed, their numbers actually rose beginning in 1929, slowly at first, but culminating in a minor boom lasting between 1932 and 1936, the peak figure of 24,911 tricars being recorded in 1935.

Table 5: Motor Cycle Combination and Austin Seven Prices Compared 1922–1928

Year	Austin Seven (2–3 seater)	B.S.A. 550 c.c.			Triumph 550 c.c.			Ariel 500 c.c.		
	£	£	s.	d.	£	s.	d.	£	s.	d.
1922	225	142	0	0	155	0	0	125	0	0
1923	165	100	0	0	115	17	6	107	0	0
1924	155	85	10	0	107	0	0	90	0	0
1925	141	87	0	0	88	5	0	77	10	0
1926	145	74	0	0	82	17	0	71	10	0
1927	145	n.a.			67	12	6	71	10	0
1928	125	66	10	0	—			66	10	0

Prices of motor cycle combinations refer to the highest price quoted for a model of the c.c. stated. They are taken from the annual *Motor Cycle Buyers' Guide*.

obvious reasons, with the more substantial rise in real incomes beginning at the end of the decade.

In order to secure major publicity for the Seven's technical and economic performance, Sir Herbert turned his sights to achieving success in competitive racing. His policy was not to build a special car which could barely approximate to a standard model, but to maintain the car's essential design, which with only minor adaptations was suitable for sale to the public in large quantities. After dismissing the building of special, or 'freak', cars as an indefensible pastime for manufacturers, he stressed the importance of testing production models, especially as the newly designed light cars were obtaining power more and more from increased revolutions, rather than by larger dimensions in bore and stroke. High performance required rigorous testing by speed trial, and racing also attracted immense publicity,[30] so it is not surprising that when E. C. Gordon England raised the possibility of racing the Seven Sir Herbert responded enthusiastically. England, who was connected with the motor industry and already experienced in motor racing, persuaded Sir Herbert that the only way to gain public acceptance for the little car as a practical proposition would be to race it.[31]

Sir Herbert's son-in-law, Arthur Waite, drove a Longbridge-built Seven to its first victory in the Brooklands Small Car Handicap in 1923,

[30] *Motor*, 11 September 1923; Herbert Austin, 'The Future Trend of Automobile Design', *PIAE*, XXV, 1930–31, p. 272.

[31] R. J. Wyatt, p. 34.

and later that year secured first place in the 750 c.c. class in the Italian Grand Prix at Monza, the first British car to win a race on the Continent since 1914. Between the extraordinary success at the Shelsey Walsh Hill Climb in August 1922, only months after leaving the drawing board, and 1924, the Seven won premier and/or other awards in no fewer than fifty-five events, quite apart from many successes at Brooklands. At Brooklands and Montlhéry it established no fewer than twenty-two International Class H records in 1924.[32]

It soon became clear that Sir Herbert had produced a winner, both at home and in Europe, and the immediate commercial success of the Seven is ample evidence of the high reputation which was established from the beginning. The only hitch which seems to have occurred arose from difficulties with the Seven's starting mechanism. Austin agents were informed that from the Olympia Show in October 1923 the Seven was to sell at £165, inclusive of mechanical starter. However, when Show time arrived, not only were mechanical starters still being assembled but many prospective buyers expressed preferences for electrical starters, which were then only at the experimental stage. A decision was taken to supply the car minus the starter at £160, with an offer to customers to supply complete equipment for the extra sum of £5 on any new Sevens delivered from Longbridge.[33] Despite this technical imbalance the Seven sold remarkably well right from the beginning (Table 6). Favourable publicity no doubt played its part, but the expansion in car sales by something like tenfold in four years and a growth in the numbers employed by about three times during the same period required managerial ability of a high order. This was especially so in view of the continuing financial weakness on trading account well into 1923, and a persistently unhealthy, though improving, balance sheet. Before we examine production management, however, it is necessary to consider the Company's commercial performance in the context of the industry and the phase of development which it had reached in the 1920s.

Austin's commercial success was the result both of internal policies and external trends which, certainly into the mid-1920s, were favourable to most car manufacturers. The movement of sales in the U.K. market between 1919 and 1925 show that after the sharp setback in 1921 the upward trend was strong, a movement also revealed in

[32] 'The Jubilee of the Austin Seven', *Austin Magazine*, May 1935, p. 747; Lambert & Wyatt, pp. 128–34.

[33] AMC Papers, Circular 5, S. Holbrook to Austin Agents, 18 October 1923.

Table 6: The Place of Longbridge in British Production of Private Cars 1922–1939

	(a) Longbridge	(b) Austin Seven	(c) UK	(a) as % of (c)
1922	2,600	178	73,000	(4)
1923	—	2,409	71,396	
1924	9,500	4,800	116,600	(8)
1925	13,250	8,024	132,000	(10)
1926	25,000	13,174	153,500	(16)
1927	38,000	21,671	164,753	(23)
1928	43,638	24,247	169,601	25.7
1929	43,287	26,540	179,178	24.2
1930	39,375	23,739	172,335	22.9
1931	39,027	20,645	159,941	24.4
1932	42,520	21,285	187,706	22.7
1933	57,350	20,383	224,704	25.5
1934	68,519	22,685	265,672	25.8
1935	76,656	27,225	324,192	23.6
1936	76,309	24,523	367,237	20.8
1937	83,990	20,671	379,310	22.1
1938	65,295	8,089	341,028	19.2
1939	63,827	656	305,000	20.9

Source: Information supplied by British Leyland and SMMT.

exports, domestic and total sales by British firms.[34] Income expansion and the reduction in car prices were important factors explaining this trend, but the effects of war and of the 1921 depression also exercised an influence well into the decade, postponing the period when 'normal growth', due to income and price effects, prevailed. Although the duty-free boom of 1925 produces distortion, the trend in home market sales suggests that the resumption of normal growth occurred in 1925, and in so far as the imports were used for stocking up, 1924 seems to be the more likely turning point. From 1924 to 1929 sales of new motor cars in the UK rose by 37 per cent, British firms acquiring 94 per cent of the market growth, accounting for 87 per cent of home sales. Continued growth in the size of the domestic market, therefore, was of vital importance to British manufacturers, but more detailed analysis reveals a marked deceleration in the growth of the home

[34] For a detailed analysis see Michael Miller and Roy Church, 'The Growth and Instability of the Motor Industry in Britain Between the Wars', in *British Industrial Developments Between the Wars* (forthcoming 1979), ed. D. H. Aldcroft and N. Buxton.

market at least from 1927, after which the expansion of British car manufacturers' sales relied increasingly upon import replacement and exports. In 1925 foreign producers held 28 per cent of the UK car market; by 1929 this had fallen to 13 per cent.

In attempting to analyse the contribution of Austin to the commercial development of the industry between the wars it is convenient to distinguish two phases of the early growth of the motor industry, namely that dependent upon *initial* demand, and that relying upon the more characteristic long term factors of changes in real incomes and costs. By initial demand is meant simply that which was activated as 'soon as consumers who could afford to buy motor vehicles heard of their existence and realized their value to them'.[35] In this phase elasticities of income and price (or rather, motoring costs collectively, since the cost of running a car depends on the depreciation of the asset value of the car, and costs of petrol, oil, tyres, repairs, and servicing, garaging, insurance)[36] are likely to be less important, at least directly, than what might be called the elasticity of product improvement: the propensity to reallocate *existing* income toward cars as their reliability improves.[37] This elasticity of product improvement was gradually superseded over time by those of income and price, and the resulting situation has been called a 'mature' or 'fully-developed' market. Continued falls in the prices of motor cars failed to stimulate a fully compensating expansion in home sales, whose decelerating growth from the mid-1920s provoked an upsurge in publicly expressed fears of the imminence of 'saturation point' in Britain; that is, the point at which the car stock would begin to stagnate, and all sales of new vehicles be devoted to replacement. In vain did the Liberal *Yellow Book* protest that 'It is reasonable . . . to suggest that we are yet very far from saturation point.'

Groups less impressed by the disparity between the levels of car ownership per thousand population between Britain and the United States and with more precise knowledge of the situation in the motor

[35] G. Maxcy and A. Silbertson, p. 38; D. G. Rhys, p. 221.

[36] According to the estimates of E. J. B. Sieve, 'British Motor Vehicle Exports (An Analysis of the Interwar Period and Some Post 1945 Trends)', unpublished Ph.D. Thesis (University of London, 1950), p. 322, it cost about 500*d.* to run a car for 100 miles in 1929, and 339*d.* in 1937; of these totals the elements of first cost (price) as reflected in an annual depreciation charge of the life of the unit, comprised only 27 and 22 per cent respectively.

[37] And hence real motoring costs.

trade took a decidedly different view. Another sign that anxiety about the future prospects for non-replacement sales was increasing is provided by the space devoted to the 'analysis' of the imminence of saturation in the yearbooks of the Society of Motor Manufacturers and Traders.[38] This was an interpretation of the vehicle market accepted by Professor Sir Henry Clay, the Bank of England's economic adviser, and one which the trade press communicated to its readers, intensifying apprehension in the trade.[39] Analysis of the pattern of new owner sales also lends support to the view that even before the Slump the growth in home demand for cars was, in effect, a response to a new product, pure and simple; an initial demand based on income diversion. After the peak value of purchases reached in 1925, there was a continuous fall until 1932; but even by 1929 sales values had fallen by nearly one-quarter, and it cannot be without considerable significance that the peak of that decade coincided with the slowing-down of the expansion of the domestic market. Of course, this can be seen as mere arithmetic: but the very scale of the peak of 1925 in the value of the market, and the fact of the steady decline thereafter, do seem to justify the contention that the character of the market was changing. For if it was the incomes of the already better off which the motor industry was tapping before 1926, and there was a discontinuity in the market, a gap in the structure of income distribution, it becomes easier to explain the co-existence of a fall in the real average values of cars purchased of well over one-quarter between 1925 and 1929 and a rise in the real incomes of persons receiving at least £250 per annum of about 5 per cent, with a 9 per cent fall in sales to new owners.[40]

The Austin Seven was admirably designed to bridge this hiatus. The Twelve had achieved enormous success and continued to be the Company's best selling car for most of the decade, but as the gap in the market became more evident, growth in the sale of the more expensive Twelve began to fall away. The contribution of the Twelve to the Company's commercial survival in the early 1920s was vital, enabling the Company to launch the Seven and in the later 1920s to develop markets hitherto untapped in Britain, even by Ford or Morris. Rapid

[38] *The Motor Industry of Great Britain*; compare the editions published in 1926 (p. 16) and 1929 (p. 45).

[39] For example, *Motor Trader*, 4, 25 December 1929.

[40] Michael Miller and Roy Church, 'Growth and Instability', in *British Industrial Developments Between the Wars* (forthcoming 1979), ed. D. H. Aldcroft and N. Buxton.

Figure 3. Price Competition in the Market for Low Cost Motor Cars 1921–27 (model years)

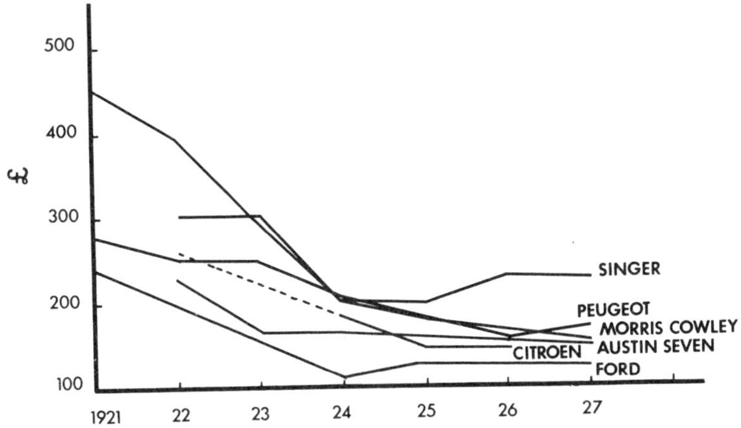

The prices used in preparing this chart are those for basic models of four-cylinder, four-seater cars quoted in the *Motor Car Index 1916–1927* (Fletcher & Son Ltd., Norwich, 1927). Singer prices refer to the 10 h.p. model 1921–24, thereafter the 10.26 model.

growth in the sales of the Seven, according to Engelbach, inspired confidence among the directors to press on with reorganization of production at Longbridge under the most difficult and financially constrained circumstances.

Yet the Austin Seven was not without competition in the section of the market at which it was aimed (Fig. 3). Among the continental manufacturers, Peugeot and Mathis competed in this small car market, but it was Citroën's 7 h.p. model which provided Austin with the greatest challenge, though the Austin Seven was both shorter and narrower by several inches than any of these competitors. Austin and Citroën cars were so competitive with each other, measured by performance and economy, that price competition became unavoidable in the battle for consumers in the early 1920s.[41] British competition was less serious. The Rover Eight, a modified air-cooled version of the pre-war Rover Eight cyclecar reintroduced in 1919, was cruder in conception and construction than other small cars, yet its performance

[41] R. J. Wyatt, p. 51.

was comparable, and, with a fuel consumption of 50 m.p.g., at least as economical to operate. Shortly after the first Austin Sevens appeared on the market in 1923, it was possible to buy a two-seater Rover Eight for £139, compared with the price of an Austin 'occasional three-seater' for £165. An important difference was that whereas the design of the Rover Eight was essentially, though not technically, a superior cyclecar, more reliable and affording greater comfort than the average cyclecar, the Austin was a 'real' car scaled down in size, with a fairly refined four-cylinder water-cooled engine of only 747 c.c. capacity; together these features achieved a highly acceptable combination of performance and economy.[42] The car's commercial success was due in part to the sheer excellence of design, which had been as true of the sturdy and endurable Twelve as it was of the Seven, while the latter's appeal was critically enhanced by its combination of high performance, low initial cost, and modest running expenses. A combination of these factors together explain Austin's success in competition with Rover and the lesser cars aimed at this market, Jowett, Belsize, and Trojan.[43] European competitors were disadvantaged by the tariff.

[42] George Oliver, *The Rover* (1971), pp. 71, 76.

[43] *Autocar*, 17 November 1922; R. J. Wyatt, p. 51; C. F. Caunter, p. 75; Cecil Clutton and John Stanford, *The Vintage Motor Car* (1954), pp. 120–3.

CHAPTER SIX

Organization, Markets and Merger Initiatives

STRESSING RELIABILITY, PERFORMANCE and low operating costs, rather than initial price (low though it was), Austin's sales campaign was relatively low key in comparison with the flamboyance of William Morris.[1] The typical Austin advertisement which appeared in the trade press and newspapers shortly after the war was essentially informative rather than seductive: 'The British Public continue to buy the Twenty on a full value for money basis and the makers are getting a fair and reasonable profit. Both sides are satisfied.' On the introduction of the Twelve, advertising copy stressed its 'good balance and proportion', comfort and convenience, and by 1925 the legend ran: 'Austin, it is agreed, means excellence', accompanied by a list of the features of Austin cars. Value for money and reliability continued to form the basis of Austin's general appeal: 'Originally designed to give utmost value for money, the Austin has never fallen short of that aim. And whilst no radical changes have been found necessary in Austin cars, improvements . . . are from time to time effected, thus always keeping the various models up to date.' By 1927, when more than 100,000 Sevens were on the road, Austin's advertising copy noted this fact, claiming that they were 'making life worth living and happiness inevitable'. The most 'imaginative' Austin copy appeared the following year, when the Company described the range of cars from the Seven to the Twenty as 'The Flying Squad': 'All Austin cars have wings, not only the well known wings emblem on the radiator but wings of speed, silence and smooth running in every part.' But the slogans which

[1] For a detailed account of William Morris's commercial policy see R. J. Overy, *William Morris, Viscount Nuffield* (1976).

typify the Austin appeal were those stressing the 'dependability' of Austin cars: 'You buy a car but you invest in an Austin. . . . Go to a third owner for proof of its lasting worth.'[2]

Only occasionally did Austin advertisements appear on the most favoured pages of the *Autocar*, whereas Morris frequently took the entire front or back page in colour to trumpet the appeal of Morris Motors. That does not show Sir Herbert's underestimation of the value of press advertising, merely that in his opinion flamboyance in advertisements was unnecessary. In 1932 he addressed an Advertising Convention in Liverpool, where he spoke of the manufacturer's dilemma in trying to strike a balance between retrenchment dictated by economic conditions and the feeling that he could not afford to economize on promotional expenditure in difficult times. While acknowledging that the press was the 'heavy artillery' of manufacturers, at the same time he warned advertisers against what he called 'boosted circulations figures and the failure of advertising costs to fall, in contrast with the productions which were advertised'.[3] After the initial launching, the Seven created its own publicity through an enthusiasm which its owners extended to it, comparable, perhaps, only to that which the Model T Ford attracted in America. The motoring press, and indeed the popular press too, described the achievements and idiosyncrasies of Austin Sevens and their drivers, a car surrounded by an aura of mirth, incredulity, and romance, coupled with, and sustained by, countless stories of its amazing economy, extraordinary durability and impressive performance.[4] Such accounts filled many of the pages of the *Austin Magazine and Advocate*, formerly the *Austin Advocate*, the Company house and advertising journal since 1911.

The sale of Austin cars depended much upon the success of distributors, and to help them to hold larger car stocks favourable credit terms were arranged with the Industrial Corporation Ltd., enabling them to borrow at 3 and 4 per cent.[5] Another measure to help boost sales was the negotiation of special insurance rates for car owners, first

[2] The quotations are from various issues of *Autocar*, *Buyer's Guide*, and from the *Austin Magazine* and *Advocate*, 1920–38.

[3] *Times*, 16 June 1932.

[4] See 'The Jubilee of the Austin Seven 1910–1935', *Austin Magazine and Advocate*, May 1935.

[5] The contract with agents stipulated that at least one car should be kept in stock permanently, and the discovery that such was not the case in many instances led to the credit scheme. AMC Papers, copy of circular to agents, 26 July 1921.

through Premier Motor Policies Ltd. and from 1921 through the Eagle Star and British Dominions Insurance Company, one of Austin's major creditors.[6] When the Twelve was launched in 1921 there was an attempt to secure exclusive dealing by making agencies for the new model conditional upon 'enterprise shown in selling the Twenty and a willingness to drop agencies for competitors'.[7]

The rapid expansion of sales from the mid-1920s led Sir Herbert to attach more attention to his distributors, in anticipation of the competition which he knew his own success with the Seven would attract. In 1927 he acquired Holland Park Hall, covering two acres, to be used both for wholesale distribution and as a service depot for the London district.[8] He also introduced various schemes to improve the repairs and maintenance service offered to customers, and to this end in 1926 Austin laid down a flat rate scheme for all Austin cars.[9] Two years later, uncertainty about market prospects explains a request that distributors should contract in 1928–29 for the same value of cars as in 1927–28.[10] The arrangement was that if at the end of 1928–29 the distributors and dealers had not individually completed the agreed schedule the Company would insist on the offenders giving up the sale of all competing lines, a threat which carried more conviction and represented more of a threat to dealers in 1928 than it had in 1921.[11] To enhance an agent's ability to stock more cars, the Austin Finance Company was formed in 1928 for the purpose of selling cars to agents on bills, a measure bringing agents greater discounts and Austin an improved cash flow. Agents paid 25 per cent deposit on the cars they bought, the remainder on bills underwritten by the Midland Bank at 5½ or 6 per cent. On condition that the Company undertook not to stockpile cars at the works in addition to the accumulation of stock carried at agents' premises under the new stocking plan, the bank loaned £500,000 to the Austin Finance Company.[12]

As part of the policy of tighter control on distributors, in 1930

[6] *Austin Advocate*, X, August 1921.

[7] AMC Papers, 26 July 1921.

[8] *Investors' Chronicle*, 10 December 1927.

[9] *Austin Advocate*, XV, 10 October 1926. A new service scheme had been introduced in 1919, following Ford's innovation in this respect the same year, but this had either lapsed or was revised in 1926. *Motor Trader*, 5 November 1919.

[10] The rate of expansion in Austin's sales fell off in 1928.

[11] AMB, June 1927, 1928.

[12] The directors were Herbert Austin and Payton. AMB, 8 February, 23 May 1928.

Sir Herbert took defensive action against the Rootes brothers' distribution agreement with the Hillman-Humber car group, refusing to renew Rootes's contract to distribute Austin cars unless Rootes severed connections with Hillman-Humber. The same action was taken against George Heath & Co., the major London distributors in whom Rootes had acquired controlling interests.[13] It may have been the resulting loss of expertise which these long established agencies had provided hitherto which prompted Sir Herbert to compensate by reinforcing the strength of the Company's sales drive. For in response to a suggestion made by the Institute of Motor Salesmanship he established the Austin Sales Training Centre at Longbridge. Organized by the Institute in conjunction with the Company, and the first of its kind, the scheme included a month's extension course of intensive training at Longbridge following the normal three months' course on motor salesmanship at the Institute's headquarters in London.[14] Training was available to Austin agents' salesmen, while for those unable to join the Centre for residential instruction the Company arranged for lecturers to visit agents' territories to inform, advise, and offer assistance in improving sales methods and, in particular, the selling of Austin cars.[15]

Sir Herbert had not always approved of sales methods in the trade, and was especially critical of price cutting through second-hand trade-ins. Deploring the price cutting of the 1920s, which he reckoned endangered the wellbeing of industry, Sir Herbert endorsed the Motor Trades Association's efforts to eliminate disorderly price competition at that time,[16] becoming chairman of a sub-committee of the SMMT in 1929 which since its formation in 1927 had sought to promote co-operation among all sections of the trade.[17] Others in the industry also drew attention to dwindling profit margins in the industry, the result indirectly, it was argued, of the 'commercial or business men of the industry', of salesmen continually seeking lower sales prices which

[13] AMB, 30 April, 28 May 1930.

[14] *Autocar*, 9 September 1932; *Times*, 2 August 1932. In 1936 Sir Herbert was elected a Fellow of Incorporated Sales Managers' Association, in recognition of his Company's service to the Association and the promotion of professionalization of sales managers in business.

[15] AMC Papers, Address by Sir Herbert Austin, KBE, to Distributors and Agents, 'Another Dependable Programme', August 1934. Following the scheme's introduction in 1932 other firms, according to Sir Herbert, had taken it up.

[16] *Times*, 28 October 1925.

[17] *Times*, 20 August 1929.

Herbert Austin at the tiller of an early cyclecar.

An early Wolseley motor car with Herbert Austin at the wheel.

Longbridge 1906.

The first Austin car trial.

The first Austin car trial in progress.

Production before moving track assembly, 1924.

An Austin Twenty Mayfair Landaulet, 1924.

An Austin Seven Tourer, with the Misses Austin, 1923.

Pictures by courtesy of British Leyland (Austin-Morris) Ltd.

created problems for the producers and ultimately for the automobile engineers. Depressed prices and profit margins were seen to discourage, if not prevent, manufacturers from reorganizing plant and introducing new methods, and for that reason Sir Herbert's preferred, but questionable, policy of orderly competition based on quality received support from others.[18] It is not surprising that Sir Herbert, as an engineer-entrepreneur, hard-pressed to sustain adequate liquidity, should have been sympathetic to this line of argument. But though nothing was to be done by any of the organizations, or by agreement between firms, the fierce price competition of the early 1920s lost impetus and the rate of price reduction declined.[19] Simultaneously, the rate of expansion of car sales in the domestic market also slowed down, in part offset by a relatively rapid, if modest, increase in exports.

Austin's performance in overseas markets was not unimpressive, accounting for 30 per cent of the value of British motor export sales, according to Sir Herbert, in 1925.[20] Recovery of the export trade had been one of Sir Herbert's declared aims after the war, for which purpose Randle Ash, formerly an independent distributor, became Austin's export director in 1922. It was he who urged the production of a specially designed colonial model of the Twelve; but Sir Herbert vetoed this proposal, arguing that the redesign of the entire chassis, which such a policy would have required, involved capital outlay and produced technical difficulties.[21] The alternative adopted was to cut prices of both the Twelve and Twenty models which spearheaded Austin's early export drive.[22] Explaining to a meeting of professional engineers in 1930 that 'none of us in this country can afford to build an essentially "colonial" vehicle',[23] elsewhere he blamed the horse-power tax for the difficulties of British motor manufacturers in export markets where big and high powered cars, uneconomic to run at home, were more suited.[24] Taxation, however, was only one of the factors

[18] E. G. E. Beaumont, 'The Influence of the Automobile User upon the Automobile Engineer', *PIAE*, XXII, 1927–28, pp. 12–13.

[19] E. G. E. Beaumont, 'The Influence of the Automobile User', p. 13.

[20] *Autocar*, 16 October 1925.

[21] Compare the unhappy experience of William Morris and the 'Empire' Oxford. R. J. Overy, p. 49.

[22] AMB, 9 November 1923; *Times*, 19 September 1923.

[23] Sir Herbert Austin, 'The Future Trend of Automobile Design', *PIAE*, XXV, (1930–31), p. 18.

[24] Meanwhile, Austin pushed sales of Austin cars to foreign tourists, at prices fixed for overseas markets, free of tax. *US Commerce Reports*, 14 May 1923, p. 421.

which may help to explain why, before the Slump, British motor car sales overseas represented so small a share of world trade in motor vehicles. The other feature of the British motor trade in the 1920s, the close concentration of sales in imperial markets, is mainly explicable in terms of sentiment or fiscal preference.[25]

* * *

It is quite possible that Austin's car exports might have been larger, had not arrangements been made in Germany, France, and the United States, to license the manufacture and sale of thinly disguised Austin Sevens in those countries. Evidently this was not Sir Herbert's view, for he stated that the reasons for the new policy on licensed manufacture were high import duties.[26] Thus in 1927 he concluded a licensing agreement with Gothaer Waggon-fabrike, in Germany, by which the newly-formed Dixi Werke Company would manufacture on a large scale and sell an exact copy of the Austin Seven in Germany and Eastern Europe, under the title 'Dixi'. The royalty of 2 per cent per car was divided equally between Sir Herbert and the Austin Motor Company. Nearly 14,000 Dixis had been sold by 1930, and production levels in the former munitions factory at Eisenach reached 350 or 400 a month, a performance sufficient to convince the Bayerische Moterenwerke (BMW) of the wisdom of taking over the company.[27]

A similar licensing agreement was reached with M. Lucian Rosengart, who resigned from the managing directorship of the Peugeot Company in May 1928, hired M. Salamon (the engineer who had designed and built the first Citroën), and commenced the manufacture of the French Baby Austin, the 5 h.p. Rosengart. In the huge Bellanger factory purchased from Peugeot, Rosengart planned to produce 60,000 vehicles a year.[28] The Company's nominal capital was 10 million francs, and the board included Rosengart himself, Henri Bancel, of the merged Chenard Walcker Company, which was to organize distribution, and Sir Herbert Austin. Unlike the Dixi, which was virtually identical with the Seven, Le Bébé differed very slightly in chassis design but quite considerably in its body, which consisted of

[25] See E. J. B. Sieve, 'British Motor Vehicle Exports (An Analysis of the Interwar Period and Some Post 1945 Trends)' (unpublished Ph.D. Thesis, University of London, 1950).

[26] *Times*, 23 February 1927.

[27] *Autocar*, 18 February 1927; R. J. Wyatt, pp. 67–8, 78.

[28] *Autocar*, 8 June 1928; R. J. Wyatt, p. 77.

a three-seater cabriolet with two separate front seats and a third set crosswise at the back. Construction was of a metal and fabric combination with steel panels up to the waist line. Eleven thousand were sold between its introduction in 1928 and 1930,[29] by which time Sir Herbert had also clinched a deal which would launch the Austin Seven on the American market.

A search for an American foothold had begun in 1928 when Sir Herbert had visited Detroit. His intention was to find an American concern which would enter into an arrangement similar to those agreed with the German and French: a licence to produce the car, designs, and a team of experts to assist in the preparatory steps in manufacture. In return, Sir Herbert wanted a directorship and a 2 per cent royalty shared with the Company. When interviewed in the United States by a newspaper reporter, Sir Herbert spoke enthusiastically, predicting huge popularity for the Seven in the USA, declaring, perhaps somewhat ingenuously: 'The car is light enough for two to lift out of the ditch.'[30] Failure to finalize a deal in 1928 led to a second attempt early in 1929, when he visited the US as SMMT representative of one of the three British companies (Vauxhall, Daimler and Austin) which exhibited at the National Automobile Show in New York. This was the first time that foreign cars had been allowed to exhibit.

Sir Herbert's advertisement in the major American newspapers invited those interested in such a deal to contact him, and arrangements were concluded within two months, with the specially formed American Austin Car Co. Inc. in Wilmington (Mass.), by which that Company acquired an exclusive licence to manufacture and sell the Austin Sevens in the USA for the next ten years, terminable if production fell below an agreed minimum.[31] Authorized capital consisted of a million shares of no par value and the American issue, amounting to £350,000, was oversubscribed at $12.50, 300,000 more being underwritten at $9. The response of the American stock market was thus surprisingly favourable in view of the sceptical reaction in the press to what, by American standards, appeared to be an absurdly small vehicle. Similar scepticism as to the suitability of the British baby for

[29] R. J. Wyatt, p. 77.

[30] *Autocar*, 3 February 1928.

[31] Sir Herbert was to receive 50 per cent of the licence fee from the American company in lieu of any royalty payable under the original licence arrangements agreed in 1922, modified in 1927. AMB, 28 August 1929.

the American market was expressed also in the British financial press. In fact the design of the American Austin differed radically from the British model, the Hayes Body Corporation tooling up for a style hitherto unknown in the American market, while Count Alexis de Sakhnoffsky was assigned the task of designing a miniature interpretation of the current popular American car,[32] 'the Bantam', as it was known. Sir Herbert's optimistic forecasts proved to be ill-founded, and in 1930 fewer than 9,000 cars were sold.[33] Whereas the Model T Ford had succeeded in breaking through the barrier of absurdity which it encountered in its early days, the Austin Bantam failed to overcome the ridicule heaped upon it from the start. The economics of the motor car, both in initial cost and operation, rendered the Bantam unsuitable for the American market, just as American cars lacked appeal for the British public. The American Austin Car Company experiment thus ended in liquidation in 1935.[34]

A more promising market for the Austin Seven proved to be Japan, where by the early 1930s the Jidosha Seizo Company, of Yokohama, had begun to manufacture a car almost identical with the French-built Austin Seven, though much inferior in construction, finish and performance. Careful scrutiny at Longbridge of a model designed to sell on the Australian market for £80 in 1933 convinced Sir Herbert that Jidosha, or Nissan as the Company became in 1934, was infringing patents covering the Seven, and proceeded to negotiate an agreement with Nissan whereby the Japanese company would in future build the cars under licence.[35] These were the origins of the Datsun motor car.[36]

* * *

Whereas the Twelve had attracted buyers at the upper end of the market for medium sized cars, the Seven appealed to economy minded purchasers, which made low cost production of critical importance.

[32] R. J. Wyatt, pp. 90–3.

[33] R. J. Wyatt, pp. 112–13.

[34] AMB, 4 December 1935.

[35] *Motor*, 27 February 1971. I am grateful to Mr. Freddie Henry for his account of this episode; by communication 2 August 1977.

[36] There is irony to be found in the coincidence between the detection of Nissan's infringement of Austin patents and the award in the House of Lords of substantial damages against Sir Herbert for breach of confidence, and a technical rejection of breach of contract, in connection with the Solcar sunshine car roof. *Times*, 19, 31 October, 8, 16 November 1933; *Birmingham Mail*, 23 May 1941.

Sir Herbert's visit to the American car factories convinced him that car making in Britain must be concentrated in fewer, larger, factories in order to compete with the Americans, whose low costs he attributed to low profit margins forced on component suppliers and to the American car worker 'who laboured twice as hard as the practice here'.[37] Volume production, albeit on a lesser scale than was to be found in America,[38] more efficient use of labour, and low cost output were the aims set for the £0.6 million investment programme begun in 1923,[39] which was to totally transform manufacturing methods and capability at Longbridge before the end of the decade. Prior to re-organization the schedules for car production were agreed at frequent intervals in small batches, the factor determining the size of the batch being Engelbach's estimates of the capital expenditure on machine tools necessary to sustain such levels. Each time the volume and composition of output was decided upon only after lengthy discussions of various combinations of product mix with anticipated costs, prices and profits of the alternatives. The investment programme beginning in 1923 marked the beginnings of quantity production at Longbridge.[40] After organization was completed, Engelbach explained to his professional colleagues of the Institute of Automobile Engineers the alterna-

[37] *Times*, 9 January 1923.

[38] In his remarks on the paper by F. Woollard (Morris Motors), 'Notes on British Methods of Continuous Production', *PIAE*, XIX (1924), pp. 453–5, Sir Herbert objected to the term 'mass production' but endorsed the need for the integrated conversion of raw materials to finished product in a continuous process of what he described as 'progressive manufacture', i.e. flow production. He argued that the large economies to be derived from line assembly could be secured from an approximate daily output of 200 cars, which was about the target capacity planned in the investment programme carried out at Longbridge in the mid-1920s.

[39] AMB, 26 May 1924.

[40] At a meeting of his professional colleagues from other motor companies in 1928, Engelbach outlined the major capital investment programme carried out at Longbridge between 1924 and 1927 and when he was asked how he had persuaded his co-directors to meet the cost of such an extensive scheme his reply was simple. He explained how he had estimated the savings to be derived from expenditure and submitted the figures in support of his proposals. On that basis his colleagues had agreed to the reorganization costing nearly £0.6 million to enable the Company to cope with an annual turnover of £4 million. He advised managers in other firms that should such a well prepared case be rejected, then resignation should follow, 'or get a new Board of Directors'. C. R. F. Engelbach, 'Some Notes on Reorganizing', pp. 523, 529.

tives which had faced the Company: either to halt production while the existing plant was remodelled, or to build and equip an entirely new plant, leaving the old factory undisturbed until completion. He described both approaches as 'heroic', the latter involving capital expenditure which few firms (and especially Austin) could face, and posing problems of managerial duplication, unless the new factory was erected immediately adjacent to the existing factory. On the other hand, to stop production until remodelling had been completed meant a loss of turnover, which again was unthinkable, given Austin's cash flow problem, and ran the risk of generating dissatisfaction and loss of morale among operating staff, with damaging long term effects. Another consideration was the attitude of agents and dealers.

Sir Herbert favoured a policy, so far as it was possible, of safeguarding standards of design and quality, of high volume production on small profit margins. Referring to the need to raise the output of Sevens, he argued at the time: 'We cannot expect to continue to get whole-hearted support from agents and dealers if we don't supply them with as many cars as they can sell . . . at the present rate of output we are only annoying our agents and customers and encouraging other firms to enter a market at present controlled by us.'[41] Constrained by financial circumstances, Austin chose the only way open to the firm, that of maintaining production and reorganizing simultaneously.[42] The principle adopted in improving internal handling and transport problems arising from operating the three separate works which comprised the Longbridge complex was that of grouping shops into more or less complete factories of their own, the products emerging from them being passed on ready for ultimate assembly in the erecting shop.[43]

Similar principles of organization were adopted in the body works as in the chassis section, machine work progressing to sub-assembly and thereafter to the body erection. Such alterations meant the abandonment of the group system of machine layout so as to enable work to proceed from machine to machine, and process to process, without any backward movement. This was the continuous flow production which had so impressed Sir Herbert in the Ford factories, the assembly line completing the system in which overhead gravity conveyers and assembly tracks played a critical part, inducing the 'atmosphere of

[41] AMB, 1 May 1924.
[42] C. R. F. Engelbach, 'Some Notes on Reorganizing', p. 496.
[43] C. R. Engelbach, 'Some Notes on Reorganizing', p. 499.

push and go' which had also evoked his enthusiasm. With the same superintendent responsible for machining, erection, and production of a given number of completed units each week (engines, gear-boxes, brake drums or axles, etc.), shortages acquired an increased importance, and difficulties due to non-delivery of one component became much more apparent and more quickly dealt with. Engelbach acknowledged that the degree of continuity in Austin's new layout was lower than that to be found in the American factories, and he explained this as due, in part, to the lack of efficient continuous furnaces needed for the hardening of steel parts, which represented a bottleneck in the line of continuous flow. Another reason was that because of the general design and the desire for the highest possible engine efficiency, Austin engines were more selectively assembled.[44]

At Austin, as in other leading motor firms, there was an increasing awareness of the advantages of well designed machine tools, and of the importance of maximizing loading positions for jigs and fixtures; of introducing hydraulic and electric power feeds, and of utilizing pneumatic or other forms of quick releasing chucks. Austin was introducing more single purpose machine tools even though the firm's car output could not keep them fully employed, some for only one-half a working week. The loss of interest on capital investment which such under-employment implied was, in Engelbach's view, offset by the assurance of full and complete operation of the remainder of the plant for all the time available in any working period, affording full utilization of labour and spreading overheads in other department. The excess capacity of the special purpose machine also offered scope for unhindered output expansion, which in turn could be expected to diminish the loss of interest on capital invested in it.

Not until the beginning of 1928 had output expanded sufficiently to justify the wholesale mechanization of chassis erection, though in the reorganization of 1924–27 moving lines, electric hand-operated hoists, pulleys and conveyors had been installed.[45] Despite the lower productive efficiency in comparison with American factories, Longbridge

[44] This was the common practice, according to Engelbach, in British motor car factories using aluminium pistons for selection in accordance with the individual engine bores; the difficulty in maintaining boring tools to exact diameters made it less expensive to adopt this practice than to insist on exact dimensions of individual cylinder bores. C. R. F. Engelbach, 'Some Notes on Reorganizing', pp. 502–5.

[45] C. R. F. Engelbach, 'Some Notes on Reorganizing', pp. 506–8.

had become the first British motor works with a moving assembly line, or 'mechanically driven track', for the assembly both of chassis and car bodies.[46] By that time the importance of possessing a best-selling car is clear from Sir Herbert's statement that a factory working to 85 per cent capacity could only just pay its way, and that reasonable profits required an output level of 95 per cent capacity.[47] In 1931 the foundry was re-equipped and reorganized on the advice of A. J. Brandt & Co., an American company connected with the manufacture of Austin cars in the United States.[48]

The introduction of labour-saving conveyors accounted for much of the drastic reductions in overhead charges, which sequential production on a quantity basis was designed to achieve. The ratio of overhead charges to the cost of productive labour, expressed as a percentage, fell from 241 in 1922 to 161 in 1924, and to 96 in 1927. Over the same period, the number of employees per car per week fell from 55 in 1922 to 20 in 1924, to 10 in 1927. Sales turnover rose by fivefold, the labour force by more than threefold, and profit by more than fourfold.[49] Clearly, the sheer volume of output brought about rising labour productivity and reduced the incidence of overheads, and Austin's commercial policy was also related to the rapidly rising turnover. But labour utilization also contributed to improved efficiency, and Engelbach was convinced that the Company had devised a unique working structure which encouraged greater efforts from employees, evidence of which was the rise in average earnings which increased by 72 per cent between 1922 and 1927.[50] This was the result, in part, of sheer mechanization and the greater output per operative which it made possible, but it owed something, also, to incentive systems based on a norm, the abolition of overtime, and the introduction of a timed piecework average with bonus payments on actual results (expressed as time saved) exceeding the norm.

In those cases where in any week results fell short of the standard,

[46] *Times British Motor Number*, 12 March 1929; C. R. F. Engelbach, 'Some Notes on Reorganizing', pp. 506–8. Mr. Freddie Henry recalls that even by 1924–25 the entire plant was linked with mechanized transfer lines. 'Even wheels and tyres rolled straight off the Dunlop lorries and down a conveyor which selected two per side of the track ready for fitting.'

[47] *Investor's Chronicle*, 14 January 1928.

[48] AMB, 24 June 1931.

[49] C. R. F. Engelbach, 'Some Notes on Reorganizing', p. 509.

[50] Ibid., pp. 509–12.

identified, for example, as a failure to supply material, a breakdown in tools, or error in jigs and fixtures, the matter was referred to the appropriate superintendent or production manager. Operatives who were deemed inefficient were 'weeded out', and foremen or chargehands considered to fall below standard were removed to different work 'or dealt with otherwise'.[51] The new system necessitated the grading of each job by the amount of skill required, consequently the rate necessary to pay an operator became the basis for wage bargaining at Longbridge. Each grade of skilled and semi-skilled workers, youths, and females was subdivided into three grades, and non-pieceworkers, labourers, superintendents and others, were paid on an output basis, more or less commensurate with the average piecework earnings of productive labour[52] and with no upper limit. Five years' experience of this system, unique in the motor industry, convinced Engelbach of its superiority compared with all others,[53] and its effectiveness was due in no small measure to the structure of production management in which Engelbach could delegate control to Hannay, the production manager responsible for fifteen or sixteen workshop superintendents, each of whom was in command of between five hundred and a thousand workmen. These were subdivided into sections of about two hundred, answerable to foremen; below them chargehands were in immediate control of groups of between twenty and thirty men.[54]

Matching the control of the workforce at the shop floor level was the exercise of efficient costing in the office, ensuring the compilation and dissemination of statistics and knowledge of factory affairs weekly, monthly, and year by year. Budgeting, forecasting, and diagnosis of changing costs were the supporting apparatus for managerial control over all departments.[55] Indeed, the increasing importance which he attached to costing may well explain Sir Herbert's agreement to

[51] Ibid., p. 510.

[52] Staff received an output bonus based on monthly production of cars. Thus, if a member of the staff received $1\frac{1}{2}$ units of bonus and was given a rise to 2 units, the extra $\frac{1}{2}$ unit did not cost the company as it was deducted from the bulk bonus allowance, the deduction of the $\frac{1}{2}$ unit being spread over all those receiving the bonus. C. R. F. Engelbach, 'Some Notes on Reorganizing', p. 512; Perry Keen (Austin Motor Co.), Letter to *Times*, 31 May 1926; also by communication with Mr. Freddie Henry.

[53] C. R. F. Engelbach, 'Some Notes on Reorganizing', p. 522.

[54] The description is that of Mr. J. R. Edwards, who joined Austin in 1928 as a toolmaker, later to become Managing Director. By interview, 12 July 1977.

[55] C. R. F. Engelbach, 'Some Notes on Reorganizing', p. 513.

address the annual conference of cost and works accountants on that subject in 1925.[56]

Costing analysis led Sir Herbert to propose that savings of 50 per cent could be obtained if the firm manufactured more castings and purchased fewer from outside suppliers. Engelbach examined this possibility over a period of eighteen months between 1923 and 1925, and argued that the striking improvements in productivity were due in large measure to the practice of employing unskilled labour which the new investment programme made possible. At the same time, the adaptation of unskilled labour to semi-skilled tasks was a relatively slow process, and he counselled against a switch away from outside suppliers until manufacturing capacity under the new system was enlarged sufficiently to cope with the rapid increase in demand occasioned by the immense popularity of the Seven.[57] Unanticipated though the effects of the sudden rise in the sales of Austin motor cars may have been, in effect they forced the Company to rely more, not less, on outside body suppliers, especially from 1927 when the fashion for fabric bodies enhanced the value of specialist coachbuilders. When the fabric fad receded, Payton defended a policy of continuing to rely on the coachbuilders for special bodies to meet the needs of particular consumers, while Longbridge concentrated on making standard bodies. Such a policy helped in achieving the reduction by one-third in the production cost of car bodies during the investment programme of the late 1920s.[58]

* * *

Investment rose sharply during those years; but financial constraints continued to determine the ability of the firm to keep pace with the market and the capital expenditure required.[59] Hence the complaints by Austin agents of insufficient supplies of Sevens in the mid-1920s.[60] In 1924 Sir Herbert had particularly pressing reasons why he wished to

[56] *Times*, 2 May 1925. In 1932 Sir Herbert opened an exhibition of new British machines for 'mechanical accounting' and his was one of the first firms to use it. *Times*, 18 April 1932.

[57] AMB, 25 February 1925.

[58] AMB, 29 August 1929. Sir Herbert had favoured the manufacture of all Austin bodies at Longbridge. *Autocar*, 3 February 1928.

[59] AMB. Thus, for example, in April 1926 Engelbach outlined an investment programme amounting to £86,475, but approval was granted for only £6,000, pending the decision of the Board.

[60] AMB, 9 May 1924, 15 September 1926.

see these constraints disappear, for each Seven produced yielded a royalty personal to him, besides which he, together with his wife, owned more than half the ordinary share capital,[61] and dividends on ordinary shares had not been paid since 1919. Cumulative preference shareholders were owed several years' arrears of dividend.[62] The balance sheet at 30 September 1924 showed an accumulated debit balance of £1,438,403.[63] Consequently it is understandable that he should have shown enthusiasm for a proposal advanced in 1924 by Dudley Docker, of Vickers, that the Austin, Morris and Wolseley motor firms should merge, so providing a solution to the financial weakness of Austin and Wolseley and creating an enlarged production base more suited to mass production. Morris, on his part, feared that there would be considerable risk,[64] even with the inclusion of the 'admirable plant which could be provided by the Wolseley Company, for the organization would be so great that it would be difficult to control and might tend to strangle itself'.[65] Sir Herbert's suggested arrangement was one which would have transferred control of all Austin's share capital and place Morris virtually in command of the Morris-Austin-Wolseley merger, a concern in Sir Herbert's view 'capable of meeting any competition likely to be met in the near future', and at the same time removing two of Morris's strongest commercial competitors. The suggestion, however, proceeded no further than the letters exchanged between the two men, owing to Morris's preference for direct ownership and control and independence and his declared 'firm aversion of being responsible for other people's money'.

Sir Herbert turned, reluctantly, elsewhere – to America. Throughout the early and mid-1920s he continued to manoeuvre in an attempt to secure amalgamation with an American company. In July 1925 he reported to his co-directors that after a visit to the United States by invitation of General Motors, he had discussed such a possibility with that Company's Finance and Executive Committee. General Motors' offer was £1.3 million cash for the Austin Motor Company's ordinary

[61] Companies House, 'A' file, 133747, Austin Motor Company, Vol. 5 (1925), Vol. 17 (1930), Vol. 24 (1935).

[62] *Times*, 2 September 1925.

[63] *Times*, 17 September 1925.

[64] The letters are quoted in Lambert & Wyatt, pp. 153–4.

[65] Past and present chairmen and managing directors of B.M.C. and B.L.M.C., please note.

share issue at a 20 per cent discount, the cash to be used for paying off the Fourth Debenture stock and the outstanding debt to the British Government, thereby leaving Austin free from any debenture charge. Sir Herbert was enthusiastic and received the support of the other largest shareholder, Harvey du Cros.[66] Sir Herbert and James D. Mooney (for General Motors) signed a declaration of intent 'to persuade our respective companies to enter into the agreement', which by then included an undertaking not to create any fresh mortgage debentures for five years, and that General Motors would nominate its own representatives 'taking care generally to preserve the British character of the Board'.

Payton led Engelbach and Neal, an accountant and external member of Austin's board, in opposing the scheme, largely because they shared an optimistic view of the Company's future.[67] The dissenting directors favoured a considerably more modest capital reconstruction scheme and avoiding American acquisition.[68] Sir Herbert issued his own personal circular to shareholders in which he stressed the significance he attached to the mobilization of capital the scheme would secure by placing huge net assets behind the shares, whereas all alternative proposals would have placed a large debenture debt ahead of them. He also intimated that the majority of the Austin directors were to have been British.[69] Sir Herbert was too late, for General Motors had

[66] Companies House, 'A' File 133747, Austin Motor Company, Vol. 5.

[67] In part their difference of opinion was over the writing down of the Company's capital, how large that (and therefore the sale price) should be, and how the losses incurred in the process of writing down should be distributed as between ordinary and preference holders. This was the negative element in their opposition, but their statement to shareholders argued that after allowing nearly £220,000 for maintenance and depreciation, net profits for the current year would exceed £500,000, and that prospects for future trading were such as to warrant optimism. AMB, 9 July, 21 August, 14 September 1925.

[68] *Times*, 17 September 1925. The offer actually made by the visiting Americans, and quickly withdrawn, was a writing-off of a total deficiency on the balance sheet of £1,662,500:

250,000 7 per cent cum. prefs. to be reduced to 19*s*. (5 per cent) and converted to 6½ per cent tax free acc. pref. shares;

1 million 6 per cent tax free pref. shares to be reduced to 15*s*. (25 per cent) and converted to 6½ per cent acc. pref. shares;

1.5 million deferred ords. to be reduced to 6*s*. 8*d*. (66 per cent) and converted into 6½ per cent cum. prefs.;

600,000 ords. to be reduced to 6*s*. 8*d*. and converted into 6½ per cent (66 per cent) acc. prefs.

[69] *Times*, 17 September 1925.

already withdrawn its provisional offer. At the Austin agents' dinner at Olympia in October 1925 Sir Herbert explained why Austin did not 'marry the lass', General Motors: 'Well, her dowry was quite substantial, but my relations didn't like her, and therefore the engagement had to be broken off. I thought it would be safer for me to marry her than someone else, also that co-operation could have been better than competition. The future might prove that I was right, but as the scheme has been abandoned I have resolved to do everything humanly possible to prove I was wrong. . . .'[70] Already Austin's suppliers had promised credit of up to £1 million and the bank also expressed willingness to extend financial support if needed.[71] But Sir Herbert's quest for a wealthy connection continued, and when Wolseley was put up for sale in 1926 he decided to bid for his old company.

There is a remarkable similarity between the post-war weakness of the two companies since their growth as munitions producers in the First World War. The reorganization for peacetime manufacture by Wolseley had necessitated substantial investment financed by a large debenture issue in 1919, at the height of the post-war boom. Like Austin's post-war history, the effect of the iron moulders' strike and of trade depression in 1920–21 further retarded the resumption of manufacture in any volume, a situation exacerbated by a weak cash position. In such a context it is not surprising that the Wolseley managers had failed to introduce a motor car which would have attracted sufficient sales to see the Company through this difficult period, and, despite financial support from Vickers, the Company fell into the hands of the Official Receiver in 1926. By that time, Sir Herbert and his new co-directors had engineered Austin's recovery, the purgative effects of Receivership enabling the Company to exploit Sir Herbert's genius as a designer.

Without the financial strength of Morris, an amalgamation of Wolseley with Austin had made little sense in 1924, but by 1926, with Austin's trading profits increasing rapidly and with the immediate prospect of a capital reconstruction and a return to a clean balance sheet, Wolseley's well-equipped works and workforce, together with a chain of loyal agents, offered real benefits to Austin. There was also the understandable attraction for Sir Herbert of gaining control of the old firm which had played such an important part in his early career,

[70] *Times*, 13 October 1925.
[71] AMB, 15 September 1925.

and which he had left in regrettable circumstances. But William Morris settled the matter simply by outbidding Sir Herbert, partly in order to prevent Wolseley from falling into Austin's hands.[72] There seems to have been no systematic plan to fill out and rationalize his own organization, for although Morris was particularly attracted by the commercial potential of the Wolseley six-cylinder engine, it was left to the Wolseley Company to finance and develop the new model.[73] Indeed, during the period of intensified competition between motor manufacturers during the Slump, at a time when the reorganization and expansion programme at Longbridge from the mid-1920s was enabling Austin to challenge Morris Motors, Morris's failure to integrate the Adderly Park Works of Wolseley with Cowley at Oxford proved to be a source of weakness in the Morris Motors organization.

Undaunted, in November 1926 Sir Herbert renewed his overtures in a letter to Henry Ford, though precisely what kind of co-operation he sought he did not specify. He outlined briefly the argument for building a car possessing the characteristics of the Austin Seven for the British and European market, the difficulty of his own Company in keeping pace with demand; he also drew attention to Ford's indifferent performance in Britain, referring in particular to the high tax and fuel consumption. 'I understand from our people that they have been examining a large number of presses that are to be sold shortly at your Manchester plant, and I am told that the sale of the Ford car in this country has dropped to a very low point. I do not like to hear of any firm going back in its production and I feel confident that if this market had been tackled differently a year or two ago, the business at Trafford Park might have been turning out at least 100,000 vehicles a year, and perhaps even considerably more. . . . I am afraid you might consider it an impertinence on my part if I were to suggest that we might collaborate together in the British market and in the British Dominions and Colonies to our mutual advantage.'[74] The reply was courteous but non-committal, and the matter dropped.[75] The ability

[72] Sir Miles Thomas, foreword to Lambert & Wyatt, p. 12.

[73] Leonard Lord later recalled that the Wolseley managers, of whom he was one, told Nuffield what they intended to do and that there was no interference. Andrews and Brunner, Notes.

[74] FMC England, Dearborn, Detroit, Acc. 285, Box 444, Sir Herbert Austin to Henry Ford, 10 November 1926.

[75] Diebold to Sir Herbert Austin, 26 November 1926; Sir Herbert Austin to Henry Ford, 14 December 1926.

Table 7: Capital Structure, Profit and Dividends, 1922–1939

Year	(a) Up capital employed (i) Ordinary	(ii) Cumulative preferred and preferred ordinaries	(iii) Debentures*	(b) Profit after maintenance and depreciation, taxes and debenture interest	(c) (b) as % of (a)(i) and (a)(ii)	(d) Dividends on ordinary shares, %
	£	£	£	£		
1922	600,000	2,750,000	1,696,047	78,564	2.3	
1923	600,000	2,750,000	1,722,101	205,334	6.1	
1924	600,000	2,750,000	1,349,300	161,174	4.8	
1925	600,000	2,750,000	1,339,737	447,851	13.4	
1926	600,000	2,750,000	1,500,000	330,508	9.9	
1927	150,000	2,000,000	1,460,360	115,639	5.4	
1928	150,000	2,000,000	1,416,447	243,025 (15 months)	(9.0)†	
1929	150,000	2,000,000	1,368,302	559,788	26.0	20
1930	150,000	2,000,000	1,316,636	384,341 (7 months)	(30.0)	60 (actual)
1931	150,000	2,000,000	1,262,374	489,232	22.0	100
1932	150,000	2,000,000	1,208,220	390,387	18.0	25 plus 25 bonus
1933	150,000	2,000,000	1,100,000	506,798	23.0	25 ,, 75 ,,
1934	150,000	2,000,000	1,100,000	661,280	30.0	25 ,, 75 ,, ‡
1935	622,459	2,000,000	1,100,000	623,928	29.0	25 ,, 25 ,,
1936	622,459	2,000,000	1,083,670	553,573	21.0	25 ,, 25 ,,
1937	622,459	2,000,000	1,066,520	555,577	21.0	25 ,, 25 ,,
1938	622,459	2,000,000	1,048,530	362,158	13.0	25 ,, 5 ,,
1939	622,459	2,000,000	1,029,640	344,720	13.0	

* From 1922 bank loans were secured on debentures.
† Figures in brackets are twelve-month estimates.
‡ Plus capitalized bonus of 300 per cent.

of Austin to expand was to depend upon its own resources, the willingness of suppliers and bankers to supplement internal funds, and the patience and willingness of shareholders to make some contribution by forgoing part of the Company's accumulated indebtedness to them.

Between the failure of the scheme to merge with General Motors and the abortive approach to Henry Ford, the Austin directors had tried to ease the burden of the Company's indebtedness by funding the whole of its existing debenture liability commitments. The First Debentures had been wholly redeemed in 1924, but still outstanding in 1925 were £225,000 of the Second Mortgage Debenture and £90,000 of the Third.[76] In January 1926 the whole outstanding debenture debt was converted into £1.5 million 6.5 per cent First Mortgage Debenture Stock, issued at 97.5 per cent, a flotation which also allowed for £290,000 to be available for working capital. Throughout 1926 and the first half of 1927 attempts were made to devise a reconstruction scheme which could secure a three-quarters majority among shareholders, a scheme which would remove the remaining deficit from the balance sheet and clear the way for a resumption of dividend payments.[77] A rearguard action, fought since 1921 by dissentient shareholders reluctant to see their assets substantially written down, eventually ended in July 1927.

The Austin capital was written down from £3.35 million to £2.15 million, with the nominal value of 20 shillings preferred ordinary shares written down to 10 shillings. The rate of dividend on preferred ordinary shares was raised from 10 to 20 per cent, and by so doing preserved shareholders' current entitlements (Table 7). Not surprisingly, at the AGM in December 1927 the Company's finance director declared: 'It is in every sense of the word a clean balance sheet.' Sir Herbert endorsed this, adding: 'Gentlemen, I believe we are back to the good old times.' Seven years' arrears of interest on the Company's 7 per cent preference capital was announced in December 1927, together with a dividend for the current year.[78] Without

[76] AMB, 21 December 1927.

[77] *Times*, 9 August 1926; 5 January, 9 July 1927. One shareholder urged others to cast aside their attitude of suspicion towards the directors 'and give them a chance to get on with the Company's business', a sentiment which received support in the meeting. *Investors Chronicle*, 22 January 1927.

[78] The significance of this reconstruction and payment of arrears was that the annual charges against the Company, with claims prior to those of preference and ordinary shareholders, were reduced to less than £200,000, but which amounted to 50 per cent of the Company's trading profit in 1924–25. Mean-

reservation the *Investors Chronicle* described the Company's financial recovery since 1924 as 'outstanding'.[79] In 1930 Sir Herbert brought welcome news at last for other holders of ordinary shares, whose dividend of 20 per cent was the first cash payment to this group since December 1918.[80]

while holders of 6 per cent 'B' preference shares who continued to press for payment of the mounting arrears owing to them, received the first instalments in 1928, and the last in 1930. *Times*, 21 August 1926; 10 December 1927; 29 March, 20 December 1928; 27 February 1930.

[79] *Investors Chronicle*, 10 January 1926.

[80] *Times*, 27 February 1930. Dividend payments between 1914 and 1918 were as follows: 1914, 2 per cent; 1915, 6 per cent; 1916, 10 per cent; 1917, 10 per cent. A bonus of 200,000 ordinary shares was issued in 1919.

Part Four: Slump, Competition and Growth

CHAPTER SEVEN

Opportunities for Expansion: Austin's Response

WE HAVE ALREADY DRAWN ATTENTION to the factors which contributed to a slowing down in the rate of expansion of the British market for cars in the late 1920s, even before the Slump. Between 1927 and 1929 home sales by British firms grew by rather less than 10 per cent, and this despite an appreciable amount of import replacement.[1] So great was the fall in imports in 1929 and 1930 that home sales by UK firms actually rose in a falling market, but a depression in home sales from 1930 to 1931, reinforced by falling exports, reduced the total sales of British firms.[2] This relative stagnation in home sales lasted until 1933, before the fall in the costs of producing and using cars, together with the simultaneous rise in real incomes, finally proved sufficient to transform the British market for motor cars into one with 'mature' characteristics; the phase when ownership would percolate down what William Morris referred to as 'the pyramid of consumption', and replacement purchases account for a major proportion of sales in the market.[3] But that phase did not originate during the Slump, for while

[1] From 1927 to 1929, total sales by British firms rose by only 10 per cent, of which import replacement took 23 per cent, the growth of the home market 44 per cent, and exports the very large share of 33 per cent.

[2] Michael Miller and Roy Church, 'Growth and Instability' in *British Industrial Developments between the Wars* (forthcoming), ed. Aldcroft and N. Buxton.

[3] Maxcy and Silberston, p. 38; Morris, quoted by Andrews and Brunner, *The Life of Lord Nuffield* (Oxford, 1955), p. 120.

it is true that replacement demand was not postponed, sales to first-time buyers collapsed. This picture should be contrasted with the years between 1932 and 1937, when new owner sales rose more than three-fold. Overall it appears that even sizeable reductions in car 'prices' failed to induce the more affluent to purchase cars in the late 1920s, when the real average value of new cars sold fell by more than one-quarter between 1925 and 1929; whereas despite the absence of such falls in 'prices' in the 1930s, when real average value of new cars sold declined by only 8 per cent, the middle classes nonetheless invested real income windfalls in motoring.[4]

Consumers' responses to the Slump do indeed seem to have accorded with the imperatives of economic rationality. The decline in new owner sales from 1925 can be interpreted as reflecting a hiatus in the market, for in the phase of initial demand, the status of the car as a quasi-luxury item persisted. But the stability of replacement sales does not mean that existing owners were unaffected by the recession. On the contrary, the *types* of cars which sold best in the Slump demonstrate the rationality of hastening replacement, scrapping old models, and buying new designs which were cheaper both to purchase and to run. One factor encouraging this trend was the reintroduction of the petrol tax in 1929 and another the Budget increases of 1931.[5] Development in motor car design and production was more important, for the desire for economy coincided with the availability of small saloon cars, which offered lower fuel, taxation, and general costs, without much loss of comfort, reliability or performance.

It was this development which contributed to the buoyancy in the sale of light cars, and especially the Austin Seven, during the Slump (Table 6). Total new registrations of cars in the UK fell from 169,000 to 144,000 units between 1929 and 1931. Registrations of cars of 11 to 16 h.p. fell from 81,000 to 63,000, and cars of 17 h.p. and over from 29,000 to 21,000 units.[6] In 1927 one-quarter of new registrations were cars of 10 h.p. or below; by 1929 the proportion was one-third, and 60 per cent by 1933.[7] Indeed, it was Sir Herbert's Austin Seven which originated this trend, already discernible before the Slump, tapping a

[4] Roy Church and Michael Miller, 'Growth and Instability'.

[5] Though surprisingly, while acknowledging the likely stimulus this would have on small car sales, Sir Herbert condemned it as a handicap to car exporters. *Times*, 4 October 1932.

[6] Registration figures refer to years ending on 30 September.

[7] Roy Church and Michael Miller, 'Growth and Instability'.

Figure 4. Car Production/Sales of Austin, Morris (Cowley) and Ford 1922–39

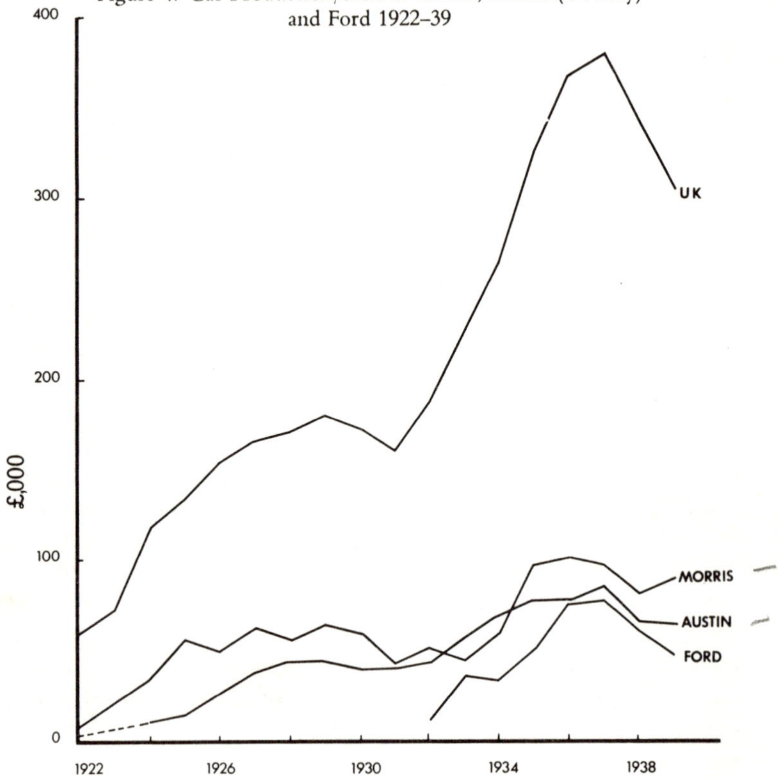

The sources for the Austin estimates before 1928 are various: *Autocar*, 6 September 1929; Austin Minute Book, 22 August 1923 (target for 1924), Austin Minute Book, 26 August 1925 (target for 1926); *Autocar*, 3 February 1928. The Ford figures have been provided by the Ford Motor Company, and those of Morris to 1935 are from Andrews & Brunner. The Morris estimates for 1936–39 are those of Michael Miller. The UK figures are those published by the SMMT.

whole new series of real income strata for car ownership by virtue of a breakthrough in the efficiency of production and in the commercial appeal and effectiveness of the product itself.

Stagnation in the home market coupled with the dynamism evident in the low horsepower class produced the combination of circumstances which signalled a new round in the competitive battle between Morris and Austin, beginning in 1928 (Fig. 4). Announcing a price reduction of Austin cars in 1928, Sir Herbert declared: 'It is a continuation of our previous practice of passing on to the purchaser at the earliest possible moment the advantage we are able to obtain by increased turnover, and improved production methods.'[8] He omitted to mention the decision announced by William Morris only three months before, in May 1928, to introduce the Morris Minor. With half of the Company's output by that time consisting of Sevens, Austin's position was vulnerable. Hitherto, Austin's principal British competition in the market for small cars had come from Singer, the third largest British motor company,[9] Triumph, and Jowett, but none possessed the financial resources which Morris's could command. His entry into the low horsepower class posed an altogether new situation. Morris's strength had lain in producing the best, the cheapest, and most popular single model in the best-selling market of the 1920s; family cars of medium size and price for a market in which Austin's reputation and sales depended on the Twelve, and that of Morris on the considerably cheaper Cowley and Oxford models. Prior to the disconcerting signs in 1928, the smaller horsepower market can have held few attractions for William Morris. In 1927 his Company had produced 61,632 cars, whereas in 1928 estimated market demand in the small light car range below 10 h.p. was about one-third of that figure. Thus, had Morris introduced a light car before 1928 he ran the risk of losing some of his own Cowley sales. The acquisition of Wolseley and the Adderley Park factory in Birmingham and the conversion into a public company may also have delayed Morris's entry into the market for really small cars.[10]

Despite its reputation as a basic economy model, the Austin Seven was not the cheapest car in its class and it was never Sir Herbert's intention that it should be, as he explained in 1932: 'For the past thirty-three years, except for World War I, I have been building motor cars of a dependable quality and selling them at moderate prices. The prices have always been a little higher than those of competitors and this little extra has provided for that higher quality and general satisfaction which the possession of an Austin car gives.'[11] Thus in 1928 the chassis price of the Seven was £99, the tourer £145 and the closed saloon £166, which compared with the cheap Singer Junior at £140,

[8] *Times*, 14 August 1928.
[9] *Autocar*, 1 November 1929.
[10] R. J. Wyatt, p. 74.
[11] *Times*, 9 September 1932.

Table 8: Sales, Production and Profit 1922–1939 (September years)

Year	Sales turnover £	Net trading profit as % of sales	Output in numbers	Profit per unit of output £
1922	1,653,440	6.0		
1923	1,943,018	15.5		
1924	3,087,135	13.2		
1925				
1926				
1927	(7,679,776)*	(10.5)		
1928	8,789,776	8.4		
1929	8,403,718	9.1	46,562	16
1930	7,405,925	8.7	36,682	(30)†
1931	6,767,775	15.0	42,817	24
1932	6,755,217	12.2	36,526	23
1933	8,622,831	11.0	53,186	18
1934	10,520,773	11.4	62,292	19
1935	11,331,425	10.4	77,171	15
1936	11,187,624	10.3	70,458	16
1937	13,283,074	9.3	89,745	14
1938	10,430,553	8.5	64,053	14
1939	10,976,762		76,482‡	

* Estimate.
† Based on estimated profit over twelve months.
‡ Excluding commercial vehicles.

and the Triumph Super Seven at £149 10*s.* 0*d.* Singer and Triumph prices remained roughly the same for 1929, with both the new Morris Minor and the Austin Seven priced at £125, and the closed saloon Seven at £135.[12]

Sir Herbert acknowledged that already there were light cars on the market priced lower than those of Austin, but that Austin cars were still in great demand; nonetheless, as a precautionary measure he announced price cuts, and was followed in this by Morris and other manufacturers competing in the same range.[13] Within weeks of Sir Herbert's price cuts they had been restored, and although we have found no evidence to explain why the directors changed their minds, the rapid growth in export sales may have suggested that price reductions were unnecessary to maintain turnover. William Morris, how-

[12] November prices, *Autocar, Buyers' Guide*, 1929.
[13] R. J. Wyatt, p. 75.

ever, less dependent upon his own organization for cost reductions than Austin, and presumably having pressed his suppliers to accept some of the cuts, was able to adhere to the new lower prices. As a result, the basic price of the Morris Minor was £5 less than for the equivalent Seven (Fig. 3). So buoyant was the demand for Austin cars during the Slump that, despite the sharp fall in profits in relation to output, profits in relation to turnover seem to have risen more sharply than was the case for other firms (Table 8). Thereafter, Austin's steady profit performance compared favourably with the fluctuation and decline at Morris Motors after 1930.[14]

Meanwhile, Austin sought to justify the turnabout in pricing by informing dealers that since the Autumn Motor Show the Company had been persuaded by agents and customers of the need to make detailed improvements, including a better quality of upholstery, more efficient door hinges and locks, and Triplex glass as standard in all cars.[15] In the following year, the Austin directors had to respond to another gesture by Morris when towards the end of 1930 he announced his intention to produce an economy two-seater Morris Minor, or tourer, for £100. Payton wanted Austin to take up the challenge by being the first to produce a two-seater for less than £100. His suggestion was to offer a complete two-seater Seven at £99, but the collective decision was to plan to make a one hundred guinea model, and to cut prices of existing models of improved quality.[16] Not until 1933 was a two-seater Seven quoted as low as £105,[17] but Sir Herbert's effective commercial answer to the open two-seater Morris Minor for £100 was not the two-seater or tourer for £122 10*s.* 0*d.*, but the four-seater Seven de luxe saloon for £130.[18]

The Morris–Austin rivalry of this period marked the beginning of a novel policy at Longbridge, though it was of brief duration in the early 1930s. By changing the outward appearance of the car slightly each year the Austin directors hoped to maintain customer loyalty so as to withstand the growing competition from other makers.[19] To

[14] Maxcy and Silberston, pp. 157–8. See also below, p. 142.

[15] Circular quoted, R. J. Wyatt, p. 86.

[16] AMB, 17 December 1930.

[17] Fletcher & Son Ltd. 'Motor Car Index 1928–39 (R. P. Brighton, 1964).

[18] R. J. Wyatt, p. 115.

[19] R. J. Wyatt, p. 88. In 1932, on the suggestion of E. L. Payton, Sir Herbert worked on a design for a 7 h.p. two-seater to sell at 100 guineas. AMB, 17 December 1930, 27 July 1932; M. Sedgwick, p. 268.

Sir Herbert this was a matter for regret, as he explained to distributors in 1934: 'The public demand for change does not always allow us to derive the full benefit of settled design. No sooner are we in full swing with current models than we have to turn our thoughts and energies to redesigning the body or chassis in an endeavour to meet – or anticipate – the public's ever changing moods.' The redesign of Austin body lines by fitting a newly designed radiator shell, the introduction of sweeping lines, lengthened bonnets, and the elimination of projecting fittings, represented a modernization long overdue, and in the following year Sir Herbert decided to make 'a bold stand against the fetish of change for change's sake', promising that the 1935–36 models would remain virtually the same, except for certain minor improvements. 'Changes which do not bring with them any solid advantages in comfort, pleasure, or safety, entail expenditure which absorbs money and [which] is not then available for an increase in quality or reduction in price.'[20] Another contribution to price stability was the agreement made in 1933 between Sir Herbert, Lord Nuffield, Sir Percival Perry (Ford), R. W. Maudsley (Standard), Sir John Siddeley and Colonel John Albert Cole (Humber and Hillman) not to reduce prices for the following season.[21]

Price maintenance proved difficult when faced with alterations in the prices of raw materials, and proliferation of models and variants became the typical response to frustrated expectations in the motor industry in the 1930s, even though Sir Herbert himself was not always enthusiastic about such a policy.[22] It is interesting to note that the creation of the Austin Ten in 1932 followed discussions among the directors on how best to respond to the apparent sales potential of a car at a price range between the Seven and the Twelve. Payton suggested the installation of a four-cylinder engine in a Twelve Six chassis using the same body, thereby obtaining the advantages of lower running costs due to lower fuel consumption and less tax. Engelbach recommended using a Seven incorporating a larger engine. Initially Sir Herbert had disputed the wisdom of adding a further Ten to the

[20] Address by Sir Herbert Austin, KBE, to Austin Distributors and Agents, August 1934, 'Another Dependable Austin Programme'; AMC Papers, AGM, October 1935.

[21] AMB, 28 June 1933; *Directory of Directors* (1933).

[22] For example, in 1932 the directors discussed the advisability of building a 12 h.p. engine for the Twelve Six h.p. chassis in order to meet competition from the Morris Cowley, but Sir Herbert insisted on a price cut on the existing model instead. AMB, 27 April 1932.

already existing range of Tens on the market, and had advocated merely a reduction in the price of the Austin Twelve Six. But a few months later, in January 1932, Sir Herbert conceded that despite the additional investment outlay necessary for the introduction of a completely new model, the falling purchasing power of consumers justified the launching of a four-cylinder 9 or 10 h.p. car as a replacement for the Twelve Four.

Once that decision was taken £45,000 capital expenditure received immediate sanction, with the result that the Austin model was in full production even before the Hillman Minx itself, or the Morris reply.[23] Moreover, Sir Herbert's new car, the Austin Ten, proved to be an immediate success, and quickly joined the Seven in dominating the Company's sales in the mid-1930s (Fig. 2). From 1932 to 1937 Austin car output increased from 42,520 to 83,990 private cars, and in 1933 and 1934 Austin was, if briefly, the largest British manufacturer of private cars. During the dynamic years from 1932 to 1935 the Company produced over 100,000 Tens of the 1932 design,[24] and a further 94,000 Sevens, a venerable but still viable product. All other models made provided only one-quarter of Austin sales.

* * *

The sales performance of Austin in the early 1930s owed much to the Company's success in overseas markets, a success which it shared with other leading British car manufacturers. From 1929 to 1931 the British share of world trade in cars and chassis increased from 7 per cent to 13 per cent; it exceeded 28 per cent in 1932, falling to 25 per cent in 1933. The resurgence of American competition reduced the share to under 17 per cent in 1934 and 1935, but in 1936, and again in 1938, about 18 per cent of world exports came from the United Kingdom. On the average, then, of the years of 1934 to 1938 British exports retained over twice their pre-Slump share of world car exports, a considerable achievement in the face of renewed American competition and the emergence of a thriving German export trade. For despite the substantial reduction in the volume of world trade in motor vehicles, even in 1931 the British *share* of the most important of the

[23] AMB, 23 September, 25 November 1931, 27 January 1932; M. Sedgwick, *Cars of the 1930s* (1970), p. 137.

[24] A fillip to the sale of Sevens, Tens and Twelves was provided by the introduction of light van bodies beginning in 1931–32. Chairman's speech, AGM, October 1932.

Big Six markets increased. The reason is obvious: in general, sales of cars fell, but imports of British cars fell *less* than did imports from the United States and Canada.

A combination of factors explains why British motor manufacturers in general, and Austin in particular, should have performed relatively well in export markets, in the Slump. Sir Herbert was convinced that it was the small utility car which saved the British export trade during this period.[25] A further factor to which Sir Herbert attributed some significance was the shift of allegiance among overseas distributors away from American cars, which they had stocked heavily incurring considerable losses, to British cars and sales methods.[26] Austin also made special efforts to promote sales in the early 1930s. In 1932 what was described as a 'gentleman's agreement' was reached with the Willys Overland Crossley Company which was to sell cars in Germany. Two per cent of the commission on retail price was to be spent upon national advertising, and Austin was to begin racing in that country. A measure of the importance attached to developing the German market is the offer price of an Austin Seven manufactured to de luxe specification, completely equipped, at £84 16*s*. 9*d*. net ex works, which was 33 per cent discount off the list price.[27]

In 1934, when the Slump export boom was petering out, Austin abolished the bonus system for its distributors, incorporating the bonus in the discount which was increased to a flat 30 per cent rate off home retail prices.[28] Some of Austin's suppliers also contributed to the

[25] In a letter to *The Times* he praised Sir William Morris for his worldwide export drive, mentioning in particular the 8 h.p. model, and referred to his own Company's experience. 'There are markets where the number of new registrations of cars which bear my name at times exceed those of any other manufacturer in the world. No small proportion of these are of the small – or as I would prefer to term them, the economic and utility – class and I rejoice to find that my friends and competitors, Morris, Singer, Standard, Triumph and others are sharing in the fruits of an extraordinary rapid appreciation in many markets of the utility – and in these very difficult days of the economic – aspect of the characteristic (small) car.' *Times*, 5 January 1931.

[26] See above.

[27] AMB, 25 May 1932. When Sir Herbert was on the Austin stand at the opening of the Berlin Motor Show in 1935 Herr Hitler told him that he had used a 'Seven' in the early days of his movement. *Times*, 18 February 1935. Two years later Sir Herbert joined with Sir Percival Percy, Lord Nuffield, Leslie Walton (of Vauxhall) and W. Rootes in urging the British Government to prevent the entry of subsidized German car imports. AMB, 11 October 1937.

[28] AMB, 25 July 1934.

Company's export strategy in 1933, when they agreed to grant special rebates for parts fitted to export models, so as to enable Austin to peg prices in export markets.[29] British manufacturers escaped the crushing recession at home which affected both the United States and Canadian industries, and the *Economist* found that to have been an important factor explaining the vastly improved competitive position of British cars overseas, for American producers were disadvantaged by the increased relative weight of overhead charges. Another contributory element was the stimulus to exports given to the British manufacturer by the abandonment of the Gold Standard.[30]

To these determinants of the relative prices of British and American cars were added a set of factors affecting both motoring costs and the ability of consumers to pay them. Probably most important in increasing the demand for small cars, in the design and improvement of which Britain had been most prominent, was the need for economy as incomes fell: a need which was as temporary as the British exchange advantage and any cost advantage due to the spreading of overheads, and which can therefore help to explain the loss of competitive edge suffered by British cars even after 1933. In this context the conclusions reached by Sieve are helpful: 'The main attraction of the British car undoubtedly lay in the sphere of operating costs. The British car catered for overseas motorists whose incomes did not suffice to run a large North American car.'[31] The result was that as an 'inferior' substitute the market *share* of the United Kingdom car 'invariably increased during the depression of 1929–31 and fell off somewhat thereafter'. Although the levels of income per capita had some influence on the British shares, they 'could not primarily be explained in terms of income'. Similarly, relative initial prices had some impact, but the most important single determinant of how well British cars did in important imperial markets was the movement of relative motoring costs themselves.[32] Outside the Empire, of course, different conditions of costs and preferences obtained, and it seems likely that, given the competitive losses suffered by British exporters to Europe from 1933, the exchange factor should be accorded a higher status. Movements in

[29] This concession probably amounted to about £20,000. AMB, 26 July 1933.
[30] *Economist*, 15 October 1932.
[31] E. J. B. Sieve, 'British Motor Vehicle Exports (An Analysis of the Interwar Period and Some Post 1945 Trends)', unpublished Ph.D. thesis (University of London, 1950), pp. 290–1.
[32] E. J. B. Sieve, p. 291.

the exchanges certainly complicated life for British manufacturers. For example, in February 1931 the Austin directors seriously discussed whether they should accept wheat and wool in exchange for motor cars in the Australian market. Concessions made to Australian distributors, granted temporarily to ease the problem, meant that in 1932 each Seven chassis was losing £50 a week.[33]

But if exports triggered the recovery in 1932, home demand dominated the boom of the 1930s, which occurred on a considerably greater scale than that of the 1920s. By the 1930s the fall in car prices and real motor costs, combined with rising real incomes, had proceeded far enough to stimulate once again a vigorous growth in the market. Between 1931 and 1937 nine-tenths of the increase in home consumption (which more than doubled) was secured by home producers. Export sales, still contributing significantly to growth and thereby demonstrating the ability of British exporters to retain footholds established in overseas markets during the Slump, absorbed 27 per cent of the growth of the total sales of British companies. The share of exports in British firms' sales thus increased from 12 to 21 per cent between 1931 and 1937.

[33] AMB, 25 February 1931; 25 May 1932.

CHAPTER EIGHT

Austin, Nuffield, and Government

THE POST-SLUMP YEARS had brought a resurgence of imports into the expanding home market. The relative deterioration of the trading position of British car manufacturers from the mid-1930s is attributable to the disappearance of the various factors which explained their improved position during the Slump. As the United States industry accelerated out of the Depression, competition from American cars in overseas markets reduced the British gain in those countries. Devaluation of the dollar enhanced the competitive edge, both in imperial and in European markets, and British exporters found it especially difficult to hang on to the latter. *The Economist*, however, was critical. Speculating on the relationship between home and export trade in 1934, *The Economist* commented that 'it seems probable that the extraordinary prosperity of the home market has led British manufacturers to concentrate their efforts upon obtaining as large a share of it as possible to the detriment of the more difficult and less remunerative export business',[1] which by 1936 had to a large extent become, according to *The Economist*, 'a cut price market, used by companies to compensate for seasonal slackness in home sales, gaining by spreading overheads over a larger output and not by profits on exports *per se*'.[2]

Motor manufacturers pointed to what they considered to be a more important reason to explain difficulties in export markets, namely, the rising trend of raw material prices, which produced frequent complaints from British motor manufacturers in the mid-1930s. Even in 1933 Sir Herbert was predicting higher car prices as a result of increases in the price of essential raw materials by between 5 and 15 per cent,[3]

[1] *Economist*, 13 October, 19 October 1934.
[2] *Economist*, 17 October 1936.
[3] *Austin Magazine and Advocate*, August 1933.

and expectations of further increases were aroused by the introduction of a government import licensing scheme in accordance with an agreement between the national federation of British steel makers and the International Steel Cartel. Having formerly defended their own industry's protected position, Lord Nuffield and Sir Herbert were nonetheless quick to condemn the steel makers' collusion under shelter of the tariff organization with the avowed intention of fixing prices,[4] which they both assumed, correctly as it turned out, to be at higher levels than hitherto.

'There is a steel and iron ring around us in this country', Lord Nuffield thundered in November 1935, claiming that, as a result, British motor manufacturers paid more than one-third as much again for their steel compared with American car makers.[5] The Pressed Steel Company and Austin were both reported to have expressed dissatisfaction, too, with the quality of British sheet steel which, though on average excellent, was alleged to lack uniformity.[6] Reflecting on the steel makers' actions, Lord Nuffield later described the situation as 'an absolute ramp. Big cigars and nothing to do.'[7] Meanwhile, Sir Herbert left rhetoric to the Oxford man and proceeded to prepare plans to enter the business of making steel himself. So began the Tunstall Steels episode, which in the liberal free trade press was presented as a determined attempt by Sir Herbert to free British motor manufacturers from the price tyranny of the protected British steel industry.[8]

* * *

Sir Herbert's first approach to the steel makers had preceded the agreement between the British Iron and Steel Federation and the International Cartel, for it was in the summer of 1934 that he, together with Payton, requested a reduction in the price of steel supplied to the Company.[9] They suggested that British steel manufacturers, jointly,

[4] J. C. Carr and W. Taplin, *History of the British Steel Industry* (Cambridge, Massachusetts, 1962), p. 559 (hereafter cited as Carr & Taplin).

[5] *News Chronicle*, 18 November 1935.

[6] Bank of England Archive, Securities Management Trust, SM2, 120/1. Skinner to Norman, 10 October 1935.

[7] D. L. Burn, *The Economic History of Steelmaking 1867–1939* (Cambridge, 1940), p. 495.

[8] *News Chronicle*, 18 November 1935.

[9] Bank of England Archives, Securities Management Trust, SM2, 120/1. Myers to Norman, 31 October 1935.

should install an up-to-date strip mill of American type, which would enable them to sell to the motor manufacturers sheet steel at a price and quality comparable with that available to American car makers. In a letter to Sir Andrew Duncan, newly appointed chairman of the BISF (nominated by Montague Norman at the Bank of England), E. L. Payton reminded him of previous warnings made to the steel makers: 'If in the near future you can satisfy us that those interested in the manufacture of steel sheets will constitute an organization free and unfettered by the handicap of association with other branches of the steel trade and capable of concentrating on the efficient and economical production of steel sheets, then we are prepared, even at this late stage, to consider whether we can meet you. . . . If the reorganization is only to consist of cartels and rings, the benefit to national trade, labour, and consumers is NIL.'[10] A refusal to consider these proposals led Sir Herbert to consult independent American experts who, on the basis of British data, reported favourably on the possibility of a British enterprise manufacturing sheet steel by American methods, initially for the use of the British motor trade.[11]

Late in 1935, proposals for the formation of Tunstall Steels as a limited company with a nominal capital of between £300,000 and £800,000 were in circulation in the press. In October came the announcement that the new company, in which Sir Herbert and E. L. Payton were the major shareholders, was to acquire a fifty acre site in Wolverhampton,[12] and that deposits had accompanied the order for the new mill. A secret memo from Sir Andrew Duncan to Montague Norman pointed out tartly that the reason why Sir Herbert was able to enter the sheet steel trade was the profit earned under tariff protection, 'whereas the sheet steel industry is in the main an exporting industry dependent upon low price and maximum load. While the sheet industry is striving to rid itself of redundancy . . . it is now threatened by a firm in a comparatively sheltered trade. Austins are both adding to the difficulties of the community and abusing the privileges which they receive from it. They cannot claim to be acting in the interests of car users, for the amount of sheets in a car is *c.* one

[10] Bank of England Archives, Securities Management Trust, SM2 120/1. E. L. Payton to Sir Andrew Duncan, 7 November 1935; Carr & Taplin, p. 503.

[11] AMB, AGM July 1936.

[12] Bank of England Archives, Securities Management Trust, SM2, 120/1, Myers to Norman, 10 November 1935; *News Chronicle*, 18 November 1935; *Times*, 19 November 1935.

fifth of a ton, and a reduction of £3 or £4 in price would have a negligible effect. Moreover the dividends paid by Austins belie their claim on this account.'[13]

The Bank of England's view, that Sir Herbert was being unreasonable, was shared also by Myers, Austin's stockbroker entrusted with the Tunstall flotation, who under the influence of Montague Norman kept the bank informed of Sir Herbert's plans. Myers wrote to Norman to tell him that 'there would be no utility in my denying the Company financial facilities because for the sum of money required the Austin Company has twice that amount of loose cash and could obtain credit anywhere'.[14] Meanwhile, frustrated by Austin's press propaganda, Sir Andrew Duncan attempted to persuade the steel makers to consider the erection of new plants on lines based on American practice, though it was Montague Norman who stage-managed these negotiations from the wings. In November 1935 he wrote to Myers: 'I, too, am trying to do whatever is possible to give Sir Andrew Duncan a chance to show that the animal in his care is not a leopard but a chameleon.'[15] An emergency meeting of the Federation eventually agreed to a solution which would enable Austin to obtain requirements on a basis to meet its complaints.

Sir William Firth was to purchase Ebbw Vale, including a quota for fine sheet steel of about 25,000 tons, which could supply Austin's entire requirements, and freedom 'to price either direct or by share participation'. It was also agreed that Sir William would install the latest plant for his tinplate, which would automatically look after sheets, '. . . so that Austin's needs for price and quality will be met'.[16] Discussions between Sir William Firth, Sir Herbert and E. L. Payton confirmed such an arrangement, though the Austin directors rejected the option of price discrimination in their favour through share participation.[17] In December, Montague Norman wrote to Myers, thanking him 'for thus helping to provide this bright spot amid much obscurity and for having provided it through that essential though unpopular method of co-operation'.[18] In fact, the new steel plant was

[13] Bank of England Archives, Securities Management Trust, SM2, 120/1, Myers to Norman, 10 October 1935.

[14] Ibid., 31 October 1935.

[15] Ibid., Norman to Myers, November 1935.

[16] Bank of England Archives, Securities Management Trust, SM2, 120/1.

[17] Ibid., Sir Andrew Duncan to Skinner (Bank of England), 20 December 1935.

[18] Bank of England, SM2, 120/1, Norman to Myers, 23 December 1935.

slowly constructed and slow to go into production, and as raw material prices in general continued at high levels while the boom lasted well into 1937, Sir Herbert once more began to criticize the steelmasters' restrictive practices as a contributory inflationary factor[19] which inevitably affected the motor industry's competitive position.

While it is true that the gains made both in traditional and new markets during the Slump were not completely dissipated thereafter, the higher share in world trade came under challenge from the mid-1930s, not only from America but increasingly, if less directly, from the German industry. But the many complaints of British industrialists about the level and progressiveness of taxation, about freight rates, and about unfair competition, should not conceal the extent to which the relative export failure of the later 1930s was due to factors within the control of British industry. By that time the Big Six producers provided the overwhelming proportion of cars exported; but the entrepreneurial failures, by making small runs of diverse lines of output, by frequent model changes, by the opportunities for cost reduction lost by the mechanism of competition through model diversification which had emerged by the 1930s, cannot but have had even more destructive consequences in neutral markets.

In an address to the Midland Branch of the National Union of Manufacturers in 1929, Sir Herbert had called for co-operative effort in the export of motor vehicles, but demanded from the Government as a condition 'definite assurance of a stable fiscal policy'.[20] Schemes for an export combine, with independent firms providing one line each in a complete range of exports backed up by joint sales and servicing facilities, were mooted, but without success. Like Lord Nuffield, Sir Herbert repeatedly stressed the importance to be attached to export performance, and had criticized any legislation, particularly horse-power and petrol taxation and restrictions on speed, considered to have discriminated against the use of larger vehicles in the domestic market. Unlike Lord Nuffield, Sir Herbert chose not to experiment with a 'colonial car', though export models were built with higher ground clearance than those for sales in Britain. A variety of organizations offering many different types of car to markets in sparsely populated areas was not a formula for export success, and it compared unfavourably with the American strategy of local assembly and manu-

[19] Carr & Taplin, pp. 572, 576; *Times*, 12 October, 21 October 1937.

[20] *Times*, 12 November 1929.

facture at levels of efficiency and in sufficient volume to make economic the holding of adequate stocks of components in widespread markets. To imitate the Americans required a greater shock than the Slump provided, and one which involved not just a growing British share of a small trade, but substantially larger volumes of sales. Not until the Second World War did that occur.

* * *

In the home market Sir Herbert faced the effects of a counter-attack which his Company's notable success since the mid-1920s had at last provoked, first from the Morris Minor, the Standard Eight and Ten and the Hillman Minx, followed in 1932 by the Ford 8 h.p. model, manufactured at the gigantic new Dagenham plant. Morris's answer to the Seven had been the Minor, but the results were unspectacular despite its magical basic bargain price of £100. The Seven's relative crudity proved insufficient to seriously diminish its long established reputation for reliability and durability, a fact which was reflected in its share of more than half the new car registrations in the 8 h.p. class in 1932, even though the *de luxe* model was comparable in price with the Morris Minor.[21] The latter's performance suffered from an excessively heavy engine and frame, defects eliminated in the later Morris Eight, incorporating a larger extra-long stroke engine.[22] It was the Ford Eight, introduced in 1932, which made most impact upon the market for the Seven. Incorporating synchromesh gearbox, something entirely new for a small car, and transverse front and rear springs, the four-door saloon was priced at £135 and the two-door version at £120, directly comparable with Austin in price. At the same time, the registration figures for 1931 had revealed the growing relative demand for 10 h.p. cars, and faced with the fall in Seven sales in 1932 Sir Herbert had announced the four-door Austin Ten Saloon priced at £168.

In 1930 Sir Herbert himself had remarked on the serious curtailment of Seven sales caused by its bigger and heavier bodywork which persistent overloading and fashion demanded.[23] But the trend continued, as the Tens made inroads into Austin sales. Hence the elongation

[21] M. Sedgwick, pp. 269, 273.

[22] I am grateful to Mr. Freddie Henry for this information.

[23] Sir Herbert Austin, 'The Future Trend of Automobile Design', *PIAE*, XXV (1930–31), p. 13.

and greater width of the 1932 *de luxe* model,[24] followed in the 1933/34 model by the introduction of a new four-speed gearbox, improved transmission, and standardized rear tanks, mechanical pump feed, and longer wheelbase.[25] Meanwhile, Sir Herbert's initial opposition to the idea of introducing the new Austin Ten disappeared in the face of falling sales, with the result that the first entirely new model in the popular class since 1922 proved to be a highly effective competitor in that most rapidly growing section of the domestic car market.[26] Described by Sedgwick as having been in 'the best square-rigged Longbridge tradition', nonetheless it incorporated six-volt coil ignition, mechanical pump feed, thermo syphon cooling, and cable-operated brakes,[27] and it was bought in large numbers (Fig. 2).

Having failed to achieve the expected inroads on Austin sales, the Morris Minor was joined in 1934 by the important new Morris Eight, which in design and performance epitomized the differences between the two companies. A new three-bearing 919 c.c. side-valve engine was combined with electric pump feed, hydraulic brakes, shock absorbers, three-speed synchromesh gearbox, and a top speed of 60 m.p.h. The roomy saloon bodies and attractively styled two-seater and tourer models also set a fashion imitated at Longbridge, Dagenham, and Canley. Both in technical equipment and styling, the Morris cars of the 1930s were in advance of other British makers, and the history of Austin cars, in particular after 1927, reveals lagging design only remedied at last in 1939. Michael Sedgwick's knowledgeable comparison of the technical characteristics of competing models to the mid-1930s leaves no doubt about the conservatism of Longbridge during that period. Apart from elongation in 1931/32, alterations were so minor that their appearance underwent little change, the largest Austin cars still wearing 'bodywork suitable for the top-hatted brigade'.[28] Sir Herbert considered that comfort and practical considerations had too long been subordinated to appearance and stream-

[24] M. Sedgwick, p. 269.

[25] M. Sedgwick, p. 269.

[26] The other new model to be introduced was the six-cylinder Austin Twelve, which was first produced in 1931.

[27] After postponement of any change in design on the insistence of Engelbach, Payton and Neal, Sir Herbert's alteration of the straight top line windscreen was adopted in the 1936/37 models. AMB, 24 October, 20 December 1934; 2 April 1935.

[28] M. Sedgwick, p. 268.

lining, a regrettable development since the early 1920s.[29] Not until long after Vauxhall and Morris had adopted overhead valves as standard did Austin follow their example. Austin brakes were mechanically actuated and although Sedgwick maintains they were not totally reliable this has been denied, the explanation for Sir Herbert's apparent conservatism in not adopting hydraulic braking (like Morris) being a preference to wait for a more reliable system, which Girling later introduced and which Sir Herbert took up.[30] Sir Herbert's attitude towards consumer preference is aptly illustrated in his response to criticism of the new Austin Sixteen. Two Austin engineers suggested that his design allowed insufficient head room. 'Public, public', he replied, 'you give them head room, and they want a low roof, give them a low roof and they want head room, they don't know what they do want.' In fact, Sir Herbert promptly devised a two-piece propellor shaft to give a low flat floor.[31]

The new models of 1933/34, as we have seen, began to remedy these deficiencies and began to exhibit symptoms of modernity, especially in 1934 when the familiar Austin radiator shell, associated with the Company since the beginning, was superseded by a newly designed curvaceous shell and lengthened bonnet – once more against Sir Herbert's inclinations, but as a concession to the apparent public demand for a more modern streamlined appearance. The year 1934 also saw the introduction of the first £100 Austin car, a two-seater Seven called the Opal, and the only model to retain the traditional flat radiator shell.[32] Austin's overall sales improved, but its share of the total output fell slightly, as Morris, Ford, and Standard pushed their 8 h.p. models hard (Fig. 4). In 1935/36 the Seven's most serious competitor, the Ford Eight, was reduced to £115 for the cheapest model, compared with the Austin Ruby saloon at £110. This situation altered the following year, when Austin prices were increased to £125 for the Ruby, while Ford unveiled its 8 h.p. model at the Motor Show with a price tag of £100, the first four-seater saloon car to be offered so

[29] See his comments in the discussion of the paper by W. O. Kennington, 'The Utilitarian Aesthetics of Automobile Body Design', *PIAE*, XXIX, 1934–35, p. 67. C. R. F. Engelbach favoured designing a body first and chassis second, a concession to comfort which not even Sir Herbert would consider.

[30] I am grateful to Mr. Freddie Henry for this information.

[31] By communication from Mr. Freddie Henry, 6 April 1978.

[32] R. J. Wyatt, p. 137. The other Sevens were the Ruby Saloon (£120), and the Pearl Cabriolet (£128).

Table 9: Price Competition in the Market for Cars, 1928–1939 (Model Years)

Year	Austin Seven £	Morris Minor £	Morris Eight £	Ford Eight £	Singer Eight and Nines £	Standard Nines £	Morris Ten £	Austin Ten £	Standard Ten £	Ford Ten £
1928	125				140	190				
1929	130	125			140	185				
1930	122	125			165	185				
1931	118	100	152		150	195				
1932	110	115	122		150	155	165	155		
1933	112	110	—	120	159	159	165	158		
1934	108	110	120	120	162	152	165	158	192	
1935	112		118	120	162	145	172	158	195	135
1936	120		118	100	165	135	172	160	189	135
1937	115		126	100	149	145	185	185	169	135
1938	112		132	115	149	152	185	175	172	145
1939	122		128	120	149	129	175	175	169	—

Prices used in preparing this chart are those quoted in the *Motor Car Index 1928–1939* (Fletcher & Son Ltd., Norwich, 1939).

cheaply (Table 9). Customer loyalty withstood the price change for two years before Seven sales suffered a serious setback, and the huge expansion in total sales of motor cars in Britain was not reflected in the relatively stable production of Austin Sevens (Table 8).

Sir Herbert decided that since the model had finally lost its dominance in the baby car market the Company should produce a slightly longer car to compete in the 8 h.p. class, to be called the Big Seven. He explained to agents and the press at Longbridge at its launching in the summer of 1937 that the Big Seven was an addition to the Austin family and did not in any way supersede the famous Baby, but the Big Seven four-door saloon duly superseded the Baby in the season following, in 1938. This was a longer, larger, motor car with a 900 c.c. engine mounted on the familiar triangular chassis frame, and priced at £145 on its introduction to the market in November 1937,[33] just as a new recession was beginning to bite. In the spring of 1939 the Seven (and Big Seven) ceased production, and a new Eight was introduced with an up-to-date mechanical specification and body style (Table 10). By the outbreak of war, the Ten and Twelve models had also been refurbished.

* * *

While the Seven and the Ten were Austin's best sellers by far in the 1930s, the venerable Twelve four-cylinder model, dating back to 1921, continued in production. Its appeal to private car buyers waned, but the Twelve's utter dependability continued to attract international recognition, if for no other reason than through its successful domination of the London taxi-cab market in the 1930s. During the 1920s, Citroën, Beardmore, and Unic had supplied most of the cab companies, but revised regulations laid down by the Public Carriage Office in 1929 offered renewed opportunity for competition in manufacturing lower and more streamlined cabs, in contrast with the high, boxy, old-fashioned appearance of those already on the streets. Every single major taxi builder brought out a new design between 1928 and 1930, notably Citroën, Beardmore, Unic and, significant newcomers in a depressed market for private cars, Morris in 1929 and Austin in 1930.[34]

Indeed, in a lecture to professional automobile engineers in 1930 Sir Herbert had referred critically to the 'archaic type of vehicle' used

[33] R. J. Wyatt, pp. 161–3.

[34] G. N. Georgano, *A History of the London Taxicab* (Newton Abbott, 1972).

Table 10: Prices of Selected Austin Motor Cars, 1919–1939 (Model Years)

(£)

	Austin Seven		Austin Ten	Austin Twelve		Austin Twelve Light Twelve Four, saloon model)	Austin Twenty			
Year	(2-seater)	(Saloon 4-seater)		(Heavy Twelve Four)	(Saloon model)		(4-cyl. model)	(Saloon model)	(6-cyl. model)	(Saloon model)
1919							495			
1920							695			
1921				550			695			
1922	225			550			695			
1923	165			450			595			
1924	155			375	475		595			
1925	141			355	455		525			
1926	145			340	350		495			
1927	145	165		275	350		450	550	525	
1928	125	135		255	315		425	495	525	595
1929	130	140		245	320		395	425	530	
1930	122.10	130		250	275				525	
1931	118	118		275	268				498	
1932	110	115	155	268	265	178			515	
1933	112	128	158	255	275	188			595	
1934	108	120	158	265	275	198			650	
1935	112	125	158	275		188			650	
1936	120	131	160			190			650	
1937	115	125	185			220				
1938	112	122	175			215				
1939	122	137	175			225				

Prices refer to the model year but are taken from the quotations included in successive issues of the *Autocar Buyers Guide* which appeared immediately preceding the Motor Show in October of the preceding year. No account is taken of price changes during the course of the year. All prices refer to basic models.

on London streets, pointing to the need for a really comfortable model.[35] Initially the Austin was not licensed for London because its turning circle was too great to meet the legal requirements, though modifications in the same year of its introduction as a taxi-cab saw Austin Twelve Four cabs on the streets of London as well as those of Manchester and other provincial cities. The appearance was conventional, with upright steering column and no front door on the near side, but despite its unspectacular entry into the trade it gradually established predominance, the 'Grand Piano', or 'Upright Grand', maintaining a reputation for dependability to which gradual improvement, rather than innovation, in taxi-cab design also contributed.[36] All bodywork was specially built by outside firms, mainly by London coachbuilders, and most were landaulets, the rear portion of which could be opened in summer.

Austin cabs won popularity at precisely the period when the use of taxis grew rapidly. Even in 1930 the Austin taxi-cab accounted for one-half of new registrations in London, but the total was only 540. The total number of new registrations in London in 1933 was 962, of which 834 were Austins, a dominance which was maintained during the continuing growth period of 1936, and indeed in the recession which followed.[37] As a proportion of Austin's total sales, of course, the taxi-cab trade was minuscule, but it was precisely the qualities which led to its virtual monopoly of that trade which also explains the Twelve's continuing popularity long after the conventional style of 1921, when it was first launched, had gone out of fashion. Apart from the longer stroke engine installed in 1927, as in the Austin Seven, to cope with increased body weight, and modifications which were necessary to ensure some degree of modernity, the Twelve-Four resembled its prototype until its replacement in 1935 by the new light Twelve-Four, introduced to compete with Cowley.[38]

Modifying the Twelve-Four in order to capture the taxi-cab trade may be seen as symptomatic of the characteristic response by motor manufacturers to disappointed expectations; namely, to diversify the

[35] Sir Herbert Austin, 'Future Trends in Automobile Design', *PIAE*, XX (1930–31), p. 11.

[36] G. N. Georgano, p. 104.

[37] G. N. Georgano, p. 106, where the figures are given for 1930–38. New registrations of hackneys in the entire UK numbered 10,002 in 1930, and 4,068 in 1933. SMMT, *The Motor Industry of Great Britain* (1969), Table 17.

[38] M. Sedgwick, p. 271.

range structure by rapidly increasing the number of models and variants offered. At its peak, this surge of market-covering by Austin resulted in the simultaneous existence of eight engine types (compared with eighteen from Nuffield), five chassis types, six different wheelbase lengths, and fifty-one body variations, with the attendant implications for the exploitation of economies of long runs.[39] Furthermore, in addition to a new luxury Twenty-Eight, replacing the Twenty, in 1938, Lord Austin announced a new range of commercial trucks comprising 30 cwt., two and three ton models, despite the insistence of Payton that commercial vehicle manufacturers were finding the trade unprofitable.[40]

It seems unlikely that the situation was as bad as sales brochures[41] would suggest, however, for these were more concerned with psychological appeal, whereas the economic importance of a product range depended upon technical complementarity. In fact, Austin concentrated upon a range of about half a dozen cars throughout the 1930s, and produced additions simply by the expedient of combining basic components in various ways. Thus, for 1934 the Company offered an 8 ft. 10 in. chassis with three different engines of 12, 14, and 16 h.p. A classic example is provided by the 900 c.c. power unit of the Big Seven, which was transferred to a new chassis for the 1939 Eight; this incorporated up-to-date mechanical specifications and body style to match the refurbished Tens and Twelves available on the market on the outbreak of war. Consumer convergence, however, ensured that actual production was concentrated on two models in the 1930s (Table 11). Austin's car model policy is compared with those of Nuffield and Ford in Table 12, which shows the numbers of different models and engine capacities produced during the years of maximum model differentiation.

The rapid growth in sales and the convergence upon two models raised policy problems for the directors, for in order to meet demands from the Company's distributors production levels rose steeply, outrunning capacity. Engelbach reckoned that the Company was losing more than £60,000 a year by subcontracting bodywork to outside suppliers. Indeed, at that time 55 per cent of the net sales value of

[39] M. Sedgwick, pp. 267–9.

[40] AMB, 4 February 1938; *Times*, 11 October 1938.

[41] Even those of Austin's which in 1932 offered no fewer than twenty-six body styles altogether.

Table 11: Number of Different Models and Engine Capacities of Austin Cars, 1919–1939

	1919	1920	1921	1922	1923	1924	1925	1926	1927	1928	1929	1930
Basic models	1	1	1	2	3	3	3	3	4	5	4	4
Engines	1	1	1	2	3	3	3	3	4	5	4	4

	1931	1932	1933	1934	1935	1936	1937	1938	1939
Basic models	4	5	7	7	7	8	7	7	8
Engines	4	5	7	9	9	8	6	7	7

Source: Fletcher & Son Ltd., Austin entries from *Motor Car Index 1916–1927* (Norwich, 1927) and *Motor Car Index 1928–1939* (reprinted Brighton, 1964).

Table 12: Models and Engine Capacities Produced by Austin Compared with Nuffield and Ford (Model Years)

	1929	1931	1933	1935	1937	1939
AUSTIN						
1 Basic models	4	4	7	7	7	8
2 Engines	4	4	7	9	6	7
NUFFIELD						
1 Basic models	13	16	23	22	15	17
2 Engines	10	8	12	18	8	10
FORD						
1 Basic models*	2	2	4	3	4	4
2 Engines	2	2	4	3	4	4
(* Different models†	1	1	3	3	3	3)

† i.e. different chassis, by disregarding of different engine options (e.g. the A and AF models) or utility models.

Source: Fletcher & Son Ltd., *Motor Car Index, 1928–1939* (reprinted Brighton, 1964).

Austin's output came from outside sources.[42] That was the justification for his proposal, made in 1932, that £60,000 should be spent on pressing plant, conveyors, and buildings for the manufacture of an extra 12,000 motor bodies a year. Sir Herbert supported Engelbach, but Payton was anxious to increase cash reserves, and it was agreed that a compromise £40,000 investment should take place for the purpose outlined by Engelbach.[43] This movement away from dependence on components supplied from other firms was overtaken by continued expansion in sales, and whilst Longbridge was almost certainly more of a manufacturing operation than Cowley or the Vauxhall works, nonetheless outside suppliers continued to play a critical role in production.

At the level of the industry as a whole, Barna estimated purchases of components and materials to have accounted for 56 per cent of home produced value in the early 1930s, and the Census of Production data suggests that a considerable diminution of the self-sufficiency of individual establishments occurred between 1930 and 1935. Elsewhere it has been argued that so far as individual motor manufacturers were

[42] AMB, 12 October 1931.

[43] AMB, 26 October 1931.

concerned, such a trend, which ran counter to the economies to be derived from indivisibilities, was of critical importance in determining the outcome of competition among the few.[44] The availability of efficient outside specialist supplies offered external economies, though not on equal terms, to the major motor companies.[45] Such a system of industrial organization allowed not only the big spenders, Ford and Vauxhall, to join Morris and Austin as leaders, but also Standard and Rootes, firms whose modest resources yet attractive designs and efficient enterprises enabled these companies to establish themselves as serious competitors among the Big Six.[44]

* * *

Another relevant factor conducive to the growth of the new competitors was the continuance of protection, a policy almost unanimously endorsed by British motor manufacturers since its introduction in 1915. Sir Herbert was no exception as his pronouncements in 1924, when Philip Snowden introduced his experiment in free trade, showed. In his capacity as a member of the Birmingham Branch of the National Union of Manufacturers, in April 1924 Sir Herbert convened a meeting of his employees to discuss the issue; 5,200 voted in support of a resolution for urging the retention of the duties, with thirty opposing votes and 680 workers absent on holiday.[46] The resolution and the voting figures were recorded and sent to the Chancellor of the Exchequer. Arguments presented in favour by Sir Herbert were to be repeated often; that since the duties were imposed in 1915 employment at Longbridge had risen fourfold; that despite higher wages and higher

[44] See Roy Church and Michael Miller, 'The Big Three; Competition, Management, and Marketing in the British Motor Industry 1922–1939', *Essays in British Business History* (1977), edited for the Economic History Society by Barry Supple, pp. 163–87.

[45] For example, Joseph Lucas quoted prices of electrical components in roughly inverse relation to the size of orders. Roy A. Church, 'Innovation, Monopoly, and the Supply of Vehicle Components in Britain, 1880–1930: The Growth of Joseph Lucas Ltd.', *Business History Review*, LII (1978), p. 241.

[46] The forms issued to foremen and chargehands to complete were framed in such a way as to encourage support for the duties, the only information considered of sufficient relevance to include being the increase in the number of workmen and staff at Austin between 1914 (without the duty) and 1923 under the McKenna duty. It was baldly stated that 'Since the duty was imposed employment in the trade has never been greater, and if the duty is abolished wages will fall and unemployment increase'. AMC Papers.

taxation car prices had been reduced to the benefit of the consumer; and that the removal of safeguarding would be followed by higher prices, high unemployment, lower wages and a drop in exports.[47] The argument was generalized when he addressed a meeting of employees and workers at Birmingham Town Hall in June, though on that occasion he declared that the motor trade did not need protection, and that if the duties were removed gradually over a three-year period the industry could dispense with preferences entirely.[48]

In fact, a softened line proved unnecessary, for the duties were reintroduced, whereupon in July 1925 Sir Herbert spoke at a meeting of Midland manufacturers, seconding a resolution demanding a widening scope for the safeguarding policy to afford relief to other industries similar to that which the Government had extended to the motor trade on revenue grounds.[49] Rarely did Sir Herbert distribute praise to Government, and a characteristic tone was struck in his address to the same Midland Branch of the National Union of Manufacturers in 1929: 'The manufacturers have too long been kicked from pillar to post by politicians whose ineptitude has only been equalled in many cases by their irresponsibility.' He called for assurance of a stable fiscal policy at a time when the removal of the McKenna Duties once more seemed a feasibility.[50]

As the Slump deepened, Sir Herbert continued to defend the duties and condemned the Government's increased tax on petrol as a deterrent to the British manufacturers' drive for exports by encouraging the British motoring public to turn to small cars to a still greater extent, when the high powered vehicles were, in normal times, the preferred choice in the major British markets overseas.[51] Elsewhere he attacked motor taxes as taxes on necessities, 'for the small car is but another instance of the luxury of yesterday becoming the necessity of today'.[52] He also suggested that the motive behind an increased petrol tax was to assist the railways to compete with road transport.[53] Such allegations

[47] *Birmingham Post*, 23 April, 10 May 1924.
[48] *Times*, 26 June 1924.
[49] *Times*, 24 July 1925.
[50] *Times*, 22 October, 12 November 1929.
[51] *Times*, 28 April 1931, 4 October 1932.
[52] Sir Herbert Austin, 'Facts and Figures that Prove that Light Cars are Making History', *Light Car and Cycle Car*, 11 December 1931.
[53] In 1939 he criticized the rise in car tax, for favouring the purchase of smaller cars. *Times*, 6 April 1939.

were repeated, and in 1938 he described one penny extra on the petrol tax as 'the last straw on the camel's back', even though he admitted that the addition was not likely to stop people buying cars.[54]

In 1932 his remedy for unemployment was an immediate reduction by £1 million in the budget deficit, coupled with a consumers' 'spend now' campaign, for which the Mayor of Birmingham received his commendation.[55] Sir Herbert was also an advocate of a 'buy British' policy,[56] and an appropriate slogan appeared on Company stationery in the 1930s: 'Buy British goods and help to reduce unemployment.' None of these ideas on economic policy was novel, but he felt strongly that economists and financial experts had hitherto failed to solve the problem of cyclical depressions. He thought the words 'depression' and 'slump' should be removed from the vocabulary of economic debate and he called for a commission of experts, bankers and economists to join with industrialists to suggest that steps should be taken to prevent the 'recurrent man-made cycles'.[57]

Even as he spoke, the rearmament programme was beginning to influence levels of investment and employment, and Lord Austin, who was a central figure in the Government's Shadow Factory Scheme, acting as Chairman of the Shadow Aero Engine Committee, was involved from the beginning. Through the Committee, it was largely his responsibility to co-ordinate the work of the six shadow factories, which he did until shortly before his death in 1940.[58] He had been approached initially in the spring of 1936, and in May of the same year Austin became the first Company to enter into a contract with the Air Ministry for the erection of a shadow factory.[59] The agreement also provided for the production of 900 Fairey Battle airframes and engines over a period of three years.[60] His disastrous experience of government contractors during the First World War helps to explain why Lord Austin (as he became in 1936) took such pains in discussing precise details of remuneration to avoid a repetition, and it was he who

[54] *Times*, 23 April 1933, 17 April 1938.

[55] *Times*, 13 April 1932, 7 February 1933.

[56] 'Sir Herbert Austin KBE, His Life Story', *Autocar*, 13 September 1929.

[57] *Times*, 20 January 1937.

[58] M. M. Postan, *British War Production* (1952), p. 418; *Times*, 25 May 1940.

[59] Early negotiations and preparations at Longbridge are recorded in the Minutes of the Aeroplane Committee, AMC Papers, 6 April to 10 November 1936.

[60] W. Ashworth, *Contracts and Finance* (1953), pp. 150–1; T.161/986, S90764, Air Ministry Memo No. 3.

suggested a bonus for economies made in production.[61] Tiresome though at least one of the civil servants found his efforts to improve the terms of his contract, Sir Herbert continued to press for a better deal.[62] Ministers and civil servants regarded his style of negotiation to be distinctly unorthodox and difficult to handle. Senior civil servant Swinton observed that Sir Herbert behaved in negotiation like a managing director and seemed to assume that Neville Chamberlain possessed similar powers of decision to those which he commanded. Chamberlain objected so much to the notion of contracts being set as personal bargains that he refused to attend a meeting of contractors, describing it as a 'poker party'.[63]

The final agreement accepted by Sir Herbert personally was £50,000 in the first year for experiment and preparation; £50,000 in the second year, against which were to be set payments per machine in that year and later; £200 for each machine produced and accepted; and a bonus on savings in cost as compared with a basic figure to be agreed later in the light of experience, the bonus being 12.5 per cent on savings up to £300 per machine and 17.5 per cent on any further savings. Lord Austin also insisted on the inclusion of a break clause, whereby the Government could be deemed to be in breach of contract if Rootes, the other airframe assembly shadow factory, received better terms than Austin. Cost estimates for construction and equipment of the factory were revised upwards in the course of negotiation from £1,350,955 to £1,515,645, and the initial workforce in aircraft production was nearly 10,000.[64]

Lord Austin criticized the Government's decision to purchase American aeroplanes in order to expand supply more rapidly and urged government departments concerned with 'mobilization' not to interfere with industry. He wanted them to decide quickly 'and then frankly tell industry what they want and how they want it'.[65] Aircraft

[61] The formula to consist of a lump sum management fee related to turnover plus a percentage bonus on reduced costs. T.161/986, S40764, Swinton to Herbert Austin, 9 March 1936.

[62] T.161/986, S40764, Runtl to Sir Warren Fisher, 23 April 1936.

[63] T.161/986, S40764. Report of TISC meeting 19 June 1936. When the parity issue was first raised in May there was some suspicion that Rootes and Austin were colluding in order to improve the terms, and that the decision of Rootes to break off negotiations in response to Austin's demands for parity was a calculated step in the bargaining progress; Bridge to Runtl, 11 May 1936.

[64] William Hornby, *Factories and Plant* (1958), p. 241.

[65] *Times*, 14 June 1938; Lambert & Wyatt, p. 163.

production did not hamper the Company's commercial progress in the immediate pre-war years, and following a recession in 1938 car production at Longbridge surged upwards, stimulated not only by price reductions but also by the belated appearance of a new 8 h.p. model which replaced the Big Seven in February 1939. A new Ten was introduced three months later, followed by a new Twelve only days before the outbreak of the Second World War.[66] Months later, Lord Austin resigned from the chairmanship of the Shadow Committee. After a bout of pneumonia in February, he died of a heart attack in May 1941.[67]

[66] Companies House, 'A' File 133747, AMC, report of AGM; Lambert & Wyatt, p. 162. For the details of the new range see M. Sedgwick, p. 272.
[67] Lambert & Wyatt, p. 167.

CHAPTER NINE

Investment, Profitability and Labour Relations

AUSTIN'S SALES LEADERSHIP was short-lived, and coincided with a period when the enlarged and more efficient capacity resulting from the investment programme in the 1920s enabled the Company to exploit the faltering progress of Morris Motors, whose investment levels fell markedly between 1928 and 1934. That was the period when the investment in land and buildings in the mid-1920s and the associated indivisibilities allowed Austin's output to grow rapidly without further substantial net investment until the mid-1930s (Table 13). By this time the massive investment by Ford at Dagenham elicited a considerable rise in capital expenditure by Austin and Morris in defence of their market shares against the American firm.[1]

After the investment programme during the Slump, when Austin's net assets increased by more than any other car maker except Ford, the Company's net assets grew least, Ford excepted. Between 1929 and 1938 only the net assets of Humber, among the Big Six, grew less than those of Austin.[2] Rates of return on assets employed and on fixed assets, show the relatively stable record of profitability after the financial traumas of the early 1920s (Table 14), a steadiness which Maxcy and Silberston's comparative analysis on a slightly different basis also

[1] Michael Miller has calculated end-year estimates of net investment (in £ millions) for Morris and Ford on a comparable basis:

	1929	*1930*	*1931*	*1932*	*1933*	*1934*	*1935*	*1936*	*1937*	*1938*
Austin	0.02	0.10	0.17	0.10	0.10	0.16	0.15	0.22	0.31	0.01
Morris	0.06	−0.04	−0.10	−0.06	−0.06	0.14	0.25	0.15	0.24	0.03
Ford	0.50	1.60	2.50	2.80	0.30	0.10	0.10	0.40	0.60	−0.50

[2] Maxcy and Silberston, Table 9.

Table 13: Growth of Fixed Assets and Net Investment 1918–1938

Year	Fixed assets £	Net investment	Year	Fixed assets £	Net investment
1918	869,418		1929	2,097,943	21,535
1919	1,754,858	885,440	1930	2,199,517	101,574
1920	1,832,456	77,598*	1931	2,364,820	165,303
1921	1,910,054	77,598*	1932	2,464,224	99,404
1922	1,867,923	−42,131	1933	2,565,486	101,262
1923	1,814,551	−53,372	1934	2,729,477	163,991
1924	n.a.	n.a.	1935	2,877,770	148,293
1925	1,433,984	n.a.	1936	3,097,061	219,291
1926	1,477,829	43,845	1937	3,403,121	306,060
1927	1,687,434	209,605	1938	3,518,049	114,928
1928	2,076,408	388,974			

* Estimate.

Net investment is defined as additions to fixed assets, excluding tools, calculated from company balance sheets. The figures are end of financial year estimates.

reveals to have been in contrast with the experience of other major competitors from 1929.[3]

Table 14 also shows the steadily improving cash flow after the crisis of 1920–21, the adoption of high depreciation rates, the costs of capital reorganization, and the fixed interest commitments preventing the Company from paying ordinary dividends until 1929. Thereafter, a generous appropriation to reserves added to the call on cash flow.[4] The

[3] Maxcy and Silberston's estimates in Table 6 refer to the ratios of *all* income (net of all charges except taxation) to net tangible assets, using the definition of Moodies Services Ltd. The numerator, therefore, includes non-trading sources of income, and losses; but whereas these were certainly important in an accounting sense they are less significant from the standpoint of trading performance. This is better indicated by the ratio of trading profits, after the deduction of maintenance and depreciation allowances only, to the book value of land, buildings, plant and equipment.

	1931	*1932*	*1933*	*1934*	*1935*	*1936*	*1937*	*1938*	*1939*
Nuffield	32.3	37.3	18.1	27.9	55.4	66.6	52.0	36.0	54.2
Ford	—	—	5.3	10.0	9.8	9.6	8.6	6.2	22.5
Austin	38.6	27.4	30.5	37.9	33.9	30.7	29.9	17.4	(22.3)

In fact, Michael Miller's estimates, shown above, lead to the same general conclusions, with Austin recording a relatively steady level of profitability for most of the 1930s, though on average at lower levels compared with Nuffield. Ford, the other major producer, showed a very low rate of return until 1939.

[4] See Appendix 3 for a detailed breakdown of funds provided by operations between 1922 and 1939.

Table 14: Profits and Assets Employed, 1922–1939

Year	(a) Profit before tax and interest (£000s)	(b) Net trading profit (Gross profit less tax and depreciation) (£000s)	(c) Net profit (Profit less tax, less maintenance and depreciation and debenture interest) (£000s)	(d) Net tangible assets* (£)	(a) as % of (d)	(b) as % of (d)
1922	222.4	90.9	78.6	3,236,330	6.9	2.8
1923 (9 months)	381.6	301.1	205.5	3,470,446	(1.47)‡	(11.6)
1924	470.9	406.9	161.2	3,381,787	13.9	12.0
1925	748.9	684.8	447.9	2,970,195	25.2	23.1
1926	648.4	594.4	330.5	3,477,018	18.6	17.1
1927	962.5	806.7	116.0‡	3,485,433	27.6	23.1
1928 (15 months)	861.3	738.7	243.0	3,438,524	(20.0)	(17.2)
1929	1,297.4	761.3	560.0	4,034,414	32.2	18.9
1930 (7 months)	858.2	645.6	384.3	3,927,425	(37.5)	28.2
1931	1,376.2	1,018.5	489.0	4,296,572	32.0	23.7
1932	1,078.1	821.0	390.0	4,269,128	25.3	19.2
1933	1,188.4	946.6	507.0	4,327,530	27.5	21.9
1934	1,505.2	1,198.5	661.0	4,725,426	31.9	25.4
1935	1,469.1	1,174.1	624.0	5,052,839	29.1	23.2
1936	1,496.7	1,157.9	554.0	5,191,730	28.8	22.3
1937	1,665.1	1,235.6	556.0	5,408,204	30.8	22.8
1938	1,282.8	834.8	363.0	5,297,259	34.5	15.8
1939	1,609.6	1,079.9	345.0	5,381,645	29.9	20.1

* Defined as assets (excluding goodwill) less liabilities.
† Figures in brackets are based on twelve-month estimates.
‡ This figure is after 'special provisions' and is affected by the reconstruction scheme. Before special provision the figure was 406.5.

rates of return shown in Table 14, both before and after financial commitments, indicate a sound managerial performance. The average (and relatively stable) rate of profit before tax, interest, and depreciation as a percentage of net tangible assets exceeded 20 per cent between 1924 and 1939.

Since the close of the First World War Austin had laboured under the burden of over-investment in fixed assets, much of it in the form of land and buildings (Appendix 3). A similar combination of over-investment in fixed assets and watered capital, which became inevitable when the Company entered the hectic post-war boom, had resulted in the spectacular bankruptcy of Wolseley in late 1926. For Austin such a situation meant that although the balance sheet value of fixed assets did not reflect increases in productive capacity, progress of this kind was revealed by the diminishing indebtedness, when book and real values of assets converged in the 1920s as output grew. Thus the increment on total fixed assets in 1919 was £0.89 million, and an additional estimated £0.15 million in 1920 and 1921. The value of the Company's fixed assets fell thereafter, before being obscured by financial reconstruction. Then came the massive £0.6 million investment programme which that facilitated in 1927 and 1928.

One particularly impressive aspect of Austin's history in the 1920s is that, unlike many other British firms, its capital stock continued to grow. Many lesser firms which had failed to solve the problems of over-valued assets, the legacy of the post-war boom, experienced sporadic negative net investment. This contrast also suggests that financial problems presented British manufacturers with persistent difficulties, which Lord Nuffield had often stressed in alluding to the success of his own enterprise. In the 1920s Austin's dire liquidity position had forced the Company into the stock market following the issue of £1 million 6 per cent cumulative preference shares in 1919, with £1.5 million 10 per cent preferred ordinary shares in 1920, and £1 million 7 per cent debenture stock in 1921. But the relative failure of these issues, and the continuing reluctance of the banks to support the Company on a long term basis, meant that only a reduction in capital and a return to profitability could provide the sources of funds necessary to secure the firm's long term future and cash returns to shareholders.

The reduction of authorized capital from £5 million to £3.8 million, and paid-up capital from £3.35 million to £2.15 million in 1927 had been secured by writing 10 shillings and 15 shillings off each

Figure 5. The Austin Profit Record 1922–39

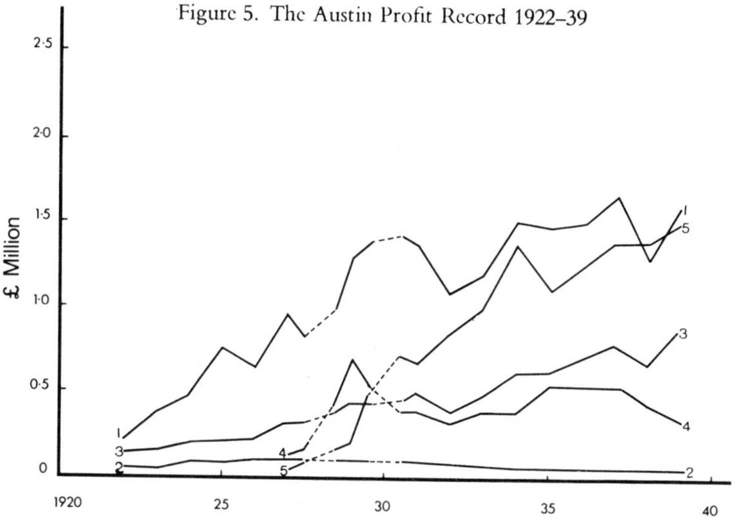

Key:

1. Profit before tax, maintenance, depreciation and debenture interest.
2. Taxation and debenture interest.
3. Maintenance and depreciation.
4. Distribution to shareholders.
5. To reserves and change in balance carried forward.

Source:
Profit and loss accounts, Austin Motor Company. Until 1927 profits which might otherwise have been allotted to reserve or carried forward were appropriated to offset the huge debt which between 1921 and 1926 was reduced from £1.88 million to £1.37 million. In 1925 £0.73 million was the cost of capital re-organization and a further £0.29 million in 1927. Discontinuities in 1928 and 1930 are explained by the abnormal length of the period to which the figures for those 'years' refer. Further detailed analysis of the profit and loss accounts are to be found in Appendix 3.

of preferred ordinary and ordinary shares respectively. Thereafter, capital was increased to £5 million by the 1,200,000 unclassified shares of £1.[5] By the early 1930s the Company was retaining approximately one-third of net earnings, in addition to depreciation which averaged

[5] In 1930 the issued preference shares and B preference shares of £1, preferred ordinaries of 10 shillings, and ordinary and A ordinary shares of 5 shillings were converted into stock. In 1934 475,000 of the unissued shares were subdivided into 1.9 million A 5 shilling shares.

round about 10 per cent of profit after tax (Fig. 5 and Appendix 4). Compared with the financially untroubled firms of Morris Motors, Standard, and Vauxhall, Austin retained a relatively low proportion of net earnings, though from the mid-1930s the gap narrowed, as Austin's ratio remained much the same whereas that of the others diminished.[6] While the reason for this change in the late 'thirties had to do with the history of the other firms, Austin differed in this respect before the late 'thirties because of the Company's relatively high gearing,[7] which postponed an even more rapid investment programme and contributed to the continuing presumption that despite the firm's favourable financial position conservative finance was imperative.

Internal funds remained the only source financing Austin's growth and development, and the firm's newly found financial strength owed much to the conservative financial policy pursued consistently by E. L. Payton.

Even after the Company had cleared the colossal indebtedness of the 1920s, the directors' explicit intention was to amass large reserves. A sinking fund capital reserve had already accumulated £167,270 by 1930, but the target was to create a total capital reserve of more than £1 million out of profits. The extraordinarily high figure of £1,129,000 held in cash was explained by the universal motor trade practice of cash settlement with suppliers in order to secure their confidence;[8] Austin customarily paid more than 80 per cent of its creditors, principally suppliers, within seven days.[9] In an interview with the Midland Bank Manager in 1932, Payton explained that for a 'precarious' business like the motor industry it was necessary to maintain a £1 million reserve to meet any contingency, and he was considering increasing that figure to £1.25 million.[10]

At the same time, Payton asked for a standby credit on a £500,000 bank debenture to be available at any time in the event of a bad year,

[6] Maxcy and Silberston, Table 7. Austin's preference shares and debentures were approximately seven times as large as ordinary shares before 1927, and comprised an even greater proportion of capital after the ordinary share reduction effected by reconstruction.

[7] Even in the 1930s profits were applied to paying a cumulative 7 per cent on preference stock, a cumulative 6 per cent (tax free up to 6 shillings in the £) on B preference stock, a non-cumulative 20 per cent (10 per cent up to November 1927) on preferred ordinary stock.

[8] AMB, 29 October 1930.

[9] Ibid.

[10] MBA (509), Midland Diary, 14 October 1932.

or a failure in Austin car sales in particular.[11] The Bank Manager's response is recorded in his diary: 'I told Mr. Payton that with the excellent organization and economies upon which their business was conducted it appeared to me that if the Austin Company lost money, all the other motor companies would have got into such a state that they would probably all be down and out, and I could not visualize at the present time the state of affairs in which the Austin Motor Company would be likely to require advances for the reasons he had mentioned.'[12] Another indication of the turnaround in the relationship between the Company and the Bank is the entry recording the agreement with Sir Herbert to offer a more favourable interest rate on the £100,000 deposit 'in order not to upset the friendly relationship which exists'.[13] At last, the problems of liquidity and capital accumulation were solved at the Austin Motor Company.

* * *

The supply of labour had presented Austin with considerable difficulties during the early years of the firm's history, especially during the war and in the immediate post-war boom. Thereafter, the problem of securing labour eased, but the increasing mechanization of production proved to be a source of friction, for innovation brought with it the threat of substituting semi-skilled and unskilled labour for skilled workers and the introduction of rate fixers as part of the search for more efficient utilization of capital and labour. These were the issues which had brought about a strike of the Tinplate Sheet Metal Workers and Braziers Society at Longbridge in 1921,[14] but the increasingly difficult trading conditions and the lack of support from other workers probably prevented its success for it seems to have petered out.

In the autumn of 1923, however, by which time trade had picked up and Longbridge in particular began to move into high production gear, methods of payment and dilution of labour became central issues. When an attempt was made to introduce new piece rates without consultation with the shop floor representatives, they protested. The

[11] Payton's expectation was for profits to fall in 1931–32, despite the increase in car sales, for prices had been cut to compete, and a larger proportion of sales were accounted for by the smaller models. MBA (509), Midland Diary, 14 October 1932.

[12] MBA (509), Midland Diary, 7 July 1932.

[13] MBA (509), Midland Diary, 14 October 1932.

[14] *Town Crier*, 4 March 1921.

Austin management invited officials of the National Union of Vehicle Builders to examine the rearrangement and to settle the matter.[15] The outcome, according to the union journal, was a complete vindication of the men's opposition and capitulation by the Company. Austin 'gracefully gave way and promised not to offend in future'. The Birmingham correspondent referred to the considerable inflation of the union's prestige at Longbridge as a result, and predicted a return to the strength held by the union prior to the engineering lock-out of 1922. Since that time only the woodcutting machinists and the vehicle builders had possessed anything approaching effective organization: 'Northfield with its great Motor Shop, the Austin, is one of our most hardly hit ones under the mass production system, and therefore needs the most watchful care in protecting our labour for the skilled men.'[16] The growth in the size of the labour force at Longbridge explains why the Company was seen as the ultimate target for organization by the unions (Table 15).

Under conditions of rapidly expanding trade, however, the men demonstrated a preference for independent action, and in 1924 the skilled body makers successfully resisted the introduction of semi-skilled workers to cope with tasks customarily regarded by the men as skilled. They struck, in contravention of the trade union agreement, and achieved a settlement through direct negotiation with the Austin managers. It was agreed that if the men's union, the National Union of Vehicle Builders, could supply twelve skilled men to meet the Company's needs, then Austin would employ them instead of removing work to the semi-skilled shops. The men also received reassurances of consultation in future should rearrangement of work in this way be considered. The dispute lasted for only two days and was resolved before the union officials had time to become involved.[17] Unfortunately the details of negotiation leading to a system of wage payments increasingly based on payment by results have not been found, but in January 1926, looking back on recent difficulties at Longbridge, the branch secretary observed that negotiations and settlements through him and through shop committees had worked very well indeed.[18]

[15] *Journal of the National Union of Vehicle Builders* (hereafter *JNUVB*), November 1923.

[16] *JNUVB*, March 1924.

[17] *JNUVB*, Vol. 2, March 1924.

[18] *JNUVB*, Vol. 4, January 1926.

Table 15: Estimates of Numbers Employed by Austin 1905–1939

1905	270	1924	5,300
1907	400	1926	8,000
1912	1,500	1929	13,500
1914	2,300	1930	12,023
1916	6,093	1933	14,500
1918	16,000	1934	17,000
1919	20,000	1935	19,000
1922	8,000 (2,300)	1936	20,000
		1939	20,000*

* Including 2,000–3,000 aero workers.

Sources:
Various, including *Autocar*, J. S. Critchley, *British Motor Vehicles* (1912), *The Red Book of Commerce* (1913), but where possible AMB and Austin Motor Company publications. Where conflicting estimates are given, that quoted nearest to the year to which the estimates apply are recorded here. The largest discrepancy was between the figure quoted for 1922 by Sir Herbert Austin in the *Autocar*, 6 September 1929, when he recalled that the numbers employed fell at one point to 2,300, while the prospectus at Companies House (file 133747) recorded 8,000 workers at Longbridge in 1922. The precise *months* to which the figures refer might explain this significant difference, due to the marked seasonal variation in employment characteristic of the motor industry.

A few months later, the editor of the *Austin Advocate* wrote to *The Times* explaining the effectiveness of the Longbridge system of payment by results, a system in which a forty-seven hour week was standard, overtime was discouraged, and encouragement given to high earnings by dispensing with limits on the basis of job norms and time saved.[19] The absence of major friction in this period of rapid growth is attributable, most likely, neither to the efforts of the trade unions, who could count only on a very low membership at Longbridge, nor to an unusually enlightened approach by Austin's chairman.[21]

Sir Herbert's suspicious attitude towards the trade unions was well known, and the events of 1926 demonstrate clearly both the Company's strength as a high wage firm and a respected employer, and as an unambiguous opponent of organized labour, at the same time pursuing an 'open shop' policy.[22] For during the General Strike about 400

[19] Perry Keene claimed that the result had been a higher wage bill for the Company, but also increased production and larger profits. *Times*, 31 May 1926.

[20] *JNUVB*, Vol. 4, July 1926.

[21] Perhaps the key was a sound negotiating relationship between Engelbach, who was responsible for devising the wages system at Longbridge, and the shop committees.

[22] *Times*, 3 April 1929.

volunteers and special constables were recruited from the Longbridge workforce, their duties consisting of ensuring continuity and safety of gas and electricity supplies and the protection of the Austin Works. Sir Herbert was cheered enthusiastically at a reception held in the factory while the Strike was on, to which he responded by welcoming 'the loyalty and spirit of co-operation which the work people assembled had shown and which he felt was shared by the entire Longbridge workforce'.[23] On the whole he was correct. Thirty wood machinists struck for a day, and striking toolmakers had more, though still small, effects on production at Longbridge. As for the vehicle workers, whose union was the strongest at Longbridge, union officials instructed those who struck to resume work.[24] Returning strikers were found employment 'as conditions allowed and when the Company required them', the phrase prompted by policy set by Engineering and Allied Employers Federation, to which Austin belonged.

There is a suspicion that the General Strike may have brought about a deterioration in labour relations at Longbridge. Three years later, by which time the Longbridge workforce had increased from about 8,000 to more than 13,000, Austin faced its most serious strike ever, when the introduction of a new grading system associated with Engelbach's reorganized production methods and the adoption of flow production met with fierce opposition. On 20 February 1929, negotiations between management and men had produced agreement on the conditions for a more widespread and intensive application of the new system, but what was alleged to have been a harsh interpretation of the agreement, and tardiness in implementing concessions, led to a strike among a section of the workpeople, beginning on 25 March. The *Times* reporter noted that a further factor precipitating strike action was the effect of the revised wage scale in increasing earnings possible for the lower grades but at the expense of a possible fall in *average* wages to about £4 weekly, mainly due to a reduction in the agreed basic rates in the engineering shop where many of the workers in the higher grades were employed.[25] Five thousand of the 9,000 workers were reported to have been dissatisfied with the proposals, and a strike committee was formed to organize a 'stay in' and a refusal to actually work.

[23] *Austin Advocate*, 17 July 1926.

[24] R. P. Hastings, 'The General Strike in Birmingham 1926', B.A. Dissertation, University of Birmingham, 1960, Birmingham Reference Library, *The Nine Days in Birmingham, The General Strike 1926* (1976), p. 23.

[25] *Times*, 3 April 1929; *JNUVB*, Vol. 7, April 1929.

The managers' response was to close the factory and to refuse all negotiations until the men returned to work after the week-end, and then to negotiate only with trade union officials. The latter advised the few members they had at Longbridge to accede to this request, which they did, but the non-union men, comprising the vast majority on strike, continued to stay out. Although the strikers were threatened with dismissal, not until the fifth day of lost production was agreement reached through union officials to hold a meeting of management, union, and non-unionist representatives, to discuss the detailed working of the 20 February agreement.[26] After assurances that there would be no victimization, the Strike Committee together with about 1,500 men and women supporters who continued to oppose the principle underlying the new wages agreement, followed the other three or four thousand strikers' return to work.

The Times reported the strike as a victory both for the Company, whose basic position was upheld, and for organized labour. For despite the influence of Bowen, the ex-miner from South Wales who led the strike only six months after joining the Company, the five or six thousand workers who followed his lead failed to secure even a hearing until they conceded defeat.[27] Not surprisingly, the trade unions sought to press this point home in a drive to increase membership at Longbridge. A report from the Midlands organizer to the *Journal of the National Union of Vehicle Builders* urged renewed efforts to organize car workers at Longbridge, after the strike itself led to an addition of 150 members of that union and the establishment of several shop committees: 'It is gratifying to chronicle these developments, as at one time it seemed as if the dry bones of Trade Unionism at "The Austin" would never be revitalized. A good deal of time and effort has been expended here.'[28]

Meanwhile, after officials had negotiated with the firm, the Engineering Employers' Federation, and worker representatives from various departments, they eventually succeeded in persuading management to withdraw the intensified grading system, and to revert to the old method of piece work, the general effect of which was to raise minimum wage rates for about 500 semi-skilled workers. Management also agreed to recognize fully the principle of mutuality in rate fixing, and to consult workers more. Finally, the Austin managers agreed to

[26] *Times*, 1, 3, 4 April 1929.

[27] *Times*, 5 April 1929.

[28] *JNUVB*, Vol. 7, April 1929.

recognize shop stewards, and provided a room in which the newly formed Shop Stewards' Committee could hold regular weekly meetings.[29] The local newspaper aligned with trade unionist and labour views, *The Town Crier*, which had refrained from reporting the unofficial strike until it was over, concluded: 'If the Austin Management learn the lesson that employers need the trade unions almost as much as its members in order to ensure they are faced with *responsible* forces and negotiators, it will not be difficult to achieve one hundred per cent membership.'[30]

Such optimism proved unfounded, for the intervening depression and the high unemployment levels which accompanied it was conducive neither to trade union expansion nor resistance to the growth of semi-skilled labour in motor production, the least organized among car workers. Even the Shop Stewards' Committee became moribund. In the mid-1930s it was estimated that at least three-quarters of the labour force at Longbridge and Cowley were semi-skilled.[31] Also relevant is the relatively high percentage of women workers employed in the motor vehicle trades in Birmingham, in comparison with the national picture.[32] These factors, rather than the 'failure' of the 1929 strike, explain the continued weakness of organization at Longbridge. Indeed, The Austin Unity Song, composed for Austin dealers and Longbridge workers in 1930, with lyrics by Collie Knox and music by Vivian Ellis, is claimed to have reflected the true spirit of Austin workers.[33] It may be so, yet in 1936 a strike with causes almost identical with those which had led to the 1929 strike occurred, when 5,000 body workers struck to resist the introduction of lower piece-work prices,

[29] *JNUVB*, Vol. 7, May 1929.

[30] *Town Crier*, NS 497, 12 April 1929.

[31] *JNUVB*, Vol. 15, October 1938; Dick Etheridge in R. A. Leeson (ed.), *Strike, A Live History 1871–1971* (1973), p. 154; *JNUVB*, Vol. 13, 1935.

[32] The figure for women employed in the 'Motor car, motor cycle, cycle and repairs' was 19 per cent for Birmingham compared with 7 per cent for the U.K. in 1924. Comparable figures in 1937 were 16 per cent and 8 per cent. Michael Beesley, 'Changing Locational Advantages in the British Motor Industry', *Journal of Industrial Economics*, VI (1957), p. 47.

[33] It was played and sung by dealers at the annual distributors' banquet. By interview with ex-Austin apprentice Mr. Freddie Henry, 8 November 1976.

> Unity of Purpose is our watchword by day,
> In all we do and say, marching on our way.
> Holding it before us as through life we go along,
> Hear the happy throng. Sing the Austin song.

first for the new Ten body, followed by similar adjustments for the Twelve body.

Once again, a non-union strike committee was formed, this time initiated by the Communist Party, who organized the strike, appointed pickets, and liaised with trade union officials whose recognition by the management provided the striking workers with their only link for negotiation. The strike lasted only a couple of days, the Company's ultimatum to sack all workers who failed to resume work being withdrawn, after a workers' deputation assured Engelbach of a full resumption of work after the week-end pending a discussion of the disputed rates. Sir Herbert warned that while the strike could now be regarded as over it might not be possible to employ the full number of workers until production was back to normal.[34] Frustrated by the exposure of their weakness at Longbridge, the Austin workers were criticized by the NUVB: 'Such strikes would be far more effective if the workers concerned would realize the need for trade union organization before the trouble starts. Indeed, if they were members of a trade union all the time it is unlikely that Employers would use such methods as cause these outbursts from time to time. Sporadic strikes and hastily improvised negotiating committees can never be as successful as solid and continuous trade union membership with the efficient shop organization that can be established.'[35]

Trade union recruitment at Longbridge did grow during the strike but also revealed inter-union rivalry, as the NUVB, the Amalgamated Engineering Union and the Transport and General Workers' Union each sought an increase in membership.[36] An article in the *Town Crier*

We stand united with Austin as our aim.
Our path is lighted with progress for the flame.
No shirkers, all workers,
All playing the game for goodwill and fame.

Shoulder to shoulder, Secure against a fall.
Bolder and bolder, we'll try to conquer all.
We'll fight for, do right for, the good of our name.
We stand united with Austin as our aim.

Loyal co-operation is the test of brotherhood.
Working as men should. For the common good.
Each for all our motto as the race of life we run,
Striving all as one. Through the years to come.

[34] *Times*, 14 November 1936, 16 November 1936.
[35] *JNUVB*, Vol. 14, October 1936.
[36] *Town Crier*, NS 894, 20 November 1936; *JNUVB*, Vol. 14, April 1937.

accused trade union officials of excessive preoccupation with recruitment while failing to provide strike leadership at Longbridge. Each union issued leaflets and circulars claiming the right to speak for the workers, and after the strike two of the unions held separate meetings simultaneously adjacent to the factory.[37] Not surprisingly, the next issue of the *Town Crier* included letters from Longbridge workers urging the newspaper to convene a meeting of trade union officers to plan and co-ordinate organization at Austin and to call shop stewards together in order to revive the Austin Shop Stewards' Committee.[38]

Two years later, 6,000 highly skilled technicians at Austin's aero works struck to secure wage rates comparable with those paid in other aircraft factories, an anomaly which should have been rectified had the men been regraded, as promised, when they switched from car to aircraft production. Again, as in 1936, the strike was unofficial, organised by an *ad hoc* strike committee, though receiving sympathetic support both from the unions and from the local Labour Party. Again it was an official trade union initiative which persuaded the strikers to resume work and to negotiate. No fewer than six unions monitored the progress of negotiations with management, and the outcome was an increase of up to 15 per cent on basic rates.[39] Thus, the Austin policy of refusing to negotiate either under strike threat or with non-union representatives once again succeeded in bringing the Longbridge strikers back to work after only a brief stoppage, an approach which also involved playing off the shop floor workers and political elements against the unions. So long as the unions remained in competition, and so long as their level of recruitment remained relatively low, Sir Herbert relied each time on an initial promise of negotiation and nothing more, coupled with a refusal to bargain under duress.[40]

Nowhere is there any suggestion that Austin victimized strikers, though as the motor trade was a seasonal trade, lay-offs certainly made victimization, if it did occur, almost impossible to detect. For production workers employment was much less secure than for tool makers, research and office staff, for the summer time before the Show was almost always slack, leading to short time and suspensions.[41] It may not

[37] *Town Crier*, NS 894, 20 November 1936.

[38] *Town Crier*, NS 895, 27 November 1936.

[39] *Town Crier*, NS 87, 2 September, NS 988, 9 September 1938; *JNUVB*, Vol. 15, October 1938.

[40] *Town Crier* referred to it as procrastination. *Town Crier*, NS 987, 2 September 1938; *JNUVB*, Vol. 15, October 1938.

[41] By interview, Mr. J. R. Edwards, 12 July 1977.

be so surprising, therefore, to discover that the NUVB found workers at Longbridge unwilling to allow union officials to take up their personal grievances over grading and working conditions with management; though the reasons for this may have had a positive aspect, for the Company's claim that the average 'all on' wage at Austin was higher than where hourly wage rates were paid went unchallenged – even by the *Town Crier*.[42] The Company's experiment in profit sharing, introduced in 1932, can have persuaded few trade unionists to alter attitudes towards their employer, for the scheme involved the purchase of shares, albeit on favourable terms, and was open only to employees with a record of twenty years' continuous employment with the Company. Of the 44,500 shares allocated to employees by 1935, 38,310 had been accepted, mainly by office and sales staff.[43]

Sir Herbert regarded his Company as a model employer and his own observations at Longbridge over the years formed the basis for a review of working conditions and the attitudes of workers over the previous fifty years, broadcast in 1934.[44] He referred to the unhealthy, dangerous and uncomfortable conditions of working common in his youth, when work often began at 6 a.m. when the doors were locked until the work was finished. He remarked on the process by which mechanization and the modernization of factory construction and workshop practice had since turned the average worker into an ultra-craftsman, compared with the factory worker before 1900. Improved working and living conditions, and the creation of an entirely new monied class of workers earning an income of £250 per annum he attributed mainly to machines, partly to the efforts of trade unions, and partly to those employers who had shown the way by setting a good example. While he closed his broadcast on an optimistic note ('the character of the British worker was never higher, neither is it inferior to any workers of the world'), he warned against the restrictive influence of trade unions. Restrictive practices of the kind which hampered individual effort, he thought, were particularly strong in the post-war period 'when nobody appeared to want to do a real day's

[42] *JNUVB*, Vol. 12, No. 73, 1934.

[43] AMC Papers. List of employees eligible to buy 'A' ordinary shares, 12 February 1935; Total shares allocated, 8 May 1935.

[44] Herbert Austin, 'Modern Industry and the National Character', 26 February 1934. The transcript is on microfilm in the BBC Archives, Portland Place. In October 1935 E. L. Payton told shareholders that the Company was paying substantially higher wages to piece-workers than was provided for by the National Agreement. ACM, 11 October 1935.

work', and against which he felt confident a reaction was beginning among the young. In an address to the National Union of Manufacturers in 1923 he declared that American workers worked twice as hard as their British counterparts.[45] Sir Herbert remained an advocate of longer working hours, and argued the case against the introduction of a forty-hour week at a Rowntree Conference of Works Managers, Directors and foremen at Oxford in 1933.[46] He maintained that trade unions must adjust their views to adapt to modern industrial developments, in their own interest as well as to the benefit of British industry.[47]

These sentiments throw little light on the particularities of life and labour at Longbridge during the period, but they do reflect a consistent attitude to labour. Inevitably labour disputes surface in the columns of the press, the trade and union journals, and the minute books; harmonious labour relations do not, or if they are the subject of comment, it is usually by management and consequently attracts scepticism. Policy at Longbridge was that of an open shop, management negotiating with trade unions even though membership was weak; but despite evidence to the contrary, Sir Herbert gave no credit to the constructive role of the NUVB in settling labour disputes at Longbridge.

[45] *Times*, 9 January 1923.

[46] See his remarks on the paper by F. Woollard, 'Some Notes on British Methods of Continuous Production', *PIAE*, XIX (1924), p. 454; *Times*, 5 October 1935.

[47] The BBC had agreed to broadcast a reply by William Ferrie, a member of the NUVB who was employed in a London motor works. According to Ferrie, however, the draft which he submitted was altered. 'Particularly I was incensed at their demand that I should put across that the slogan "Workers of the world unite", is not a revolutionary slogan.' He refused to drop his 'H's and 'to speak as they imagine a worker does', and as a result the broadcast did not take place. Instead, Ferrie wrote his own reply to Herbert Austin which was published by the Workers' Bookshop Ltd. In this pamphlet he disputed the extent of the improvement in working conditions and living standards and attacked the Bedaux system and the demoralizing effects of an eight-hour day working at a conveyor belt. He expressed regret at the disappearance of 'old' craftsmanship and the erosion of direct relationships between employers and workmen. William Ferrie, *The Banned Broadcast of William Ferrie* (1934).

CHAPTER TEN

The Managers

WHEREAS IN THE 1920s the Company's chief problem was the supply of capital, by the late 1930s the renovation of human capital required attention. Austin was a large public company, but the achievements of its venerable founder had been so remarkable, and his dominating influence on the style and decisions of the managerial triumvirate had been exercised for so long, that leadership succession might have posed a serious problem had it not already been solved by Lord Austin, three years before his death. At the Annual General Meeting in 1929 a shareholder had remarked upon Sir Herbert's ownership of half the shares in Austin, as a corollary of which, claimed the wag, 'He is not only the Chairman . . . but the Mikado. He touches a button and a director jumps up.'[1] The reference was to A. C. R. Waite, formerly Austin's racing driver, who in 1927, after a period as superintendent of the finished car department, had been appointed manager of the Austin Distributing Company in Australia at the age of thirty-seven, and was a director of the Austin Motor Company.

Arthur Waite was Sir Herbert's son-in-law, and this explains the sarcastic exchange which temporarily raised the temperature at the Annual General Meeting. Sir Herbert's own son, Vernon, who had been groomed for managerial succession, was killed on the Western Front in 1915, and the effect upon his father had been acute and protracted.[2] But the suspicion that his son-in-law was to inherit the chairmanship was unfounded. Indeed, it would have been totally uncharacteristic had Lord Austin's spiritual and effective successor been other than a highly professional engineer, which explains the pattern of

1 AMB, June 1929. Preferred ordinary shares carried with them severely restricted voting rights.

2 Lambert & Wyatt, p. 108. An obituary of Lord Austin referred to his plan to retire at the age of fifty (1916) and leave his share in the business to his son. *Birmingham Post*, 24 May 1941. Another contemporary who knew Lord Austin

his son's education. Brother Harry was plainly unsuited to become more than a shop superintendent during his lengthy employment under Herbert's direction, first at Adderley Park and subsequently at Longbridge.[3]

One possible candidate was E. L. Payton, aged sixty-one, Deputy Chairman since 1928, the man chiefly responsible for the Company's financial success since 1921 and who was to become Chairman for a brief period after Lord Austin's death. Engelbach was another possibility, but again he was of the same generation. In 1938 he was sixty, did not enjoy good health, and was almost blind. On account of age, however, neither could offer a long term solution to the succession problem. Within Longbridge there seemed to be no obvious successor to Sir Herbert, and his temperament seems to have been entirely inappropriate for grooming the kind of successor eventually chosen. One of Austin's agents reckoned that 'one of his greatest failings was his anxiety to do everything himself and his unwillingness to allow his colleagues to undertake any responsibilities which they would willingly have done. . . .'[4] Perhaps he was always too confident in his own abilities in any matter to do with design and production engineering to be able to prepare his own people to assume the highest level of responsibility.[5] Or perhaps he chose deliberately to recruit from outside Longbridge.

Wherever the truth lies, once Lord Austin had encountered Leonard Lord, then aged forty-one, the Longbridge baron must have had few doubts that Lord was the man, not only for Engelbach's job but ultimately for his own. After his retirement as Works Director early in 1938, Engelbach continued to serve on the Board, and although he gave no press interviews his wife told a reporter that her husband had resigned voluntarily and that he had always been keen to encourage new blood.[6] The Austin Minute Book records Engelbach's willingness

---

reckoned that 'he seemed to feel the loss more keenly as the years went by'. Quoted in Lambert & Wyatt, p. 170.

[3] See below, p. 180 and also Lambert & Wyatt pp. 52 and 113.

[4] J. H. Barnett, formerly Austin agent in Wolverhampton, questioned shortly after the death of Lord Austin quoted in Lambert & Wyatt, pp. 176–7.

[5] I am grateful to Mr. Freddie Henry, formerly an Austin apprentice and on the Longbridge staff for many years, for the information conveyed by interview 8 November 1976, and on which this paragraph is based.

[6] Lord Austin declined to comment on the newspaper report which also claimed

to resign on condition of satisfactory monetary compensation.[7] He left of his own accord, but probably prompted by his co-directors.

Lord's qualifications for his new position went far beyond the 'priceless gift of youth' on which Payton dwelt when announcing his appointment to shareholders, for Lord could claim much of the credit for the revitalization of Cowley in the mid-1930s, wresting from Longbridge the major share of British motor car production and raising profit levels at Morris Motors.[8] Having already transformed Wolseley, Nuffield made Lord the effective supremo at Cowley, and it was he who was largely responsible for the revolution in model range, production methods, sales and profit performance of the Oxford company in the mid-1930s. Lord had dominated Cowley – his genius as a production engineer combined with a talent for design and a flair for business organization made him perhaps the outstanding figure in the British motor industry by the 1930s.[9] The manner of Lord's departure from Cowley and his entry to Longbridge throws light not only on Lord but on Sir Herbert, too. When Lord had been appointed to the Cowley position by Lord Nuffield, he had promised that he would stay at Cowley until Morris had regained the leadership in the motor industry, and that he would only consider leaving after one year of peak output and profits. Settling Lord's salary each year proved to be an embarrassment to both men, for Lord would ask for whatever Nuffield thought he was worth, rather than a precise figure, and each time he had felt that the resulting salary was an underestimate. The crisis occurred in 1936 when it became clear that Nuffield, who was merging his privately run businesses, including Wolseley, MG, and Morris Commercial, wanted Lord to run the entire Nuffield empire. In return for this, Lord asked for a share in the business, and a refusal was followed by Lord's decision to resign, travel, and recharge his mental batteries. Although subsequently Nuffield made some amends when he appointed Lord to manage the Special Areas Trust at a salary considerably in excess of that which he had received as managing director of Morris Motors, Lord stayed out of the motor industry until his move to Longbridge in February 1938.

that Engelbach himself had nominated Lord as his successor. *Birmingham Gazette*, 8 February 1938.

7 AMB, 4 February 1938.

8 Michael Miller and Roy Church, 'The Big Three', pp. 163–87.

9 There is a brief portrait by Frank G. Woollard, 'Sir Leonard Lord, KBE, A Personal Assessment', *Motor*, 6 July 1955.

By that time, feeling his age and with no obvious successor to run Longbridge, Lord Austin sent for Leonard Lord, who recalled later that he had been taken round the plant where he succumbed to the seductive smell of oil. Once it was established that Lord was agreeable in principle to joining the Austin Board, Sir Herbert pre-empted discussion of salary by remarking that as the Board wished Lord to do his job Lord should be paid the same as himself. There was no mention of a figure, but Lord accepted the offer as entirely satisfactory; it was, as he put it later, 'Austin with whole jackpot'. His reminiscences also suggest that Lord preferred Lord Austin to Lord Nuffield, and not only because of their contrasting attitudes to salaries. Longbridge, he recalled, was run by Austin who was an engineer and a practical man, who knew all his people, all of whom were in the jobs they could do. Whereas the Nuffield empire was built on buying, Longbridge was an engineering factory proper.[10] Thus, at the age of forty-one, Lord replaced Engelbach as Works Director in 1938, becoming joint managing director and vice-chairman with Payton, following the death of Lord Austin in 1941. When Payton retired in 1945 on medical advice, Lord became managing director and chairman of the Austin Motor Company.

In certain respects the circumstances surrounding Lord's entrance on the Longbridge scene resembled closely the conditions of his earlier move to Cowley. Austin had ceased to move with the times, its cars had acquired a slightly antique air, and the problem of succession to an ageing founder without an heir was common both to Morris Motors and to Austin. Once more Lord assumed his role with a commitment and vigour, telling Sir Miles Thomas, a senior executive with Nuffield at that time, that with Longbridge as his base his intention was to take Cowley apart, 'brick by bloody brick'.[11] Lord shared some of Lord Austin's style of earlier years, making frequent visits throughout the works, but whereas Austin's tours were at speed Lord's progress around the plant was relaxed, with hands in pockets and cigarette

[10] These impressions are based on notes of an interview with Leonard Lord by P. W. S. Andrews made available to me by Elizabeth Brunner, to whom I am most grateful.

[11] Sir Miles Thomas, p. 181. It is interesting to note that when Lord became Chairman and Managing Director of Austin in 1949, the Board agreed to give him the equivalent of £100,000 under an agreement binding him not to enter into the motor industry elsewhere in the world during the rest of his life. *Coventry Evening Telegraph*, 22 November 1949.

dangling from his lips. Lord proved to be in sharp contrast with the shy and sensitive Engelbach, a kindly and cultivated man, who was rarely ever seen on the shop floor.

Within months of his appointment, Lord had so gained the confidence of Lord Austin that he assumed a leading part in the introduction of two new cars, the Big Eight and the Ten,[12] and it was Lord who promoted Ricardo (Dick) Burzi, an Italian stylist recruited from Lancia in 1930, to whom was given a free hand in body design. Tough talking by Lord to Lord Austin led to the premature retirement of the chief designer, Hancock, and John Hannay, the production manager, both of whom had been at Longbridge since the foundation of the Company, Hancock having been with Herbert Austin at the Wolseley Sheep Shearing Machine Company.[13] Thus the turbulent Lord made an immediate impact at Longbridge, and referring to Austin managers at an Austin Ex-Apprentices Dinner held in January 1939 he told Lord Austin: 'You'll need a couple of coaches to take them away before I've finished.' Not surprisingly the washroom graffiti at Longbridge reflected the misgivings of an apprehensive staff: 'Oh Lord, give us Engle bach.'[14] The Longbridge gerontocracy which had ruled the firm since 1921 was coming to an end. Lord galvanized Longbridge as he had transformed the Morris plant in the mid-1930s, and his success eventually led to the merger of Austin and the Nuffield empire with the acerbic Lord ultimately as its emperor.

To people inside the Company, inside or outside the motor trade, Sir Herbert was 'the Old Man'. To many outside the Company but inside the trade he was 'Pa' Austin, the father of the British motor industry, a nickname reflecting not only his pioneering in the 1890s but more especially his fame as the procreator of the Baby Austin Seven.[15] More than one person has described him as possessing boundless energy, who in the years following the First World War was invariably at the office long before other workers, and whose departure from it was typically accompanied by 'doors swinging to and fro and a rush of air in the hallway'. Sir Herbert was like 'a tornado, who used

[12] The chassis units had been developed by Hancock's team under the close scrutiny of Lord Austin before Lord's arrival.

[13] By communication from Mr. Freddie Henry, 6 April 1978.

[14] By communication with Mr. Freddie Henry, 6 April 1978.

[15] I am grateful to Mr. Freddie Henry for this information, by interview, 8 November 1976. Stanley Edge as interviewed by Jonathan Wood, 'The Birth of the Austin Seven', *Thoroughbred and Classic Cars*, August, 1977.

to tear around the works and offices'.[16] Courteous and benign, it was rare that he lost his temper, though he could irritate his colleagues by occasional irascibility or lack of tact. He seems to have been a man without social pretensions, and according to his daughter accepted his peerage in 1936 with reluctance.[17] Between the wars he drove an old, but immaculate 'one-off' 'Fifteen' Tourer with a Twelve body, changing to a Sixteen Saloon which incorporated the new Austin Hayes transmission, first introduced in 1932.[18] He arrived at Longbridge typically shabbily dressed and wearing a square crowned bowler hat, the effect of which was to accentuate the angularity of his features and the squareness of his build.[19] He appears to have received the respect of at least most of the skilled workers at Longbridge, born of the recognition that whatever the job they performed he could do it.[20] Equipped with pencils in both hands, which he manipulated simultaneously, he was a daily visitor to the workshops, and frequently to be found in the car and machine design departments; characteristically he possessed a reputation for spotting idleness and shoddy practice.[21] Sir Herbert was a man who could make, and had actually made, motor cars with his own hands.[22] Engelbach was seldom seen on the shop floor, though it was usually Engelbach who was spokesman during labour disputes; and from the time when, as a nominee of the

[16] He often stayed until 8 p.m. and frequently was to be found there on Saturdays and Sundays, too. By communication from Mr. H. W. Holbeche (ex-Austin apprentice), November 1976; Stanley Edge, 'The Birth of the Austin Seven', *Thoroughbred and Classic Cars*, August 1977, p. 16.

[17] Lambert & Wyatt, p. 157. Sir Herbert became Baron of Longbridge in the same year as he made a substantial donation towards the extension and further endowment of the Cavendish Laboratory in Cambridge.

[18] By communication with Mr. Freddie Henry.

[19] By interview with Lord Thomas, 10 August 1976, and with Mr. Freddie Henry, 8 November 1976. There is a description, too, in *Autocar*, 23 August 1929; Lambert & Wyatt, p. 145.

[20] By communication from Mr. H. W. Holbeche (ex-Austin apprentice), November 1976; A. G. S. Davison, *At the Wheel* (1931), pp. 17–18; Lambert & Wyatt, p. 89. Also by communication from Mr. Freddie Henry, 6 April 1978.

[21] A. G. S. Davison, pp. 17–18; Lambert & Wyatt, p. 89.

[22] His understanding and feel for machine tools is illustrated by a story told by Mr. Freddie Henry, an apprentice in the works in 1927, who recalls assisting a demonstrator set up a turning machine of completely novel design: 'The Old Man appeared, jumped up on the platform, and pushing the demonstrator aside proceeded to operate the machine without a moment's hesitation.' By communication, 22 April 1978.

Midland Bank, he joined the Board as a financier in 1921, Payton had rarely spent the entire week at Longbridge.[23]

Visibility was all that seemed possible in a huge organization employing thousands of people, and it is not surprising that on his factory tours Sir Herbert spoke only to the 'old stagers'.[24] In any case, his essential temperament was one of detachment; he rarely smiled and, not surprisingly, presented a somewhat dour public image.[25] A reserved and reticent man, he confessed difficulty in verbal expression, while the trade press found him elusive.[26] He had set ideas, but was open to persuasion and would sometimes ask for advice even if it was rare, on works matters, for him to be proved wrong.[27] But then unlike the withdrawal symptoms exhibited by Lord Nuffield, the reasons for Lord Austin's unwillingness to be influenced by others in the Company were due not to ignorance of most things technical, but to the extraordinarily high professional standards which he represented and to the ultimate criteria he adopted in discussing business affairs: that is, whether from the standpoint of an engineer any decision or judgement was the right one. Such an approach may not have brought him popularity nor led his Company to achieve commercial supremacy in the motor industry. But that was the key to his behaviour and to the business decisions he made.

The conviction that he was right and a reluctance to compromise twice precipitated his resignation, both times on the insistence of his Board of Directors. The first occasion was in 1905, when he left the Wolseley Motor Car Company, parting company from the Vickers brothers; the other occasion, less obscure and probably more complex, was his departure from the Wolseley Sheep Shearing Machine Company in 1933. It may be relevant that at the time when Sir Herbert had been a member of the UK trade delegation to Finland in 1933 an accompanying senior civil servant, C. F. Mowier-Williams, had noted in a report that he had not found Sir Herbert a very easy man to deal with.[28] Sir Herbert's relations with Vickers many years before, and

[23] By interview with Mr. T. A. E. Layborn, 8 September 1977.

[24] By interview with Mr. Freddie Henry, 8 November 1976. See also, for the pre-First World War period, A. G. S. Davison, pp. 17–18.

[25] As did Payton, while Engelbach, too, was serious, if kindly. By interview with Mr. T. A. E. Layborn, 8 September 1977.

[26] By interview with Lord Thomas, 10 August 1976; 'Sir Herbert Austin', *Autocar*, 23 August 1929.

[27] By interview with Mr. Freddie Henry, 8 November 1976.

[28] BT 59/17 (DOT) DC 410, C. M. Mowier Williams, 'United Kingdom Motor

with his co-directors at the Wolseley Sheep Shearing Machine Company in more recent times suggest that this might well have been a valid assessment.

* * *

Herbert Austin's exit from the Wolseley Sheep Shearing Machine Company in 1933 was preceded by friction with his co-directors. The issue which provided the occasion, but not the cause, of Sir Herbert's departure was whether or not Wolseley should acquire R. A. Lister & Co., an Australian agency importing Wolseley machinery but which henceforward intended to manufacture locally. Sir Herbert, who had been in correspondence with the agency, was in favour of the proposal, and was supported by two directors. Three others had voted against to produce a tie, whereupon Sir Herbert had used the chairman's second casting vote – and not for the last time.[29] In October 1933 Sir Herbert wrote to the board referring to 'our final decision on the matter. No useful purpose can be served by further negotiation.' This provoked an immediate reaction from the dissenting co-directors, who requested Sir Herbert's resignation on the grounds that he had at some time mentioned retirement, that he had admitted being unable to spend more time on the Wolseley business affairs. They argued that as a result the Company's interests had been, and were being, sacrificed, and that the time had come to allow his colleagues 'a freer hand in its management'.[30]

Immediately preceding a Board Meeting on 21 November 1933, a special meeting of the Board was convened at which Sir Herbert was handed this letter signed by a majority of directors. After reading the contents he requested its withdrawal, at the same time giving an undertaking that he would resign. After he left the meeting the minutes were torn from the minute book and deposited for safekeeping with the National Provincial Bank.[31] In his formal resignation, dated 5 December 1933, Sir Herbert drew attention to the contrast between the fortunes of the Company during the lengthy period when it had

---

Trade Delegation to Finland 1933'. For what reason it is not entirely clear, Sir Herbert had refused to stay in the same hotel as Walton, Rootes, and the men from the D.O.T.

[29] WSSMC Papers, Board Minutes, 11 January, 17 May, 5 July 1933.

[30] WSSMC Papers, A. D. Grant, F. A. Phillips, and H. S. Hotson to Sir Herbert Austin, 21 November 1933.

[31] WSSMC Papers, Copy of Special Board Meeting, 21 November 1933.

been under his direction, with the less than flourishing condition of the firm which prevailed on his departure.[32] The minute books of the Wolseley Sheep Shearing Machine Company are not very helpful in defining his contribution to the firm after the early years when he had established his own Company. In 1909, two years before he was to become Chairman, the Board of Wolseley had voted a special fee in recognition of the time he had spent on the Company's business, of his assistance in changes in management, and of the technical advice he had given to the Board.[33] That was at a time when the nominal capital was raised to £100,000 and when Herbert Austin had been the only Birmingham based director.[34] The fact that it was not until after he left the firm that a managing director was appointed suggests that throughout his time as Chairman he had filled that central role himself, though his co-directors clearly felt that to him the Wolseley Company had become merely a surviving memory. Finally, even those in sympathy with the policy of local assembly in Australia decided to sever the bonds of sentiment holding man and firm together, and to set about retrieving the Company's position.

In the Company of his own creation, and in which he continued to be the major ordinary shareholder, his authority was diminished as a result of the financial crisis after the First World War, when the Creditors' Committee appointed Engelbach as Works Director with a seat on the Board and Sir Reginald Brade as Secretarial Director, to act together with Sir Herbert as a Board of Management. Sir Herbert's resistance to this attempt to clip his wings proved only partly successful, for the strength of his personality enabled him to dominate Engelbach, though not E. L. Payton.[35]

As part of the 1926 Reconstruction Scheme, subject to the control of the Board, the management was to be vested in a committee of

[32] WSSMC Papers, 5 December 1933. The Board decided to appoint a managing director in February 1935. He was H. J. McNamara, BSc, AMICE. WSSMC Papers, Board Minutes, 6 February, 6 March 1935.

[33] WSSMC Papers, Board Minutes, 3 March 1909.

[34] The others were Henry Grant, an Australian representative from a Sydney merchant firm, and the Chairman, P. S. Phillips, an Abergavenny tinplate manufacturer, for both were active directors who attended most meetings until his resignation in 1933. Companies House, 'F' File 29846, Wolseley Sheep Shearing Machine Company, Memorandum of Agreement, 26 January 1897. For directors' attendance see minute books of the Company.

[35] He resigned in protest against Sir Herbert's refusal to be bound by the Creditors' Committee's initial intention that the Company should be managed by managers of equal status without a director.

three, though in fact this had merely formalized the existing practice whereby Sir Herbert was chairman 'with general supervision of the company affairs', a managing director in effect; E. L. Payton, as deputy chairman, was responsible for finance,[36] and Engelbach was in charge of the works. The formality made no difference; two years later, Sir Herbert reported to shareholders that members of the Committee of Management were always in touch and in consultation, although the meetings were not held formally and no minutes were recorded.[37]

While the Company's principal problem in the 1920s was finance, Payton's counsel seems to have been at least as influential in decision-making as that of the Chairman, as the early history of the Seven, which Sir Herbert developed at his own expense, showed. Sir Herbert's stature and the dramatic improvements in the Company's financial position by the 1930s enabled him to force some of his views when he chose to do so. Thus in 1934, despite Payton's remark that most of the commercial vehicle makers were not receiving an adequate return on capital invested, Sir Herbert's opinion that the Company should enter that section of the motor industry was accepted, and in 1937 the first Austin two and one-half ton lorry went into production.[38] It is significant, too, that it was Lord Austin who conducted negotiations with the Government regarding the Shadow Factory Scheme at Longbridge.

Because of the tightness of managerial control at Longbridge and the absence of committee minutes there is no evidence other than the mostly unhelpful Board Minutes to convey the Chairman's style, though they do reveal that, unlike William Morris, the Chairman was almost always present, until shortly before his death. Perhaps as a clue the memories of Lord Thomas, a fellow member of the SMMT car manufacturers committee, and of the Motor Trade Association (a body concerned with resale price maintenance and orderly trading by agents) in the 1930s, are of some relevance.[39] Lord Thomas recalled one meeting in particular where manufacturers and agents were assembled to discuss trading practices, an issue over which opinions

[36] Companies House, 'F' File 133747, Special Resolution, 27 July 1927.

[37] In 1927 an Extraordinary General Meeting had passed a special resolution to this effect, adding a new article to the existing Articles of Association. AMB, 27 November 1929.

[38] AMB, 26 June 1934.

[39] Based on the interview with Lord Thomas, 10 August 1976.

were sharply divided. Sir Herbert began the meeting by stating his own point of view, that agents should discipline themselves in the pricing of second-hand cars and should not expect to be subsidized by manufacturers. During the lengthy and heated debate, Sir Herbert listened impassively and closed the meeting by declaring that everyone had spoken his mind, that his opening views had not been effectively contradicted, and this was the decision of the meeting. Lord Thomas, it is true, worked for W. R. Morris, but the world of the motor trade was not large, and there is a measure of truth in his description of management at the Austin as a 'pyramidical structure' in which all decisions were taken at the apex.[40] Retaining a close personal relationship with Payton, Engelbach, and subsequently Lord, the Austin Motor Company continued to be an essentially *personal* enterprise in style, but the managerial apex consisted of not one man, but three, and the major policy decisions were essentially those of Sir Herbert and Ernest Payton.

Sir Herbert Austin's managerial role was that of a man confident of his own judgement and prepared to defend his opinions, just as his ownership of slightly more than 50 per cent of the Company's ordinary share capital from the time his Company turned public until his death was indicative of his willingness to accept the risks of ownership long after the firm had lost the structural characteristics of a family firm. The continuing high proportion of capital held in the form of debentures meant that the scope for independent manoeuvre was limited; furthermore, owing to Sir Herbert's ignorance of industrial finance Ernest Payton held the purse strings from 1921, which enabled him to circumscribe Sir Herbert's decision-making powers.[41] His substantial personal commitment, by the criterion of the size of his equity shareholding, reinforced by his sheer professional stature, secured for him a considerable influence on the Company's fortunes. To an outsider it seemed that at Longbridge 'the father figure of "Pa" Austin was at the top, and what he said was law';[42] but the realities of power and responsibility within the Company were more complex.

40 Lord Thomas, 'Foreword', in Lambert & Wyatt, pp. 8–10.

41 Mr. T. A. E. Layborn recalls that Sir Herbert 'knew nothing about finance' and relied totally on Payton. In a speech made by Payton on the occasion of Sir Herbert's elevation to the peerage, Payton declared that he could remember having had only one quarrel with the Chairman of Austin. It began on the day Payton had joined the Company and was still continuing. By interview with Mr. T. A. E. Layborn, 8 September 1977.

42 Lord Thomas, 'Foreword', in Lambert & Wyatt, p. 9.

Part Six: Perspectives: The Man, the Firm and the Industry

CHAPTER ELEVEN

Personal and Professional Dimensions: Entrepreneur and Manager in Context

IN THE ABSENCE OF private papers, Herbert Austin's public reticence leaves little scope for the biographer whose imperative is to explore the mind and motivation, as well as assessing the importance, of the central figure. The biography written by his daughter in collaboration with the motoring historian, R. J. Wyatt, provides an unblemished account of an honest, gentle, generous and industrious genius. Perhaps the portrait presented in *Lord Austin The Man*[1] is over-idealized, but it is impossible to modify it with confidence in the absence of evidence relating to his personal affairs. As a young man his leisure hours were spent in drawing and in playing the violin, and apart from the occasional game of cricket played with the Works team, and motor car racing before 1914, little time was spent in recreational activities. From that time onwards work was even more relentless than in the early years of the firm's foundation, leaving time only for listening to music, especially to grand opera, and visiting the theatre. Apart from his immediate family and colleagues at Longbridge, notably his personal secretary, Bobby Hewitt, he was a remote, somewhat dour figure, preoccupied with motor cars in a lifetime dedicated to their design and manufacture.

It is impossible to do more than try to identify, as far as it is possible, his business *persona*, which explains why this biography of Herbert

Austin must comprise a part biography of the Wolseley Sheep Shearing Machine Company and a complete biography, so far as the documentary evidence which survives permits, of the Austin Motor Company, until Lord Austin's death in 1941. The picture portrayed here, therefore, is overwhelmingly biased towards an exploration of the history of his working life, but that bias, which is partly a reflection of the paucity of primary sources and the character of the materials used, imparts less of a distortion than might be supposed. For except for a brief period immediately following the First World War, when he dabbled in politics, work and closely related professional activities dominated his life.

Even in writing a business biography of Herbert Austin the documentation is so sparse that we are unable to distinguish precisely any changes which may have occurred in his approach to business during the course of his lengthy career. We cannot, for example, assess the validity of his claim to have been motivated by a social responsibility to the community, for whom progress in transportation was important. He may have believed this to have been true, and his earliest experiments with internal combustion may, indeed, have been prompted by the time spent in the Australian outback, as may his production of the first Austin Seven in 1910, and the pre-war Austin Ten, though neither brought commercial success. His approach to motor car design thereafter until 1921 hardly suggests a preoccupation with other than relatively expensive, high quality motor cars, which bore little resemblance to the serviceable, low-cost utility vehicles of the kind Henry Ford sold to American farmers.

He was prepared to exploit such profitable opportunities as might arise out of his own business activities, but there is no evidence to suggest that he was engaged in a perpetual search for material reward.[2] Except for his continued connection with the Wolseley Sheep Shearing Machine Company, all of his business ventures grew out of the motor trade. His correspondence with the Wolseley directors and with Kayser in the early years suggests rather that he held a notion of just and deserving reward for effort, and he was not prepared to accept less than that. A provision in his will also suggests that he abhorred what he referred to as 'super luxury'. He left sufficient to ensure the material security of his family during their lifetime and expressed the wish that

[1] Lambert & Wyatt (1968), pp. 158–60.

[2] W. A. Howitt, 'Impressions of Lord Austin' (1941), National Motor Museum.

should his family achieve affluence by earning it, the money should be used wisely.[3]

Forthright, serious-minded but unsophisticated, such political opinions as he uttered were almost indistinguishable from those of William Morris. Both shared conservative views, though Herbert Austin was the only motor manufacturer to become an M.P. The impetus leading to his candidature as an M.P. for the King's Norton division of Birmingham in the 'Coupon election' of 1918 was the wish to serve the national interest, a claim which, had it been articulated by someone other than Herbert Austin, might appear at worst a downright concealment of personal ambition, at best pure naïveté. If he is open to either accusation it must be the latter, and it could account for his total disillusionment after his experience of the House of Commons between 1919 and 1925.

As a leader among Midland businessmen in his capacities as Chairman of the Austin Motor Company and of the Wolseley Sheep Shearing Machine Company, he was a considerable employer of labour, while his professional standing had been recognized in his election as President of the Institute of British Carriage and Automobile Manufacturers in 1912. But it was his major contribution to the war effort which persuaded him that his experience and managerial skills should be shared with the country in the national interest. In recognition of his contribution to the war effort, he was created a Knight of the British Empire in 1917 and received the Order of Leopold, awarded by the Belgian monarch.[4] His politics were essentially pragmatic and derived from his conviction that the post-war reconstruction could best be achieved by a coalition government possessing business capacity, a 'businessman's government'. In his electoral speeches in 1918 he stressed the need for 'strong cohesive government'. He supported Lloyd George as a proven leader who could speak with the voice of the British people: 'Empire is important to us and hence the freedom of the seas to Britain vital',[5] a sentiment which is consistent with his membership of the executive committee of the Empire Economic Union.[6] *The Birmingham Mail*, sympathetic to Sir Herbert's Conservative stand, presented the other two competing candidates in the election as Tom Hacket, a co-operative candidate ('a conscientious

[3] Lambert & Wyatt, p. 171.

[4] 'Sir Herbert Austin KBE, His Life Story', *Autocar*, 13 September 1929.

[5] *Birmingham Mail*, 11, 13 December 1918.

[6] *Times*, 9 December 1929.

objector and a thoroughgoing Socialist'); and Norman Birkett, a Liberal ('out of the Cadbury stable . . . with little record of war work').[7] Sir Herbert won by a handsome majority and he was returned as a Unionist in the 1918 election, but an examination of Hansard reveals not even a maiden speech before he lost his seat in 1925.

A statement which comes closest to representing a political philosophy is to be found in a letter which he wrote to *The Times* newspaper in May 1921, commenting upon the coal dispute. 'It is surely quite time that we as a nation realised the extreme danger to our well-being of the present impossible conditions and of the vital necessity of dropping this continual agitation for equality. Equality has never existed, and will never exist, but if it did, it could only be on the level of a beast in the field and none of us, not even the most rabid communist in the country, would advocate that. Gross injustice, on the other hand, can and should be removed, if it exists. . . .'[8] Asked about his politics in 1929, Sir Herbert denied any intention of returning to Parliament again: 'I am convinced that the business men of England, including myself, are best engaged in giving the whole of their attention to their own particular jobs and thus bringing about a solution of the country's difficulties by natural means – the thriving condition of the Longbridge factory today will do more, for example, to minimize the evil of unemployment than could all my efforts on the floor of the House.'[9] These sentiments barely concealed his own inadequacies as a politician and his low opinion of politicians in general. This is clear from a letter he wrote to *The Times* in January 1931 in which he reacted to criticisms levelled against manufacturers of small cars by P. J. Pybus, M.P., for their 'cynical neglect of overseas demand for a larger car'.[10] 'If Mr. Pybus and his colleagues would treat politics as a business and see for themselves the vision which unfolds itself in the conception of the gradual development of imperial economic unity,

[7] *Birmingham Mail*, 10 December 1918.

[8] *Times*, 21 May 1921.

[9] *Times*, 21 May 1921: 'I do not wish to infer that I regard Parliament as a home for nonentities, or as a place from which no good thing can emanate. My point is that men such as myself can accomplish more outside than in. Despite this, I remain convinced that the argument promulgated in 1919 still holds good today, and that England does need to be governed in a businesslike fashion. After all, government *is* a huge business and needs to be run on lines exactly similar to those along which any small enterprise might be expected to prosper.'

[10] *Times*, 31 December 1930.

they would perhaps be of greater help in the colossal problem of creating employment, than by destructive criticism of the motor and other industries.'[11]

Counterbalancing his disregard for politicians was an unlimited admiration for engineers. Thus, in a speech given at a meeting of the Federation of British Industries in 1937 he remarked: 'Let the economists and financial experts put on their thinking caps and try to catch up with the engineers, and their slump periods, like plagues, will be things of the past.'[12] The reference to engineers, implying levels of achievement to which others should strive, is a significant clue to his general approach to life. The professional engineer was in control of that which he created or produced. Almost by definition, problems were amenable to solution, and feeling at ease in such a role, whether through engineering intuition or training, did not necessarily equip him to exercise control or even influence over economic and social problems.

Possibly it was this feeling of powerlessness in general, inducing in Sir Herbert a sense of frustration, which helps to explain his attraction to Pelmanism, a philosophy which, in its internalization of human problems and its stress on an individual's power to control his own particular destiny, seemed to accord with his own experience, providing an explanation acceptable to him of his own motivation and achievements. Perhaps it is significant, also, that his conversion appears to have coincided with the Austin Motor Company's move into the black. 'Life has taught me', he wrote in 1929, 'that nothing worthwhile is accomplished without untiring exertion and interminable application fortified and inspired by very definite purpose.' Survival and success in business, he maintained, was due to something more than 'the mere exigencies of commercialism – to some guiding force whose energy is drawn from the distant objective, to a purpose transcending the accumulation of wealth'.[13] The conception of his own purpose he traced to his time in Australia, where the vast distances separating settlements impressed upon him the importance of eliminating distance to remove social isolation. It was not long, he claimed, before he recognized his life's purpose was to motorize the world and

[11] *Times*, 5 January 1931.
[12] *Times*, 30 January 1937.
[13] Sir Herbert Austin, 'The Importance of Purpose', *Pall Mall Magazine*, V (1929), pp. 12–15.

supply the most basic form of motorized transport, a rationalization of events and developments separated by thirty years.[14]

Remembering, perhaps, the problems he had encountered in his early career, and especially in the post-war years, he later urged others to 'Get down to some bedrock need, and then spare no effort to serve it. Work will bring yet more work. Tiring days will often be followed by sleepless nights. If the purpose be strong enough, the perseverance great enough, success must inevitably attend.'[15] In 1930 Sir Herbert's photograph appeared in a *Times* advertisement on behalf of the Pelman Institute, in which he urged readers to train their minds on scientific lines by taking a course in Pelmanism in order to develop will power; 'To command opportunity and compel success every man must have a full and sure conviction of his inherent right to a place in the sun and must then train his mind to such vigour that it is capable of grappling with the problems of life as they arrive. The job for everyone is to fit ourselves for better things and then go out after them.'[16] Complacent and naïve though we may interpret these sentiments as a general philosophy, nevertheless even disregarding the element of rationalization of personal experience they do seem to offer an insight into his own motivation from the time when he began to make motor cars. He had been wounded by grief, disillusioned by his brief parliamentary career, and frustrated by what he felt to be a shift in attitudes, encouraged, he thought, mainly by the trade unions, towards a collectivism which was hindering society's adaptation to modern industrial development.[17]

Lord Nuffield described him as one of the best motor engineers in the world, whose contribution to the development of the motor industry in the early days far exceeded his own.[18] Lord Austin's professional career included the presidency of the Institute of British Carriage and Automobile Manufacturers (1912), of the Institute of Automobile Engineers (1931), and of the Institute of Production Engineers (1932–33). From 1918 he was a member, and in 1936 was elected an Honorary

[14] A few years later he attributed his initial attraction to motor car design and production to the 'hard work involved pedalling a bike up the steep hills'. *Birmingham Post*, 27 November 1936.

[15] Sir Herbert Austin, 'The Importance of Purpose', *Pall Mall Magazine*, V (1929), p. 15.

[16] *Times*, 14 January 1930.

[17] Sir Herbert Austin, 'Modern Industry and the National Character', BBC Archives, 26 February 1934.

[18] *Times*, 19 April 1934.

Life Member, of the Institute of Mechanical Engineers, a year after he had been elected Honorary Life Member of the Institute of British Foundrymen. He became President of the British Cast Iron Research Association in 1929. Other indications of the esteem in which he was held within the motor trade were his early chairmanship of the manufacturing section of the Society of Motor Manufacturers and Traders, and subsequently his election as President of SMMT (1934–35). He was a Master of the Worshipful Company of Coach Makers and Coach Harness Makers (1934), and Member of the Livery of the Worshipful Company of Carmen.[19] In 1934 he was a member of the Transport Advisory Council,[20] and in 1933 was included in the UK Trade Delegation, sponsored by the Board of Trade, which was sent to Finland to negotiate over tariffs. C. F. Mowier Williams, the senior civil servant who took note of the discussions, reported that while Sir Herbert had revealed a lack of preparedness on Finnish life, he had been impressive on technical issues, a compliment not repeated about the other members of the delegation, Leslie Walton, Vauxhall's chairman and President of SMMT, and W. E. Rootes.[21] His membership of that delegation and his appointment in 1937 as Chairman of the Shadow Aero Engine Committee are evidence of Lord Austin's reputation at Government level at a time when his age might have suggested that his potential contributions as a professional motor engineer were at an end.

Such a remarkable record of recognition and achievement is indicative of Herbert Austin's professional status and of his standing in the world of business. But only by comparing what we know about him and the companies with whose fortunes he identified, with the characteristics, careers and contributions of other leading motor manufacturers, can we try to assess his role in the development of the motor industry and to place him in the wider context of British business history.

Before 1914 Herbert Austin possessed qualities recognizable in the archetypal inventor-entrepreneur, bent on making a success of his own enterprise. The formation of the Austin Motor Co. (1914) Ltd., when ownership was thrown open to the public, marked a turning point, for especially after the war Sir Herbert's motivation appears to have

[19] *Autocar*, 30 May 1941.
[20] Lambert & Wyatt, p. 157.
[21] BT 59 (DOT) 410, C. F. Mowier Williams, 'United Kingdom Motor Trade Delegation to Finland, 1933'.

had little to do with a stereotype maximization of profit, revenue, or anything else susceptible to simple measurement. During the difficulties of the period after the reformation of the Company in 1919, as Chairman of the Austin Motor Co. Ltd. he was anxious to divest himself of his financial obligations by selling the Company to the highest bidder – against his co-directors' wishes – but ensuring that he would be retained in his position as chief executive. After the death of his son in 1915, owner-entrepreneurship seems to have held few attractions for a man in his fiftieth year, hemmed in, from 1921, by Payton, Engelbach, and the debenture holders. Creative application through invention, engineering and design, rather than the permanence of his institutional creation, probably provides the key to Sir Herbert's motivation between the wars, though within the context of the firm he concerned himself with more limited objectives. The extent to which he was prepared to sustain the Company in order to protect his position can be gauged from his continuing refusal to sell his majority equity holding in the firm. This is consistent with his wish to negotiate the Company's future, and therefore his own, on terms chosen by him. But his co-directors, commanding the professional expertise but without an appreciable stake in ownership, succeeded in vetoing any attempt to sell. Indeed, it is possible to draw the distinction in attitudes towards the Company's long term future held by founder and by managers. Accustomed to entrepreneurial leadership, after 1920 Sir Herbert became prepared to mortgage the long term future of the firm for his own relatively short term satisfaction, for in 1920 he was already fifty-four. Engelbach and Payton, who conform more to the kind of expert but 'administrative' personalities, consolidated, restructured, and institutionalized within the Austin Motor Company the original purpose envisaged by Sir Herbert before his son's death – besides, perhaps, protecting their own short term futures.

Despite the authority which his titular and equity holdings offered in theory, in practice the scope for exercising a purely autocratic style of management was, we have argued, limited. Managerial goals were not the subject of explicit discussion in the documentary evidence which survives, and beyond Sir Herbert's alleged ambition to motorize the common man, and to preserve the firm's reputation as a maker of vehicles of high quality and low cost, no more precise objectives of the firm (profit rates, for example) have been recorded.[22] Discussions by

[22] Contrast the apparent lack of formulated profit objectives at Austin with Perry's declared policy of cutting prices to a minimum 'in conformity with

the managers concentrated upon costs, profit margins, and break-even points for alternative sales levels, and throughout the 1920s finance was the determining factor which limited the maximum levels of sales, despite predictions of effective demand to justify exceeding the targets chosen.

The goals of the enterprise were imprecisely formulated, and in general Sir Herbert's views seem to have weighed scarcely more heavily in management policy between the wars than those of Payton and Engelbach. This might appear somewhat surprising in view of P. Sargant Florence's definition of Austin as one of the largest owner-controlled companies in the 1930s; for the firm not only met his criteria by having more than 30 per cent of its voting equity held by twenty of the largest shareholders, but Sir Herbert owned more than one-fifth of the voting shares.[23] That his influence on policy was not greater than it appears to have been is explicable by the Company's high gearing, and the limitation placed on the effective power of those holding equity by the prior financial claims of the debenture holders. A high grade of ownership concentration and a much higher degree of personal dominance was possessed, of course, by Nuffield and Rootes, while Ford and Vauxhall were in the hands of their parent companies in the US. Other characteristics of Austin shared by motor manufacturers generally included a small board of directors, little interlocking with other large producers, a relatively low prevalence of divorce of ownership from control, and the presence of a company 'style', not easily described, generated by the founders.[24]

Why such a style should exist is explicable only in terms of historical standards, which tended to foster the concentration of effort within a limited repertoire of activities. For Sir Herbert these were largely restricted to motor and machine tool design, quality, performance and cost; for Payton, the priority was a sound financial basis; for Engelbach, works organization and production. As a result, the shape of the learning curve at Longbridge was influenced much by these elements

---

Ford's established principle' and of fixing a limit of 10 per cent net profit. Ford Archives (Ford Motor Company, Detroit), Acc. 572, Box 18, 6 December 1929.

[23] P. Sargant Florence, *Ownership, Control and Success of Large Companies* (1961), ch. V. Austin is ranked as grade two in concentration after Morris, Ford, Vauxhall and Rootes, each of which was in the grade one category. The analysis was based on capital structures in 1936.

[24] P. Sargant Florence, ch. V.

and tended to exclude as major priorities pricing targets, administrative structures, and managerial succession. Long after Engelbach and Payton entered Longbridge it was customary to design a car before determining a price rather than designing to a target price; to adapt in response to competition or sustained complaints from Austin dealers. Innovation was seen not as a continuing industrial imperative, but as an imaginative process to be stimulated when the need arose, to combat critical adversity as in 1921, or to withstand competition as in 1932. This essentially 'conservative' strategy, which typified the conduct of Austin's affairs, is thoroughly consistent with a wish to minimize uncertainty during the Company's post-war history. This implied a desire for liquidity, the need to create a customer, the 'Austin owner', and an emphasis on flexibility in corporate strategy to a degree which left unresolved the problem of executive management succession, until the imminent retirement of the Longbridge geriatrics and a fall in the Company's market share prompted Lord Austin to approach Leonard Lord.

In conclusion, it will be instructive to try to assess Herbert Austin's contribution to the motor industry by comparison with that of William Morris,[25] for these were the men who, excluding the special case of Perry and the American Ford Company, more than any other influenced the character and course of development of the British motor industry. Herbert Austin came to dominate the scene until 1920, when he abdicated the commercial leadership of the industry which passed to William Morris. Thereafter, the public image of the relationship between the two men was one of amity, respect, and mutual recognition of the achievements each had secured for his respective firm and for the British industry.

Sharing common roots in rural society and similar parental social status, Morris and Austin attended local schools, but whereas the latter proceeded to commercial college and apprenticeship under a Scottish engineer in Australia, William Morris left his toolmaker's apprenticeship unfinished and became a mechanic. Neither seems to have been committed to any religious beliefs, unless Pelmanism, to which Herbert Austin came late, qualifies as such. Both were self-made men and both were competitive. Morris became a pedal cycle champion, and Austin was a racing driver in his own cars, but whereas that sense of com-

[25] A brief comparison of William Morris with Henry Ford is to be found in the author's review article 'Myths, Men and Motor Cars', *Journal of Transport History*, IV (1977), pp. 102–12.

petition remained with Morris, at least until the late 1920s, Austin's financial difficulties and his personal loss brought by war coloured his outlook thereafter. Austin was ten years older than Morris, establishing his own company at the age of thirty-nine. This followed his sacking by Vickers from Wolseley,[26] and in both respects, failure followed by a new start, the careers of Austin and Morris were similar, the latter establishing his own enduring car firm at the age of thirty-six. Whereas Morris later left design to his key engineer, Austin continued to play a major part in designing Austin cars until his death.[27]

Morris, who began as a dealer in motor cars, directed his efforts to the production of a vehicle designed for volume production for a sizeable middle class market, sensing the need for such a model after the evident failure of the cyclecar. Austin, however, pursued a more cautious, less imaginative policy, experimenting with cars of moderate horsepower but for a long time remaining unconvinced of the compatibility between volume production on the one hand, and on the other, quality and reliability. Perry's development of the British market for Ford cars assembled in Manchester is another case where a commercial sense was the driving force in a Company's history before 1914. Just as the severe depression of 1921 provided the cue for Morris to slash prices, so it precipitated a rush of creativity in Austin, a response which typified the difference in structure, organization and approach between the two companies.

By its very character, the adoption of assembly production by Morris forced managers to concentrate on input prices negotiated with external suppliers to an extent which was unusual and avoidable within a self-contained manufacturing motor works like Longbridge. And whereas Morris's rise to pre-eminence was based on a highly and perhaps excessively flexible system of component assembly, Austin long

[26] The note on Lord Austin written by a former Austin agent, J. H. Barnett, quoted in Lambert & Wyatt (but not referred to in the text), makes it clear that, whatever the ambiguities surrounding the reasons for, and circumstances of, his departure from Vickers, in fact Austin received a letter terminating his engagement with the Wolseley Tool and Motor Car Company. See the note reproduced in Lambert & Wyatt, pp. 176–7.

[27] By communication from Mr. Freddie Henry, 6 April 1978: 'Until (1938) the Old Man took a leading part in the design of the cars and, in addition, he was a first-class engineer. In fact he could be described as Chairman, Managing Director, Production Manager, Chief Engineer, Chief Designer, and Plant Engineer, for he was involved in all these matters from 8 a.m. to 8 p.m., Sunday and weekday!'

continued to manufacture virtually the entire car. Until the expansion from the mid-1920s, a legitimate distinction can be made between Morris as an assembler and Austin as a manufacturer, a contrast in the style of the companies to which Lord drew attention in 1952, even though the justification for such a distinction had since disappeared. The contrasting structure and organization also meant that whereas Morris's managerial role concentrated mainly on the co-ordination of component supplies and the control of a relatively small workforce, Austin became immersed in the complex problems which large scale production raised for effective internal management, a role which the Creditors' Committee in 1921 apparently thought was beyond him.

War affected Morris mainly by postponing the innovations planned in 1913, but Austin was forced to find completely new models after the war in order to survive. Wolseley failed to find a suitable car and finally collapsed in 1926 under crushing financial burdens inherited from the war. Lacking the massive resources which Vickers could offer Wolseley to tide that Company over the post-war Slump, Austin was thrust into its own crisis in 1920, and rescued by creditors, notably, if tardily, by the Midland Bank, only after a hectic and often humiliating period when Herbert Austin sought support from diverse sources. Both the Twelve and the Seven were conceived in desperation, induced by the threat of bankruptcy, and delivered by City midwives. Thereafter, Sir Herbert's unhappy financial experience bulked large in the determination of policy guidelines, and the Company's conservative financial policy, like that of the soundly based finances of Morris, was a springboard for Austin's revival.

Herbert Austin and William Morris typically regarded government intervention (protection for the motor industry excepted) and trade unions with scepticism, though to neither could be attributed a coherent political philosophy. They both shared a distrust, too, of politicians. A desire to help to impart the smack of firm government took Herbert Austin to the House of Commons for a brief and undistinguished spell, while only the most furtive and indirect flirtation with Oswald Mosley's New Party can be debited to Morris's political account.[28] Both men made money, and in 1910 the Austin family moved into Lickey Grange, with 200 acres of parkland, where Lord Austin lived until his death.[29] Yet whereas Nuffield's fortunes ran into

[28] R. J. Overy, p. 110.
[29] Lambert & Wyatt, p. 100.

millions of pounds, Austin left little more than £1 million, and the gifts he made amounted to a fraction of Nuffield's munificence.[30] The largest single donation was £250,000 for the extension and further endowment of the Cavendish Laboratory at Cambridge University in 1934, two years before he became Baron Austin of Longbridge.[31]

Difference in wealth is a reflection of the two firms' contrasting financial histories, for neither man indulged in luxury. Both remained guarded in their attitudes to the value of higher education as an ideal training for responsibility in the motor industry. Austin, it is true, devoted considerable thought and resources to the training of his own apprentices, but, like Morris, for the most responsible of all positions in his Company he made no preparations.

An abiding grief, following the death of his son Vernon, could well have contributed to Sir Herbert's reluctance to consider the problem of succession after the war, for after beginning at the work bench Vernon had completed his apprenticeship at Longbridge. Later he had spent several months gaining experience in a Swedish electrical firm, after which he was expected to take up a junior executive role at Austin, and subsequently to manage the Company, a prospect unattractive to the young man.[32] Attached to the racing unit at Longbridge, early in 1913 he had co-driven as mechanic in a prototype Austin Sports car entered for an Alpine Trial, and Herbert must have considered his hitherto reluctant son's future succession at Longbridge to be at least a possibility, and one which Vernon's death only a year later cruelly destroyed.[33] An obituary noted that Lord Austin had planned to retire at the age of fifty, relinquishing his share to Vernon.[34]

Indeed, the problem of filling the topmost position of responsibility in the two firms reveals another intriguing parallel. Morris was childless; Austin had two daughters, but his only son was killed in 1915.

[30] *Birmingham Mail*, 23 May 1941, obituary. The major donations recorded there were £5,000 to Toc H; £250,000 to Cambridge University for Scientific Research at the Cavendish Laboratory; and £7,000 to the Birmingham United Hospital for the purchase of a radium bomb.

[31] Lambert & Wyatt, p. 157.

[32] After a reluctant apprenticeship, and contrary to his father's wishes, Vernon Austin enlisted in the Army with a view to a career as a professional soldier. He left after only a year, remaining on the Army Reserve List of Officers. In the following year he was recalled to his unit for active service. Lambert & Wyatt, pp. 101–2, 109.

[33] By communication with Mrs. Z. E. Lambert, 13 February 1978.

[34] *Birmingham Post*, 24 May 1941.

Neither took steps to seek a successor from within his respective organization, though by the time Nuffield was in his fifties Leonard Lord had been given more responsibility than any other person, except Nuffield himself. There is no reason to suppose that Nuffield would have made Lord his successor, yet after his departure Nuffield appears to have ignored the problem until his own delayed retirement loomed ahead after 1950. Similarly, Lord Austin was over seventy years of age before his thoughts turned to succession and to the appointment of Leonard Lord, initially to replace Engelbach, ultimately to succeed Lord Austin himself.

Whereas Nuffield was an autocrat, whose intervention in policy-making continued in erratic fashion long after his knowledge of the industry warranted it, Austin's autocratic bent was contained by his co-directors and the stern imperative of conservative finance following the reconstruction of 1921–22, despite his initial spirited rearguard action. Firm, if largely unimaginative, control at Longbridge contrasted with the jealousies and intrigue which seem to have embittered internal relations between managers within the Nuffield dominion. Historians of business management seeking for pointers to the future will learn little from Longbridge, for it was within Nuffield's unwieldy organization that the establishment of a divisional structure was introduced. The growth of Austin meant little more in terms of organizational change than the physical growth of Longbridge, and perhaps increased strains on internal organization which were tackled only after Lord's appearance upon the scene.

In his recent biography of William Morris, Overy has argued that one of the main reasons why Morris stands out from his contemporaries was his ability to take advantage of a unique situation, the possibility of producing cars by component assembly for example, by which he 'grew great on other men's efforts cleverly presented as his own'.[35] Morris's success lay in combining a commercial flair with the ability to solve the financial problems of breaking into the sequence leading to large scale production and self-sustaining financial and capital growth. In this, Morris was also assisted by the chance differential effects of the war on potential competitors. Morris's organization, dependent upon credit from suppliers, could survive the financial blizzard of 1920, on the basis of share capital and loans of less than £50,000 made available by bankers and friends in 1919 and 1921, a

[35] R. J. Overy, pp. 124–5.

piffling amount compared with the needs of the hugely expanded Longbridge enterprise.[36]

Austin's achievement was due initially to a technical brilliance unmatched by Morris's commercial perception, a weakness which the baleful financial effects of the First World War, combined with the unfortunate public flotations of 1914 and 1919, exacerbated. His technical contributions to motor car design in the early 1920s were as important to the industry's development as those of Morris in 1913, for the Seven was a model which made possible the penetration of an income stratum that the Cowley could not reach. Delayed and demoralizing to morale at Longbridge though it was, external intervention via the capital market, with the financial reorganization and managerial renovation that followed, provided the key to Austin's remarkable success in the succeeding period to 1939. Conservatively directed, nonetheless the very stability of management policies at Longbridge was in contrast with the sometimes anarchic conditions experienced within the Nuffield empire, where the frequent and often prolonged absences of an unpredictable despot[37] were in contrast to Sir Herbert's regular daily business at Longbridge. Both the profit records and market shares of the two companies also revealed volatility for Nuffield, stability for Austin, though we do not suggest that there was necessarily a causal relationship between style of management and profit performance.

Overall, such contrasts would seem to offer a fair reflection of the respective personalities at the head of the two major British motor companies during the industry's most formative years before the Second World War. In his prime, William Morris was an entrepreneur *par excellence* whose personal contribution after the late 1920s was often less than constructive. Herbert Austin remained, until the end, the inventive engineer, whose professional achievements were widely and officially acknowledged. Leonard Lord, who knew and worked for them both, stressed that Nuffield was quite different from Austin, in that whereas the latter was a 'practical man' Nuffield's best asset was his keen appreciation of prices and cost. Basically Nuffield was 'an extremely keen buyer, going to endless trouble to get what he needed', whereas Austin was preoccupied with the practicality of making cars.[38]

Earnest, hardworking, and true to the professional standards which

[36] Ibid., pp. 21–2.

[37] Sir Miles Thomas, *Out on a Wing* (1964), pp. 157–9.

[38] Andrews and Brunner, Notes.

justified so wide a recognition, nonetheless there are signs which suggest that his managerial abilities may have reached their limit by the First World War, and it was his innovative talent as a creative engineer which in 1921 and 1922 enabled him and the Company to surmount the problems which almost overwhelmed them both. Thereafter, just as success encouraged Lord Nuffield to become a proprietor without the wish to manage, circumstances compelled Lord Austin to concede both control and managerial primacy within the firm which was his creation. Whereas Lord Nuffield's riches led him to spend less and less time at Cowley, as he involved himself more and more in wholesale charity work and public affairs, Lord Austin's temperament, business experience, age and sense of enduring grief may help to explain why Longbridge continued to absorb him almost entirely. It was truly characteristic that when Lord Austin died in 1941, at the age of seventy-four, he did so only minutes after putting his signature to documents approving the design for new cars planned to go into production after the war.[39]

[39] Lambert & Wyatt, p. 168.

CHAPTER TWELVE

Austin and the British Motor Industry

HERBERT AUSTIN IS REMARKABLE both as a pioneer in the technology of the motor car from its beginning in Britain in 1895, when he built the first British motor car, and as the sole survivor from that phase in the industry's development, designing cars successfully for more than forty years. For good or ill, Herbert Austin is the archetypal figure in the history of the first forty years of the British industry's evolution. After only slight encouragement from his employers, the WSSMC, his success in attracting financial backing for his inventions from Vickers was the turning point leading to commercial production. Indeed, his contractual arrangement with Vickers is typical of the way in which existing engineering firms tested the profitability of the nascent motor industry.

The arrangement between W. G. Wilson, like Herbert Austin an engineer-inventor, with Armstrong Whitworth was of a similar kind[1] and represented a method by which firms, both curious and cautious regarding the commercial possibilities of motor cars, sought to cope with the uncertainty and risks that accompanied the rapid changes in motor technology in the pioneering stage. The parallel between Wilson and Austin is especially intriguing, bearing in mind that both Vickers and Armstrong were important engineering firms, whose command of resources and skills implied an immense potential for the development and growth of the motor industry. The reluctance to become committed to the ideas of a single inventor with the attendant

[1] R. J. Irving, 'New Industries for Old. Some Investment Decisions of Sir W. G. Armstrong, Whitworth & Co. Ltd., 1900–1914', *Business History*, 17 (1975), p. 154.

risk of becoming identified with his errors as well as his success, might explain in part the relatively short term arrangements between the Vickers brothers and Austin. These allowed Vickers to abandon their man over disagreement concerning the horizontal engine design and to engage J. D. Siddeley on a similar basis to replace him. Four years later, Siddeley was removed as General Manager of the Motor Works and Hopwood appointed to replace him.

It was such a context of uncertainty which explains why Herbert Austin was prepared to strike out independently in 1905. Under Vickers, by 1913 Wolseley had become the largest, if one of the most unprofitable, British car manufacturers. Austin had reached an output roughly half as large as Wolseley's but twice that of Armstrong Whitworth, the other large engineering firm to have established a sizeable bridgehead in the new industry. Saul has drawn attention to the lack of substantial direct connections between the machine tool and motor trades, a feature contrasting with the American industry, and argued that it cannot be coincidental that the groups of firms which possessed no pre-motor car history at all turned out to be among the most successful survivors as volume car producers.[2]

True, Austin and Standard were new firms, Austin formed in 1905 and Standard in 1903, but while they were launched without the material resources of larger engineering companies, both Herbert Austin and R. W. Maudsley, Standard's founder, brought with them considerable engineering expertise, and, on Austin's part, an intimate knowledge of, and reputation in, machine tool engineering. These men shared other characteristics, middle class education followed by a formal engineering apprenticeship, though in social background, education, and apprentice training Maudsley's was the more distinguished, if no more effective.[3]

Of the other firms who survived to compete among the Big Six, the founders of Singer and Hillman, later to form part of Rootes, also received experience in machine building; both were at Penns, the Greenwich firm of marine engineers, followed by a spell at Coventry Machinists, before setting up as cycle makers.[4] But whereas Singer, Hillman, and later Morris, formerly a mechanic, relied much upon their engineers for developing techniques of manufacture, Herbert Austin was responsible for all the major decisions affecting design and

[2] S. B. Saul, 'The Motor Industry', p. 40.
[3] J. R. Davy, *The Standard Car 1903–1963* (1964), p. 11.
[4] S. B. Saul, 'The Motor Industry', p. 28.

production before 1921. By continuing to manufacture most of the entire car within a single plant Herbert conformed to common practice, and not until Ford introduced quantity production of popular cars based on component supplies, shortly before the First World War, did the character, scale, and structure of motor manufacturing in Britain begin to alter.

In comparison both with French and American achievements in 1914 the production performance of the British motor industry was disappointing. Saul attached considerable importance to the refusal of existing large firms, especially engineering firms, to join the industry, and to the insistence of British engineers upon making so much of the cars themselves.[5] Although Herbert's overtures led Joseph Sankey & Sons to press metal body shells for building upon wooden frames,[6] Austin's experience suggests that British engineering firms could not, or would not, supply other basic components of the quality called for in motor production. Indeed, a major reason why British engineering firms declined to move into motor manufacture in a big way is suggested by the conclusions of Dr. R. J. Irving, whose research on the records of Armstrong Whitworth showed rates of return on expensive motor production falling below those on hydraulic engineering and arms manufacture. Armstrong Whitworth was one of several of the largest engineering firms which between 1905 and 1914 diverted an increasing proportion of their resources into arms production.[7] An expanding market in international arms, together with rising levels of British defence expenditure, generated demand which led to wider distribution of orders for munitions by the British Government. The decision to manufacture arms rather than cars, it is suggested. had little to do with entrepreneurial ineptitude.[8]

Some indication of the significance to be attributed to the absence of such companies in the motor trade is provided by the fact that Vickers' investment in Wolseley reached £450,000 by 1913, when the firm was

[5] S. B. Saul, 'The Motor Industry', p. 43.

[6] Ibid., p. 36.

[7] R. J. Irving, 'New Industries', pp. 166–8.

[8] Had Armstrong decided that it was commercially worthwhile developing the motor car business with substantial investments, it seems likely that the proposal for volume car production (5,000 to 6,000 annually) made by C. R. F. Engelbach, later the production director at Austin, would not have been rejected. The references to this come from the Vickers Archive – Elswick File, envelope 172. I am grateful to Dr. R. J. Irving for drawing my attention to it.

generally regarded as one of the leaders in car production, organization and method.[9] In introducing production in large batches, Wolseley also compared favourably with Austin, which in this respect was also 'behind the times'. Nonetheless, labour productivity does not appear to have been markedly different as between the two firms.[10]

In comparison with the American industry, engineering skills and progressive workshop practice were important ingredients missing in the industry before 1914, while finance through public issues on the Stock Market was not difficult to secure – though when it was obtained in this way disastrous consequences often ensued.[11] In fact, most of the successful survivors shared the pattern of Austin's financial experience, combining personal savings and the savings of personal contacts for initial capital outlay, trade credit coupled with bank loans and overdrafts meeting requirements for working capital. Furthermore, a reputation as an inventor could attract investment from the commercial tycoons or promoters, like du Cros who invested in Austin, and Friswell who helped to finance Standard – not an unmixed blessing.

The most serious weakness in the British industry, in Saul's view, was the absence of 'commercial acumen', and the preoccupation with individuality and technical perfection, a preoccupation which he attributes largely to the training and experience of the pioneers who were strongly influenced by traditional ways of engineering.[12] Herbert Austin's approach to the market, like that of perhaps most of his contemporaries before 1921, certainly warrants such a conclusion, though W. R. Maudsley at Standard found his own preference for the production of cars in quantity for a popular market blocked by a commercial man, the Chairman, Charles Friswell, who then held a majority shareholding in the Company. Formed in 1896 with a capital of £40,000, Friswell Ltd. was one of the first motor agents, importing cars from France for sale to the British public. Subsequently its chairman-owner, Charles Friswell, acquired the sole distributors' rights for the sale of Standard cars.[13] With dominance at board level, Friswell found himself in a position to dictate manufacturing policy but he rejected Maudsley's plans for standardization in preference for small

[9] S. B. Saul, 'The Motor Industry', p. 39.
[10] See above, p. 36.
[11] S. B. Saul, 'The Motor Industry', p. 31.
[12] For a discussion of Austin in his contemporary context see above, pp. 36–41.
[13] Pollitt Papers 232/42, 398/12, Friswell.

batch production of several different models, with frequent modifications and highly priced.[14] How many more dealers were apparently uninterested in selling low-priced standardized vehicles we do not know, but in this particular instance direct contact with the market did not bring the era of mass motoring nearer. Neither did a similar agency alliance between the mercurial Australian salesman, S. F. Edge, and Montague Napier, the distinguished engineer.[15] Not until 1918 is there evidence of Austin's dealers expressing their views on the type of car they wished the Company to produce,[16] but only after his own preference was revealed to be unwise did Sir Herbert take note and design smaller, cheaper models. In this instance, Professor Saul's strictures on the inability of engineers to read the market are valid, but the manner in which volume production and sales was initiated in Britain before 1914 suggests that other factors may have been equally important in hindering the industry's development. For in the two spectacular cases where direct personal contact with the market did prove to have important repercussions for the industry other elements were also common to commercial success.

Before 1913 only one Englishman had successfully displayed a sensitivity to the commercial needs of the motoring public. He was Percival Perry, an entrepreneur in the literal sense, one year younger than Morris. After a middle class education, he had worked initially with Harry Lawson, the company promoter, developing road rights for Daimler, then left in 1894 to work in the family printing business. In 1903 he had become involved with the Central Motor Car Company, an organization set up to sell Ford products in Europe from a London base. Disagreement led to his departure, after which he persuaded Henry Ford to open a branch of the Ford Motor Company on a similar basis to Ford Agencies in American towns, which would form the spearhead of a nationwide Ford dealer organization with Perry at its head.[17] In 1911 the headquarters moved from London to Trafford Park, Manchester, where car assembly began. More than 3,000 Fords, rated at 22.4 h.p. and priced from £135, were sold in 1912, and nearly

[14] Standard Motor Company Minute Book, 8 February 1977; 5 January 1909; 5, 19, 26 April, 10 May, 14 June 1910. Charles Friswell sold his Standard shares in 1912, when S. Bettman, a Coventry businessman, became Chairman.

[15] Charles Wilson and William Reader, *Men and Machines* (1958).

[16] AMB, 6 April 1921.

[17] Mira Wilkins and Frank Ernest Hill, *American Business Abroad, Ford on Six Continents* (Detroit, 1964), pp. 23–6.

twice that figure in 1913, by which time the Company employed 814 workers.[18]

Like Perry, Morris ran a car agency, and like Perry, he sensed the existence of a potential demand for a popularly-priced car. The first Morris Oxfords were being sold at a basic price of £175 for the 8.9 h.p. model in 1913, and in the following year Morris produced more than a thousand cars, an achievement hitherto reserved for a handful of British manufacturers.[19] The relatively highly priced 'popular' car reflected Herbert's insistence on putting quality and reliability before economy and price, exemplifying that relative disregard for the commercial aspects of motor car design and production which contrasts so sharply with the approaches of Ford and Morris. Separated by eleven years in age, Morris in his mid-thirties was nonetheless a 'new man' to car manufacture, in so far as hitherto he had sold, rather than built, motor cars; whereas Herbert's experience of car manufacturing during the pioneering phase lasting over a decade seems to have created an attitude of mind belonging to that earlier era when, quite properly, sheer technical performance demanded the highest priority, and when control of the entire manufacturing process was considered vital. By contrast, both P. L. D. Perry, who took advantage of the overheads carried by the Ford plant in Detroit to launch the low priced popular car in Britain, and William Morris, by adopting the assembly principle, avoided the heavy overheads necessary for volume production. Given a rational disinterest by the armament firms in volume car production, the inclination within smaller engineering firms to manufacture, rather than to assemble, was at least as important a hindrance to mass production as their approach to the market. Lacking the vast resources of the armament firms, and wary of the motor financiers, the risks associated with the imitation of a Ford type car were such as to deter the heavy investment required for low cost production of low priced cars before 1913.

That recovery after the war depended merely upon possessing a commercially successful model in a firm's repertoire in 1914 is a possibility which the Rover Company's history eliminates. The firm's experience in the short run might have validated such a hypothesis, but only a few years after the war, Rover, as its historian notes, was in the red, the effect of competition from Morris and Austin.[20] The imme-

[18] P. L. D. Perry, 'The Ford in England', *Ford Times*, 2 (1914), pp. 234–329.
[19] R. J. Overy, pp. 6, 128.
[20] George Oliver, *The Rover* (1971), pp. 65–71.

diate response of Rover managers to the post-war conditions was to improve the Twelve in power, design and fittings, pushing the price further from the pockets of that section of potential first-time car buyers identified by the *Times* reporter in 1913. At the same time, the Rover managers tried to supply the needs of that section of the market by adopting J. Y. Sangster's prototype air-cooled 8 h.p. car, the details and price of which were announced before the end of 1919. Production of this completely new model began in 1920, when together with the Twelve production exceeded 5,000 cars, rising to nearly 6,500 in 1922.[21] By that time Austin had added the Twelve to the Twenty but Sir Herbert was still designing the Seven, the car which was a major factor in ending the success of the Rover Eight. The speed with which Rover's new model was brought into production after the war is in contrast to Sir Herbert's perseverance with the Twenty.

In assessing his decisions relating to the immediate post-war policy we may note that his choice was the only rational option open to him, ill-suited though the Twenty was to standardized volume production, for that was the model which was competitive within its range. Sir Herbert is open to criticism, however, in concentrating upon his single model policy without at the same time planning a successor to the Austin Ten. At the Rover works a completely new Rover Eight had been designed and went into production within two years of the Armistice, even before Sir Herbert had acknowledged the need for an Austin car smaller than the Twenty. Designing new cars took months rather than years, and even the Austin Seven took only six months or so to design, with a further six months to prepare for commercial production. But despite the pointers towards the future trends in car purchase provided by the immediate pre-war success of the Rover Twelve, the Singer Ten, the Standard Model S 9.5 h.p. cars,[22] and the Morris Oxford, Sir Herbert chose to ignore them, and to disregard advice from the agents selling Austin motor cars, perhaps beguiled by the similarity in horsepower of his own Austin Twenty and the Model T Ford. Only when the popularity of the larger cars was clearly affected, in part due to the economic difficulties which encouraged the shift of demand away from more expensive cars, and reinforced by the rise in prices forced upon manufacturers as a result of the horsepower

[21] Ibid., pp. 65–71, 89.

[22] In 1913 the Standard Motor Company produced the Model 'S' 9.5 h.p. 'light car', offered at £185. Nearly 2,000 chassis were produced between mid-1914 and mid-1915. J. R. Davy, *The Standard Car 1903–1963* (1964), pp. 19–21.

tax, did Sir Herbert begin to plan in earnest for the Austin Twelve, and subsequently for the Austin Seven.

We have criticized Sir Herbert's failure to acknowledge the growing importance of light cars in the market, and his total commitment to the Austin Twenty after the war. From a consideration of likely car sales he lacked a better commercial alternative in 1918, but although time was spent in improving the design of the Twenty, incorporating the American arrangement of a centrally controlled gearbox and adopting modifications derived from wartime experience,[23] he planned no replacement for the Austin Ten, which before the war had aimed at, but which failed to appeal to, would-be car owners outside the highest income groups. Undoubtedly this was an omission which rendered the Company's immediate post-war recovery more problematical, but its relative importance is diminished when considered in the context of the immensity of Austin's problems produced by the huge wartime expansion, and the imperative to proceed with peacetime production at a level more than tenfold that achieved in any year before the war.

This was the problem which faced other large munitions works possessing respectable histories of motor vehicle production, notably Wolseley, Belsize and, in its most extreme form, at Beardmore. Prominent among those manufacturing firms which were to survive in the long term and which were the quickest to adapt to peacetime production, were Singer, Rover, Standard, and above all Morris and Ford, whose production strategy of assembly offered the most room for rapid recovery from wartime conditions. Ford, Morris, Singer, Standard and Rover had each produced light cars with some success before 1914, and it was to modified versions of such models that they returned in 1919. Ford excepted, each had been involved in munitions production during the war, though none had undergone the enormous expansion which so transformed Longbridge.[24] Ford and Morris apart, Singer was next best placed for recovery, with a proven light car, a strong financial position in 1914 which enabled the Company to cope with the immediate post-war general problem of liquidity, and directed by managers eager to expand, but with caution.[25]

The immediate post-war history of Standard illuminates the peculiar problems of Austin because before 1914 the companies were similar in

[23] Lambert & Wyatt, pp. 116–17.

[24] A. Holme, 'Some Aspects of the British Motor Manufacturing Industry During the Years 1919–1930', M.A. (University of Sheffield, 1964).

[25] *Midland Daily Telegraph*, 9 October 1931.

many respects. One important difference was that in 1913–14 Maudsley had mounted the Company's first attempt at volume production of the Model 'S' Standard light car of 9.5 h.p., and this was resumed immediately after the war.[26] In terms of capitalization and output Austin was considerably larger than Standard in 1913, and the differences widened with the first public capital issues of 1914 which doubled Standard's capital to £50,000, compared with Austin's 1914 capitalization of £650,000. Both increased their issued capital in 1919, Standard to £300,000, Austin to £3.35 million, their respective problems of indebtedness and shortage of working capital being similar, except in scale. Even Maudsley's policy, following Ford and Rover before 1914, of producing a single commercially successful motor car of the latest pre-war design was not sufficient to overcome the financial burdens imposed by the effects of war.[27] Maudsley also recognized the need for a slightly larger four-seater car than the 'S' model, and in July 1921 announced the Standard Model 'SLO' 11.6 h.p. touring car, which appeared on the market simultaneously with the Austin Twelve, and proved to be an immediate success.[28] Sir Herbert Austin and Richard Maudsley, it seems, allowed much the same lag between the resumption of peacetime production and a decision upon the post-war trends in the market for motor cars. That was the rationale for Sir Herbert's persistence with the Twenty in 1919, unsuitable though it may have been for concentrated volume production, for while the Austin Ten had been the cheapest of the four basic models offered by the Company in 1914 it had not achieved commercial success comparable with other light cars then on the market. Indeed it was in an attempt to improve its competitive position that the horsepower of the Austin Ten was increased from 10.1 to 14.3, so that by 1914 the model was classified as the Austin 12/14. Advertising of the Austin light car was also in a low key. When the war ended, Sir Herbert must have acknowledged that on past record if he was to adopt a single model policy he must introduce a modified version of the Twenty rather than the Ten.

[26] J. R. Davy, *The Standard Motor Car 1903–1963* (1964), p. 21.

[27] The symptoms of financial difficulty are recorded in minutes of the Standard Motor Company during these years. In April 1918, for example, the Government owed the Company £140,000. Mortgage debentures had been issued to secure overdrafts running at £130,000, and the Government had failed to make deposits with Standard in respect of continuing contracts involving heavy expenditure already incurred. 27 April 1918, *Standard Motor Company Ltd., Minute Book.*

[28] J. R. Davy, *The Standard Motor Car 1903–1963* (1964), pp. 23–5.

Maudsley's persistence with his own more appropriately designed light car did not enable the Standard Motor Company to avoid financial difficulties after the war, small though they were in comparison with those facing Austin. Had Austin possessed a car comparable with the light cars of Rover, Singer, or Standard in 1914 his post-war problems would surely have been lessened by easing liquidity. Nonetheless, the histories of Rover, Standard, and Singer suggest that while a commercially successful motor car was a necessary condition for post-war survival it was by no means a sufficient condition for success. As for Morris, the Oxford was an imaginatively designed car with commercial appeal at the right price, but sound finance and flexible production were critical to the Company's post-war success.

Even before the war commenced *The Economist* was predicting that the boom in light car production in the autumn of 1914 would be followed by a process in which low priced American cars would force some British manufacturers to invest in really large scale production of cars, to accept lower profit margins, and to concentrate on that section of the market willing to pay not more than £200 for a vehicle.[29] The increase in Austin's capitalization when it became a public company in 1914 was to permit expansion, though there is no record of any intention to develop large scale light car production at Longbridge before 1920.[30] Perhaps, as he claimed in retrospect, he had been impressed by a 'vision' of mass motoring during his stay in Australia, but the lag between his experiments with a single cylinder Austin Seven in 1910 and the introduction of the 'baby' Austin in 1922, his commitment to a high quality and not inexpensive small car between 1910 and 1914, and the context of the design innovations embodied in the Seven, all suggest otherwise. For the Seven represented a classic example of the design of a new product to solve the problem of depression, falling sales, and serious financial pressures threatening the Company's existence. The 'critical level of vulnerability', which Checkland has suggested so often seems to be almost a necessary antecedent to a firm's adaptive response[31] was reached in 1920–21, when Sir Herbert's

[29] *Economist*, 22 November 1913, 24 January 1914.

[30] The Austin Twenty model of 1914 was a new design, 'the Sports Twenty', though war had prevented its introduction to the market. The 1919 body was 'streamlined and completely different from the pre-war models', and the entire car, incorporating features derived from wartime experience, has been described as 'entirely new in concept'. Lambert & Wyatt, pp. 116–17.

[31] S. G. Checkland's review of D. C. Coleman, History of Courtaulds, *Economic History Review*, XXXIII (1970), p. 560.

creative genius proved equal to the crisis. His engineering brilliance in designing the Twelve and the Seven at the age of fifty-five was vital for the Company's survival in the immediate post-war era, when most motor companies were undergoing severe financial difficulties. It is almost paradoxical that a crisis of such serious dimensions should seem to have been necessary to stimulate the Company's revival, for not only did it force Sir Herbert along the path towards the market for really low priced motor cars, but it also precipitated changes in managerial personnel designed to tighten control over both production methods and finance.

The common view of the effects of the war upon the motor industry is that it probably accelerated, rather than retarded, innovative development. There is little reason to doubt the validity of this conclusion. Austin's history shows this to have been true in the sense that large scale munitions production led to the adoption of repetition manufacture to an unprecedented degree, the installation of huge sheet metal presses, compressed air sprays and special hardening and heat treatment plants and an enlarged research section, thereby equipping the Company for product control and scientific choice of materials to an extent which was usually confined to armament firms.[32] But perhaps the more interesting question is whether, even acknowledging the stimulus to innovation given to motor manufacturers during the war, the British motor industry was helped or hindered in its overall development. The evidence suggests that the catalyst which provided the spur to British manufacturers was not war, but Henry Ford, who provided W. R. Morris with the model for assembly production, and later helped modify Herbert Austin's conservative views on methods of manufacture.

In 1913 more than 6,000 Fords were assembled at Trafford Park, where more than 800 people were employed. In 1914 the labour force had risen to 1,500, and sales to 12,500.[33] Though Ford relied upon imported chassis and components, the size of the labour force is indicative of the scale on which assembly was conducted in Britain even before the war.[34] By that time Ford was already using vanadium steel in car chassis for lighter weight, a practice hitherto condemned by British engineers; but its tensile strength prompted the British Govern-

[32] L. H. Pomeroy, 'Automobile Engineering After the War', *PIAE*, LX (1914–15), p. 8.

[33] P. L. D. Perry, 'The Ford in England', *Ford Times*, 2 (1914), p. 234.

[34] *Ford Times*, 1 (1912), pp. 1–6; 2 (1914), pp. 310, 329; W. Davidson, 'The Science of Bodybuilding', *Ford Times*, 2 (1914); 3 (1914), p. 18; 3 (1915), p. 375.

ment to use it in the construction of the Navy's new light cruisers from 1914. Methods of assembly imported from the US already involved moving conveyors, while in all operations of machinery and sub- and main assembly the employment of specially constructed jigs dispensed with the need for measurement by operatives. Ford claimed to have the best fitted body shop in Britain, containing advanced metal cutting and bending tools and high speed labour-saving paint-spraying equipment.[35] What was also reckoned to be the largest and most modern cold riveting plant in England lengthened the life of, and strengthened, the stamped metal parts which were substituted for woodwork to an increasing extent, and an array of advanced wood-working and automatic screen-fitting machinery reduced labour time drastically.[36] By integrating assembly with manufacture, by installing conveyors and chutes to eliminate interval loading and transport, and by introducing automatic stoving and enamelling, Ford in England produced a model of efficient operation. Moreover, right from the start, Perry sought to encourage British component suppliers to produce items of the quality needed.[37] It seems likely that by 1914 British motor manufacturers could have learned from the Trafford Park enterprise virtually all that the disruptive experience of the war would have to offer. It would have been surprising had Ford's competition in a free market not forced British manufacturers to learn such a lesson, after which others would have followed Morris in the search for volume, low cost production of cars for a popular market. *The Economist* had forecast that such a 'squeeze' was imminent early in 1914.[38]

That the lessons from experiences of wartime production might be misinterpreted is clear from remarks made by Wolseley's chief engineer, A. A. Remington, who in 1918 expressed the view that the level at which cars were economic to manufacture would be not less than a thousand vehicles, 'possibly over one or two years'.[39] In an article carried by the *Autocar* on 'Munitions Work as an Education' in

[35] *Ford Times*, 1 (1912), pp. 141–6; *Motor Trader*, LII (1911), p. 327.

[36] W. Davidson, 'The Science of Bodybuilding', *Ford Times*, 2 (1914).

[37] *Motor Trader*, LII (1911), p. 324. Also a transcript of an interview with Patrick Hennessey (Ford's purchasing manager) by Mira Wilkins in 1960 refers to this point. Ford Archives.

[38] *Economist*, 24 January 1914.

[39] A. A. Remington, 'Some Probable Effects of the War on the Automobile Industry', *PIAE*, XIII (1918–19), p. 453.

1919,[40] B. H. Davies included among his list of lessons likely to have been learned: more attention to experimental work, the maximum employment of unskilled labour, the economics of large scale production and an alteration in attitudes to engineering: 'Now price is the target, and the engineer is asked to find ways of producing a car to meet it.' He predicted that greater attention would be paid to the supply of low-priced cars in future. Research and the employment of unskilled labour had long been features at Longbridge, though war intensified both practices. The vastly expanded scale of production and the requirements of standardization and specialization, however, were the aspects of wartime operations which led Sir Herbert astray. In order to meet overheads an output was required which far exceeded pre-war levels, and due to his inability to assess quickly either the post-war trend in the market for motor cars, or to recognize the financial implications of trying to maintain high levels of production of high quality motor cars, Sir Herbert could do little at first to steer the Company away from the brink of collapse.

Wolseley's experience was similar; here the combination of the financial burdens of overcapitalization following wartime expansion and the failure to produce a commercially successful motor car eventually led to liquidation in 1926. The post-war history of Belsize, which before the war had mounted a serious bid to manufacture cars in volume and which during the war employed some 5,000 people at its massive Manchester works, is likewise one of overcapitalization, lack of liquidity and a misreading of the market.[41] Belsize was in the Receiver's hands in 1923, and despite financial reconstruction its fortunes declined, until its demise in 1930. Austin's history might have been identical had not the Creditors' Committee, and the Midland Bank in particular, adopted a firm line; for they insisted on the introduction of new managers possessing professional expertise to compensate for Sir Herbert's managerial blind spots, while fortuitously harnessing his creative engineering brilliance in designing Austin motor cars.

At the depths of the Company's ill fortunes, Sir Herbert was a fierce critic both of the Treasury and of the Banks. On the evidence of the firm's pre-war financial performance we are disposed to sympathize with his view that Treasury officials treated Austin unfairly, and by so doing exacerbated the Company's plight. But while the behaviour of the Midland Bank managers appeared unsympathetic, they were,

[40] B. H. Davies, 'Munitions Work as an Education', *Autocar*, 42 (1919), pp. 653–4.

[41] *Motor Trader*, LIII (1912), p. 324, LXXIV (1923), p. 83.

without doubt, instrumental in achieving the injection of expertise into top management which neither the speculator hitherto responsible for finance, Harvey du Cros, nor the car salesman, W. G. Randle Ash, possessed. Sir Herbert was an engineer and designer of the old school, preoccupied with the quality and performance of the product above all else; C. R. F. Engelbach's talent and interest lay primarily in organization methods and systems of production; Payton became responsible for solving the Company's colossal and complex financial problems and for the introduction of strict internal financial control. His succession to Harvey du Cros as Deputy Chairman is symbolic of the transformation in the character of Austin after 1921.

The events of 1919 to 1921, culminating in the crucial managerial reconstruction, may have been spectacular in the degree of success achieved subsequently at Longbridge, but the sequence of events was certainly not peculiar to that company.[42] In 1921 a correspondent writing in the *Motor Trader* referred to the widespread problem of illiquidity affecting the motor industry, which in several cases had led to recourse to groups of financiers willing to put up the money in return for seats on the Board and influence in other ways.[43] Standard, for example, obtained assistance from Barclays Bank in 1920, conditional upon the bank's nomination of two members of Standard's Board of Directors. One of these was C. J. Band, who was appointed Chairman, and the other was E. J. Corbett, manager of the Coventry Branch of Barclays Bank.[44] Personal intervention of this kind, however, while it increased the probability of survival could not guarantee success, and it was not until the appointment of a new managing director, Captain J. P. Black in 1929, that Standard began to emerge as one of the Big Six.[45]

At Longbridge the effects of intervention were dramatic, though

[42] The Slump of 1921 also provided the matrix for Morris to cut prices and release the mechanism of elasticity. For this reason, and because of the reconstruction of Austin, the effects of the Slump were less harmful than the high incidence of company mortality which followed might suggest.

[43] *Motor Trader*, LXIV (1921), p. 89. See similar remarks in *Investors Monthly Manual*, 52 (1922), p. 235.

[44] Kenneth Richardson, *Twentieth Century Coventry* (Coventry, 1972), p. 63.

[45] The Board of Rover called in an accountant, H. Howe Graham, to examine the Company's problems in 1932. He was co-opted as financial adviser for two years during which time he completely reorganized production. At the same time Colonel Searle, identified with the firm's difficulties, resigned in 1932. Recovery followed. G. Oliver, *The Rover* (1971), pp. 102–5.

hardly justifying the refusal by banks and other financial institutions to extend conditional assistance beyond that granted between 1919 and 1921. In retrospect, however, the Company's history in the remaining years of that decade fully vindicates the operation of the external capital market in having eventually rescued the valuable economic assets of Longbridge and ensuring, by managerial renovation, the effective economic exploitation of Sir Herbert's fertile mind. To answer the question whether the operating of the external capital market in this or other ways acted to improve the performance of the British motor industry would require considerably more research into the histories of other companies, for the respective consequences for intervention of the kind that occurred at Austin and Standard depended much upon the activities of the personalities involved, as well as upon the degree of involvement in management.

* * *

In terms of innovation and trade the performance of the British motor industry between the wars has attracted attention from historians wishing to generalize about the record of British industry in that period, thought the provisional conclusions regarding the motor industry rest on flimsy foundations. Austin's history is of special importance in this debate, accounting as it did for between one-fifth and one-third of British car output after the mid-1920s and remaining the second largest car producer in Britain. The context of a duty of $33\frac{1}{3}$ per cent on all imported motor cars between 1915 and 1939 should not be forgotten, and its protective effect on the industry, as indicated by the consequences of the brief experiment in free trade in 1924–25, acknowledged. For apart from that short period, imports of foreign motor cars were minimal in the 1920s and 1930s.

As for exports, it is neither surprising that before the Slump of 1929–31 British exports represented a small proportion of world trade, nor that sales were concentrated in markets linked to Britain by historic trading ties or fiscal preference. But whereas before the Slump the figure for car exports was less than 7 per cent of world car exports, between 1929 and 1938 British exports retained more than twice that percentage share, despite renewed competition from the American industry recovering from the Slump and the successful trading penetration by a flourishing German industry.[46] Although British car

[46] For a discussion of trends in motor exports between the wars cf. Michael Miller and Roy Church, 'Growth and Instability'.

exports fell during the Slump, in comparison with the exports of other car-producing countries the industry's relative position improved. During the recovery period exports rose absolutely but deteriorated relatively. The relative improvement during the Slump, in which the low horse-powered models of Austin and Morris were critical, occurred as a result of a favourable combination of movements in home production and prices in export markets, with changes in incomes and motoring costs in markets overseas. The disappearance of these factors during the recovery was followed by relative deterioration from the mid-1930s.

Richardson has defended the trading performance of the motor industry between the wars, maintaining that British car manufacturers performed well against competitors. But following A. H. Kahn, Alford has criticized their marketing techniques and the proliferation of models, attributing both to the pervasive influence of engineers within the industry. Such dominance and its consequences, he argues, was not conducive to sound management and was contrary to the long run interests of the industry,[47] a criticism to be found also in Graham Turner's book on the recent history of British Leyland.[48] Despite Alford's strictures on the marketing performance of British motor companies, he concedes that the effects of such weaknesses as there were did not seriously damage British motor exports. Indeed, an examination of the trade statistics shows that British manufacturers not only took advantage of the Slump when the characteristics of British popular cars of low cost, high performance, and low fuel consumption found a buoyant demand in depressed markets overseas, but that thereafter British manufacturers succeeded in retaining a significant share of world markets until the mid-1930s. From that time, the re-entry of the Americans and later the emergence of state-induced German competition[49] posed a threat to British achievement overseas.

We have suggested that due to the huge disparity between the size of British and American markets, and, given the protection of a growing market by tariff, the appropriate technology and methods of production for effective competition at home were of a kind which permitted

[47] B. W. Alford, *Depression and Recovery? British Economic Growth 1918–1939* (1972).

[48] Graham Turner, *The Leyland Papers* (1971).

[49] Michael Miller and Roy Church, 'Growth and Instability'; R. J. Overy, 'Cars, Roads and Economic Recovery in Germany 1932–8', *Econ. Hist. Rev.*, XXVIII (1975), p. 482.

competition among the few, thereby hindering concentration of resources on a small number of models, arguably necessary for successful exporting. Given the structure and composition of home demand, is it realistic to think that British firms might have performed more effectively in the design and marketing of motor cars? Alford suggests that they might, and is specific in offering the reason why they didn't; the all-pervading and inhibitive influence of the engineers, explained by reference to the 'pioneering manner in which the industry developed'.[50]

Influence and dominance are imprecise concepts, not easily susceptible to measurement. Even an examination of a single firm, concentrating upon an individual's contribution to decision-making, may fail to identify the precise relationships between managerial status and effective influence. We are unlikely to find the Boards of any motor manufacturers dominated by marketing men, but in this respect motor firms are unlikely to have differed from most other manufacturing concerns. Randle Ash was on the Board of Austin in charge of marketing, but Sir Herbert was chiefly responsible for design, while decisions on model policy were taken by him, together with Engelbach and Payton. Even though an examination of the Company's marketing policy hardly indicates disinterest, the design of motor cars tended to be conservative throughout the 1930s, but the fact remains they were popular, which suggests that the charge of disregarding the market's needs between the wars, by Sedgwick especially, is an exaggeration. How applicable is the criticism to Austin's competitors?

The spectacular rise of Morris Motors from the 1920s owed much to his philosophy of expanding sales both at home and overseas, Miles Thomas, the commercial dynamo in his twenties, pressing exports with vigour. It was by default that the thrust of Morris Motors was not wholly sustained from the late 1920s, though it was Morris himself who was largely responsible for the bewildering range of vehicles offered by the Nuffield organization in the 1930s. Singer, between the wars, was dominated by W. E. Bullock, the same age as Morris, likewise educated at a local school. He became a toolmaker's assistant and subsequently an engineer before becoming managing director. His son, W. E. Bullock, was educated at Malvern College, served an apprenticeship with Singer, and became assistant managing director in 1928, then general manager four years later. Singer's fall from the Big Three after 1928 had little to do with marketing policy, and was

[50] B. W. Alford, p. 54.

due mainly to financial over-commitment through investment in the huge Hay Mills plant purchased from Daimler, which proved too large and too uneconomic for success at that time.[51]

Standard was in the hands of the distinguished engineer, R. W. Maudsley, until the appointment of Captain J. P. Black as Works Manager in 1929. The son of a civil servant, Black received his education at a grammar school and was articled to a solicitor until the First World War interrupted his career. After the war he joined Hillman, to become first sales director and then joint managing director with Spencer Wilkes until 1928, when the Rootes Brothers took over the Company. Black's particular interest lay in production systems and works organization, and when he joined Standard from Hillman, with capital to invest,[52] it was by completely overhauling the productive organization that he achieved prominence for Standard cars and the Company during the Slump. From the time when Black arrived, the hitherto dominant influence of traditional engineering was already on the wane, and R. W. Maudsley himself appears to have approved of the changes in model strategy and policy in the late 1920s. On his death in 1934, Black, who by that time was joint managing director with Maudsley, became Chairman and managing director of Standard.[53]

For ten years after the First World War the management of Vauxhall was in the hands of its founder, Leslie Walton, a man twenty years younger than Austin, but whose Etonian education and commercial training failed to achieve more than survival for his company, until the General Motors Corporation took the firm over in 1925. An engineer with American experience, W. O. Kennington became General Manager under Walton's chairmanship for two years, after which C. J. Bartlett, an accountant trained at Bath Municipal College and hitherto managing director of General Motors' operations in England, became Vauxhall's managing director in 1929.[54] Vauxhall's policy, however, was dictated from the United States, which by concentrating on the medium priced car until 1930[55] catered for a relatively secure

[51] *Midland Daily Telegraph*, 9 October 1931; G. S. Davison, *At the Wheel* (1931), pp. 37–41.

[52] Black married Hillman's daughter.

[53] J. R. Davy, *The Standard Car 1903–1963* (1964), pp. 31–3; *Times*, 19 October 1930, 4 November 1931; Kenneth Richardson, *Twentieth Century Coventry* (1972), pp. 63–4, 100.

[54] Percy Peters and H. Thornton (eds.), *Who's Who in the Motor Trade* (1934).

[55] L. C. Darbyshire, *The Story of Vauxhall, 1857–1946* (Luton, 1946), pp. 40–1; Michael Sedgwick, *Cars of the 1930s* (1970), pp. 288–90.

market segment, though one where economies of scale were not large. Ford's English company was directed by Sir Percival Perry, the ex-Ford dealer recalled to Trafford Park in 1928, and who master-minded the removal to Dagenham in 1932 with the full support of the American parent company. Perry was quite definitely a 'marketing' man, though his initiatives were frequently inhibited by directions from Dearborn. Ford's success in the 1930s owed much to Perry's ability to persuade his American master that he knew what kind of a car a large section of the motoring population in Europe wished to buy. Finally, the takeover of Hillman Humber by the Rootes Brothers in 1928 marked the amalgamation of a potentially effective manufacturing plant and design team with successful sales organization conducted by William Rootes, a former Singer apprentice, and brother Reginald, formerly a civil servant. Each had entered his father's motor sales and service firm in 1924, a step which explains the essentially commercial orientation which characterized the Rootes manufacturing organization from the outset.[56]

A brief review of the distinctive managerial features of the Big Six companies, largely impressionistic though it must be, suggests that in four cases at least, Morris, Ford, Vauxhall and Rootes, the dominance of engineers in boardroom decisions was considerably less than complete. The exercise of commercial judgement, however, appears to have been neither sustained, in the case of Morris, nor unhampered by decisions made by the managers in America in the case of Ford and Vauxhall. Production men were probably dominant at Standard and Austin and, indeed, by default, in the Nuffield organization in the 1930s, when *The Economist* pointed to deficiencies on the part of British motor firms in export markets.[57] Entrepreneurial failures in the industry abounded, and the small success of diverse lines of output and frequent model changes were symptoms which in the 1930s had deleterious, though not disastrous, effects on the industry's ability to compete. These failings and their importance among the Big Six, however, should not be accorded great importance. To achieve a transfer of British exports to an enlarged and efficient basis similar to the Americans, with local assembly and manufacture of sufficient volume to render adequate overseas stockholding of components economic, needed a greater shock than the Slump provided. A neces-

[56] G. S. Davison, *At the Wheel* (1931), pp. 99–101.
[57] *Economist*, 13 October 1934, 19 October 1935, 17 October 1936.

sary condition for such a transformation was not just a growing British share of a smaller international trade, but a substantially larger sales volume.

To mount such a major onslaught on world markets would have required investment on such a massive scale which, perhaps understandably, British motor companies were unwilling to contemplate. The experiences of the post-war boom and its aftermath predisposed Austin and Standard to conservative financial policies, establishing large reserves to cover the event of possible future difficulties. In fact, Rootes did attempt to exploit overseas markets in a big way,[58] and his failure to achieve more than he did W. E. Rootes attributed to the basis of motor taxation, which he maintained created a market quite different at home to the type of demand encountered in overseas markets,[59] a view shared by Morris, Perry, Austin, and other motor manufacturers,[60] but which ignored the protection it extended to British car makers from American mass producers. But even at Longbridge, perhaps more under the influence of engineering minds than other major firms, the efforts aimed at furthering exports do not suggest a lack of commitment to commercial expansion overseas. Like Lord Nuffield, Sir Herbert took considerable pride in drawing shareholders' attention to their respective companies' export performance, and both possessed extensive distribution networks, with subsidiary companies and sales representatives based overseas.[61] Among the lesser firms, by the early 1930s Standard had more main distributors located abroad than in the UK, Singer had 40, and Humber and Hillman together 110.

Alford has drawn attention to the proliferation of engine types and models, following Kahn, as a sign of both a lack of direction and a development not conducive to growth in the scale of production.[62] Careful analysis of engine and model types, advertising copy, and production figures, indicates that the leading companies actually

[58] In the *Motor Trader* the new Rootes merger was seen to herald a 'foundation on which one can hope to see the development of a group in the motor industry capable of competing in world markets with powerful foreign competitors'. *Motor Trader*, XCIV (1928), p. 267.

[59] G. S. Davison, *At the Wheel* (1931), pp. 104–5.

[60] Morris tried to educate the British public to prefer larger horsepower cars suitable for North American and Commonwealth markets. R. J. Overy, p. 35.

[61] *Autocar*, 9 December 1932.

[62] B. W. Alford, *Depression and Recovery?*, p. 51.

manufactured a much narrower range of cars than others have suggested, additions being produced by the simple expedient of combining basic components in various ways. Filling those gaps in the market which the demise of the small specialist firms left behind, Nuffield was the major culprit, producing more than 20 in the early 1930s; but Austin produced only 7 models for most of that decade, while Ford made only 3 or 4.

Marketing performance, of course, was influenced by the quality of the product, which raises the question concerning the adequacy of the rate of technical innovation, both in the manufacture and design of British motor cars between the wars. On the basis of very impressionistic evidence, H. W. Richardson thought that the record was satisfactory; that the rate of technical innovation was adequate, and the industry 'not unenterprising'. Our research supports that view. Ford had introduced mechanized assembly using moving tracks at Trafford Park before the First World War,[63] and Morris, soundly financed, adopted some of these methods at Cowley in the early 1920s under the guidance of Frank Woollard, the noted production engineer.[64] Hampered by financial constraints, Austin emulated Ford in the mid-1920s, when under Engelbach's reorganization Austin became the first British motor works with a moving assembly line for the assembly both of chassis and car bodies. Singer, Standard, and Hillman were quick to follow by introducing mechanical assembly in their factories a few years later. The delay in Austin's adoption of new production methods was almost entirely due to financial circumstances, while Standard, too, experienced difficulties over finance in the 1920s which even the rapid growth of home demand between 1922 and 1927 could not overcome.

Improvements in technical design, as well as in production methods, were borrowed from the American industry. Vauxhall was responsible for first introducing the synchromesh gearbox on a popular car in 1931, independent front suspension in 1935, and unitary construction in 1938.[65] But the lag between the introduction of these innovations on

[63] As had A.E.C. in the manufacture of buses.

[64] R. J. Overy, p. 84.

[65] A telling reflection on the differences between British and American motor car designing is provided by the history of the Austin-Hayes infinitely variable transmission, a highly sophisticated mechanism patented by the American, Hayes, but which none of the American manufacturers would develop. Hayes was introduced to Sir Herbert who immediately agreed to develop the

the Austin models, and their diffusion among British manufacturers, Morris in particular, was short, even if the overall appearance of Austin motor cars tended to be behind the times.[66] By the mid-1930s, therefore, the technological basis of British motor car production was sound, even if the springs of invention were American.

There is little evidence, then, among the leaders of the motor industry of a 'lack of personnel who were adequately trained to appraise the commercial value of technical advances regardless of their country of origin'.[67] It seems likely that the inhibiting effects on exports of the relative absence of 'marketing men' holding key positions in the motor industry between the wars may have been exaggerated, and that the differences between the types of cars needed in overseas markets outside Europe, reinforced by the taxation structure and protective commercial policies of European producers, explain the relative weakness of motor exports after the mid-1930s.[68] British manufacturers held on to their enlarged share of world trade after the relative export success in the Slump, and it was only when the substantial boom in home demand occurred, beginning in 1934, that British exports of motor cars began to falter. Both *The Economist* and *The Statist* attributed this, in part, to the predisposition of producers to concentrate their efforts on the less difficult and more remunerative home market,[69] although the shifts in exchange values were also less conducive to expanding exports. In 1936 the Imperial Economic Committee drew attention to the subsidies which Italian and German car exporters were granted by their respective governments. When imports of Fiat and Opel cars began to rise sharply in 1937 Sir Herbert joined with Nuffield, Perry, Rootes, and Walton in urging the British Government to prevent further dumping, a plea also taken up by the

new transmission, which was incorporated in Austin Sixteens from 1932 and later in the Eighteens. Other British manufacturers showed no interest. I am grateful for this information to Mr. Freddie Henry, who was assigned to the project.

[66] The technical characteristics are compared in Michael Sedgwick, *Cars of the 1930's* (1970), especially pp. 268–79, 284–7, 288–9.

[67] B. W. Alford, *Depression and Recovery?*, p. 55.

[68] An example of the discriminatory effects of the tax structure is that whereas the Standard 8 of about 1,200 c.c. was taxed at 8 h.p., the Opel Olympia of 1,200 c.c. was taxed at 16 h.p.

[69] *Economist*, 13 October 1934, 19 October 1935, 17 October 1936; *Statist*, 19 October 1935.

SMMT.[70] Such general economic factors as these would seem to be more fundamental to an explanation of trends in imports and exports of motor cars after 1934 than strictures on marketing policies and the inhibiting commercial influence of engineers.

Austin is particularly vulnerable to the charge that the cars produced at Longbridge possessed an 'antique' air, less suited to overseas markets than to the competitive but diverse market at home. Exactly where responsibility lay for this situation is difficult to decide. Chapman's study of Boots demonstrated clearly that it is possible for a large discrepancy to exist between the formal structure and organization of a company and the realities of decision-making and policy formulation.[71] In this instance, although we have drawn attention to the slightly captive nature of Austin's position as Chairman and Managing Director after 1927, nonetheless regarding matters concerned with design he was the arbiter. It has been argued elsewhere[72] that the composition of the market, the structure of the industry, and the technology of volume output, as distinct from American-style mass production, rendered design of paramount importance in determining the performance of individual companies, as indeed it was in influencing overall industrial performance in world markets.

[70] AMB, 11 October 1937; *Thirtieth Report of the Imperial Economic Committee. A Survey of the Trade in Motor Vehicles* (1936), pp. 89, 98; *Economist*, 16 October 1937.

[71] Stanley Chapman, 'Strategy and Structure at Boots the Chemists', in Leslie Hannah (ed.), *Management Strategy and Business Development* (1976), pp. 93–107

[72] Roy Church and Michael Miller, 'The Big Three'.

Appendices

APPENDIX ONE

Specification of Plant Required for Motor Vehicle Manufacture on a Moderate Basis (1900)

	£	s.	d.
1 16 h.p. Gas Engine, and Fittings	250	0	0
Machine Shop			
1 2 feet by 6 feet Planing Machine	150	0	0
2 16 inch Shaping Machines	130	0	0
4 9 inch Screw-cutting Lathes—8 feet beds	300	0	0
4 6 inch Screw-cutting Lathes—6 feet beds	200	0	0
1 Chucking Lathe	100	0	0
1 small Slotting Machine	65	0	0
4 Lathe Millers	200	0	0
2 Brass Finishers' Lathes	100	0	0
1 Boring Machine	125	0	0
2 1¼ inch Turret Lathes	200	0	0
2 ⅞ inch Turret Lathes	150	0	0
1 No. 3 Tool Room Milling Machine	200	0	0
3 Plain Milling Machines	300	0	0
1 Automatic Gear-Cutting Machine	200	0	0
1 Vertical Milling Machine	125	0	0
1 3 inch Cutting-off Machine	40	0	0
4 25 inch Upright Drilling Machines	125	0	0
4 small Drilling Machines	60	0	0
1 No. 2 Universal Grinder	150	0	0
1 No. 1 Universal Grinder	110	0	0
1 Cutter Grinder	45	0	0
1 Twist Drill Grinder	18	0	0
3 Tool Grinders	36	0	0
1 Lapping Head	5	0	0
1 Brazing Hearth	5	0	0
Smiths' Shop			
8 Smiths' Hearths, Anvils and Tools	20	0	0
1 Power Hammer	75	0	0
1 Blower	8	0	0
1 Furnace for hardening	8	10	0
1 Furnace for case-hardening	7	0	0
1 Tool Forge	8	0	0
	£3663	10	0

	£	s.	d.
Pattern Makers' Shop			
1 Lathe	20	0	0
1 Hand saw	25	0	0
1 Mitreing Machine	15	0	0
Body-Making Shop			
1 Hand saw	25	0	0
1 Saw bench	35	0	0
Fitting and Erecting Shop			
30 Vices for Bench	60	0	0
2 Marking-Off Tables	15	0	0
Benches, Trestles, Belting, Files and General Odds and Ends	100	0	0
Shafting, Hangers, Pulleys etc.	100	0	0
Erection of Engine, Machines, etc.	150	0	0
Fittings for Offices, Stores, etc.	100	0	0
Preparation of premises for occupation, including Pits for erecting Shops, etc.	50	0	0
Cranes in Erecting and Machine Shops	60	0	0
General Stores, such as Bar iron and steel, Timber Oil, Waste, etc., etc., say	581	10	0
	£5000	0	0

Estimating that it would be necessary to spend £5000 on manufacture before Returns balanced Expenditure

The outlay would be:

	£	s.	d.
Cash payment to Vendor's Company	6000	0	0
Share payment to Vendor's Company	4000	0	0
Cost of Equipment, as above	5000	0	0
	£20,000	0	0
Leaving an available reserve of	£10,000	0	0

	£	s.	d.
Wages—per week			
Full-pay mechanics	64	0	0
Assistants, Labourers, etc.	53	15	0
Staff, including Manager, Draughtsmen, Foremen, Clerks, Storekeepers	31	10	0
	£149	5	0
Purchases would equal roughly	125	0	0
	£274	5	0
Establishment charges, including Directors' Fees, Managing Director and Secretary's salary, Advertising, Rent, Rates and Taxes, Patent and Other Fees, could be safely reckoned at £1,800 per year, or per week	34	12	0
	£308	17	0

It would thus be necessary to turn out 1½ cars at a net selling price (after paying Agents' Commission) of £200 each per week, to pay expenses. It is estimated that the equipment is capable of an output of between 2 and 3 cars per week, of the above value.

Source: Wolseley SSMC.

APPENDIX TWO

Estimate of Expenditure in connection with the establishment of a works for manufacture of motor vehicles at Longbridge near Birmingham—6 September 1905

Buildings and Land

These consist of a modern well-situated and built works capable of employing about 800 men and are fitted with engines, generators, boilers, piping etc. for power, lighting and heating purposes. All the buildings are also fitted with sprinklers and there is a substantial water tower and tank to supply these sprinklers.

Very little alteration would be required to make the various shops suitable and a start could be made in about 3 weeks time after taking possession. The land is freehold and contains a little over 8 acres—The purchase price for the land, works, and fixtures is about £10,000 the fixtures being valued at £2,000 —The owner will let on lease the land and buildings at about £400 a year subject to an option to purchase during 1st 3 years of tenancy, if purchased he would be willing to leave on mortgage about £5,000 at usual rates—He wishes to sell the fixtures.

Plant

To obtain a reasonable and economical output of say 2 chassis per week value £400 each—plant to the value of about £7,900 would be required and this amount would equip Tool, Grinding, Machine, Polishing, Plating, Smiths', Coppersmiths' and Erecting shops sufficient for say the 1st year's work.

Purchases

These would average about £250 weekly being probably heavier during the 1st four months than later ones.

Wages

These would average about £250 weekly being heavier during the 1st four months than later ones.

Salaries

These would average about £40 weekly and would be fairly constant.

Advertising, Exhibitions, Trials, Catalogues, Stationery—would probably cost about £40 per week.

Travelling Expenses—these might amount to £10 per week.

Insurances, Legal Charges, Rates, etc. would probably cost £26 weekly.

There would be additional expenses incurred, in getting the works in order—in purchasing office furniture and fittings, in painting of signs, in repairs, etc., etc., amounting probably to £10 weekly—The total weekly expenditure would therefore approximate £626—It would take about four months to get ready to commence deliveries so that a sum of about £8,500 would be expended in general expenses before any returns could be expected.

Assuming that the works were rented and that the owner would agree to let the fixtures be paid off by 4 quarterly instalments, and that the plant could be purchased on similar terms, at the end of the first 4 months an expenditure of about £11,000 would have taken place, after which the sales should easily equal the outgoings.

APPENDIX THREE

Austin Motor Company Ltd. Assets 1906–1939 (£s)

Year	Building, Plant and Machinery	Stock and Tools	Cash and Investments	Debtors
1906	27,073	22,985		1,748
1907	44,623	49,857		10,690
1908	50,911	57,813		18,580
1909	57,900	63,187		19,221
1910	76,184	96,936		28,614
1911	87,663	129,950		25,849
1912	110,695	178,688	9,219	31,034
1913	137,350	231,019	50,735	29,588
1914	173,851	267,908	82,692	33,420
1915	260,272	407,750	200	112,940
1916	350,644	692,535	18,213	299,923
1917	838,866	1,231,105	200	456,368
1918	869,418	1,926,586	200	456,700
1919	1,764,857	2,050,155	212,272	151,230
1920	1,986,702	1,903,361	209,789	176,978
1921	1,910,054	850,721	276,961	104,324
1922	1,867,923	791,986	417,783	60,849
1923	1,803,067	958,392	469,103	73,573
1924	1,789,001	932,187	461,184	75,308
1925	1,431,354	1,084,898	456,609	114,121
1926	1,440,375	1,002,883	871,957	88,337
1927	1,590,192	1,716,375	679,555	99,676
1928	2,076,408	1,346,204	630,477	133,080
1929	2,097,943	1,370,644	829,117	130,855
1930	2,118,132	1,166,935	1,260,714	100,911
1931	2,313,456	1,254,929	1,375,394	116,859
1932	2,436,729	1,076,058	1,383,403	121,155
1933	2,502,718	1,080,802	1,361,469	120,378
1934	2,653,361	1,311,841	1,416,471	106,674
1935	2,836,040	1,359,472	1,492,718	195,268
1936	2,936,493	1,372,395	1,496,197	164,656
1937	3,322,276	1,646,966	1,460,081	217,804
1938	3,516,304	1,271,065	1,313,648	81,695
1939	3,520,493	1,277,163	1,611,480	289,049

Austin Profits and their Disposition 1922–1939 (£000s)

	12 months to 31.12.22	*9 months to 30.9.23*	*12 months to 30.9.24*	*12 months to 30.9.25*	*12 months to 30.9.26*	*12 months to 30.9.27*	*15 months to 31.12.28*	*12 months to 31.12.29*	*7 months to 31.7.30*
Profit	+222.4	+381.6	+470.9	+748.9	+648.4	+962.5	+861.3	+1,297.446	+858.157
Charges: Maintenance	−76.4	−108.2	−138.5	−164.1	−172.4	−262.2	−323.4	−324.9	−180.1
Depreciation	−71.5	−51.4	−64.0	−61.1	−54.0	−55.8	−72.6	−104.1	−62.5
Total Maintenance and Depreciation	−147.9	−159.6	−202.5	−225.2	−226.4	−318.0	−396.018	−428.981	−242.670
Interest on Debentures etc.	−52.3	−43.0	−88.2	−72.8	−88.3	−96.5	−115.800	−88.940	−49.922
Directors' fees	−3.6	−2.6	−3.0	−3.0	−3.0	−3.0	−3.5	−1.5	−2.4
Balance	+18.6	+176.4	+177.2	+447.9	+330.5	+545.0 −100.0	+461.775	866.965	+613.092
Taxation ex reserves	+60.0	+29.1	—	—	—	—	+50.00	+172.177	+150.000
Total available	+78.6	+205.5	+177.2	+447.9	+330.5	+445.0	+411.77	+694.788	+463.092
To preference dividends	0	0	0	0	0	−105.0	299.0([b])	404.0([b])	42.9
To ordinary dividends	0	0	0	0	0	0	0	139.6	+341.4
To reserves, etc.	0	0	+15.9	−726.9([a])	0	+39.4	+52.95	+46.06	+28.82
Net balance	+78.6	+205.5	+161.5	+279.0	+330.5	+300.6([b])	+59.82	+105.128	+49.972
Brought forward	−1,883.6	−1,805.0	−1,600.0	−1,438.4	−1,717.4	0	+10.6	59.7	+76.0
Carried forward	−1,805.0	−1,600.0	−1,438.4	−1,717.4	−1,386.9	+10.6	+70.42	+164.828	+125.972

([a]) expenses of Capital Reorganization.
([b]) Before charging £290,830 appropriated for Capital Reorganization

Appendix 4 (*contd.*)

	12 months to 31.7.31	*12 months to 31.7.32*	*12 months to 31.7.33*	*12 months to 31.7.34*	*12 months to 31.7.35*	*12 months to 31.7.36*	*12 months to 31.7.37*	*12 months to 31.7.38*	*12 months to 31.7.39*
Profit	+1,376.244	+1,078.145	+1,188.440	+1,505.212	+1,469.144	+1,496.7	+1,665.1	+1,282.8	+1,609.6
Charges: Maintenance	−391.9	−292.7	−365.6	−480.2	−483.6	−530.8	−606.5	−449.9	} −891.9
Depreciation	−107.7	−101.1	−116.8	−146.7	−145.0	−173.8	−179.5	−223.3	
Total Maintenance and Depreciation	−499.637	−393.794	−482.387	−626.932	−628.596	−704.6	−786.0	−673.2	−891.9
Interest on Debentures etc.	−83.524	−80.001	−71.255	−55.000	−55.000	−53.9	33.5	−52.8	−52.9
Directors' fees	−2.4	−3.0	−3.0	−2.0	−2.0	−2.0	−2.0	−1.0	−1.0
Balance	+874.232	+681.387	+703.053	+876.280	+838.548	+790.1	+877.1	+108.7	+716.2
Taxation ex reserves	+250.000	+156.000	+125.000	+160.000	+150.000	+165.0	+250.0	+175.0	+300.0
Total available	+624.232	+525.387	+578.053	+716.280	+688.548	+625.1	+627.1	+433.7	+416.2
To preference dividends	+73.6	+72.0	+73.1	+73.3	+73.6	+73.5	+73.2	+72.9	} +346.1
To ordinary dividends	+415.7	+317.5	+434.7	+588.0	+550.4	+367.2	+345.9	+242.2	
To reserves, etc.	+51.47	+54.99	+70.39	+50.00	+32.08	+67.9	+100.000	+187.0	+18.9
Net balance	+83.462	+80.899	−1.37	+4.98	+32.468	+116.5	+108.0	−68.4	+51.2
Brought forward	+279.8	+270.5	+319.2	+357.9	+362.9	+370.8	+373.9	+303.3	+303.4
Carried forward	+363.262	+351.399	+317.83	+362.88	+395.368	+487.3	+481.9	+243.9	+354.6

Bibliography of Sources Cited

I Primary Sources

The primary records referred to are almost entirely those of the Austin Motor Company held at Longbridge in Birmingham. These records, which are small in volume, have not been catalogued but consist of two types, the directors' Minute Books (referred to in abbreviated form as AMB) and miscellaneous documents and sundry papers (referred to as AMC Papers).

At the Aston factory of Wolseley Webb Ltd.: the Directors' Minute Books of the Wolseley Sheep Shearing Machine Company (referred to in abbreviated form as WSSMCMB) and a very small amount of correspondence and assorted documents (referred to as WSSMC Papers).

Companies House: The 'A' and 'F' files of the Austin Motor Company (133747) and of the Wolseley Sheep Shearing Machine Company (29846).

Public Record Office: The records which have been useful in this study are Treasury Supply files, T.161/52 and T.161/986.

The Bank of England: Records of the Securities Management Trust S.M.2 120/1.

The Midland Bank: Class 509 (uncatalogued).

The Ford Motor Company (Dagenham): Sundry Papers.

The Ford Motor Company (Detroit): Acc 285, Box 444.

University of London (and The Veteran Car Club): The Pollitt Papers.

BBC Archives: transcript of talk broadcast 26 February 1934, 'Modern Industry and the National Character'.

The Standard Motor Company Archives (Canley Works, Coventry).

R. Carl Hicks and G. D. Babcock, Report of the Automobile Situation in the World and Europe (1927), typescript report for the President of the Dodge Motor Corporation (Detroit Public Reference Library).

II Printed Sources

1. OFFICIAL

Royal Commission on Motor Cars, P.P. 1906, XLVIII.

Committee on Industry and Trade, Survey of Metal Industries, IV, 1928.

2. THESES

A. Holme, 'Some aspects of the British Motor Manufacturing Industry 1919–1929', M.A., University of Sheffield, 1964.

D. R. Littlewood, 'The Location of the British Motor Car Industry 1880–1930', M.A., University of Leicester 1962.

J. R. Marsh, 'Birmingham Public Opinion and Economic Development 1919–1932', M.A., University of Birmingham, 1961.

E. J. B. Sieve, 'British Motor Vehicle Exports (An Analysis of the Interwar Period and Some Post-1945 Trends)', Ph.D., University of London, 1950.

3. PERIODICAL LITERATURE

To supplement the limited volume of primary sources relating to Austin's history periodical literature has been used intensively. As only a few of the references taken from contemporary periodicals originate in the form of articles and cannot, therefore, be cited specifically, the list of periodical publications consulted is presented here, together with the abbreviations used in footnotes and references.

The Austin Car Owners' Journal (Dec. 1911, No. 1–Aug. 1927, 16) thereafter *The Austin Magazine and Advocate.*
Austin Apprentice
Autocar
Automobile Engineer
Automotive Industries
Automotor Journal
Birmingham Gazette
Birmingham Mail
Birmingham Post
Business History
Coventry Evening Telegraph
Cyclecar
Directory of Directors
Economist
Ford Times
Investors' Chronicle
Investors' Monthly Manual
Journal of Industrial Economics

Journal of the National Union of Vehicle Builders (JUNVB)
Journal of Transport History
The Manifold (Austin Motor Company)
Midland Daily Telegraph
Motor
Motor Car Index
Motor Car Journal
Motor Cycle Buyers' Guide
Motor Trader
Old Motor
Pall Mall Magazine
Proceedings of the Institute of Automobile Engineers (*PIAE*)
Proceedings of the Institute of Mechanical Engineers (*PIME*)
Statist
Stock Exchange Year Book (*SEYB*)
Thoroughbred and Classic Cars
Times
Town Crier
US Commerce Reports

4. ARTICLES

Appleby, E. J. — 'The Small Car, An Outline History of the Modern Bijou Automobile', *Autocar*, 9 May 1930.

Austin, Sir Herbert — 'Sir Herbert Austin, KBE, His Life Story', *Autocar*, 1929.

Austin, Sir Herbert — 'The Importance of Purpose', *Pall Mall Magazine*, V, 1929.

Austin, Sir Herbert — 'The Future Trend of Automobile Design', *PIAE*, XXV (1930–31).

Austin, Sir Herbert — 'Facts and Figures that Prove that Light Cars are Making History', *Light Car and Cycle Car*, 11 December 1931.

Austin, Sir Herbert — 'Modern Industry and the National Character', 26 February 1934, BBC transcript.

Beaumont, E. G. E. — 'The Influence of the Automobile User upon the Automobile Engineer', *PIME*, XXII (1927–28).

Beesley, M. E. — 'Changing Locational Advantages in the British Motor Industry', *Journal of Industrial Economics*, VI (1957).

Berriman, A. E. — 'A Review of the Rating Question', *PIAE*, XIX (1925).

Chapman, Stanley — 'Strategy and Structure at Boots the Chemists', in Leslie Hannah (ed), *Management Strategy and Business Development* (1976).

Checkland, S. G.	Review of D. C. Coleman, History of Courtaulds, *Economic History Review*, XXXIII (1970).
Church, Roy, & Miller, Michael	'Growth and Instability in the British Motor Industry Between the Wars', in Buxton and Aldcroft (eds) *Instability and Industrial Development, 1919–1939.*
Church, Roy, & Miller, Michael	'The Big Three: Competition, Management, and Marketing in the British Motor Industry, 1922–1939', in Barry Supple (ed), *Essays in British Business History* (Oxford, 1977).
Church, Roy	'Innovation, Monopoly and Supply of Vehicle Components in Britain, 1880–1930: the Growth of Joseph Lucas Ltd.', *Business History Review*, Vol. LII (1978).
Church, Roy	'Myths, Men and Motor Cars', *Journal of Transport History*, IV (1977) 2.
Davies, B. H.	'Munitions Work as an Education', *Autocar*, 42 (1919).
Edge, Stanley	'The Birth of the Austin Seven', *Thoroughbred and Classic Cars*, June 1977.
Edge, S. H.	'Sir Herbert Austin, KBE, MP, During Years 1920–25', *Magazine of the Austin Seven Club Association*, publication No. 73.
Engelbach, C. R. F.	'Some Notes on Reorganizing a Works to Increase Production', *PIAE*, XXIII (1927–28).
Engelbach, C. R. F.	'Problems in Manufacture', *PIAE*, xxviii (1933–34).
Floud, R. C.	'The Adolescence of American Engineering Competition 1860–1900', *Economic History Review*, No. 1, XXVII (1974), 1.
Hancock, A. J. W.	'Lord Austin – Engineering Genius', *Motor*, 6 July 1955.
Howitt, W. A.	'Impressions of Lord Austin' (1941).
Irving, R. J.	'New Industries for Old, Some Investment Decisions of Armstrong Whitworth, 1900–1914', *Business History*, 17 (1975).
Kennington, W. O.	'The Utilitarian Aesthetics of Automobile Body Design', *PIAE*, XXIX (1934–35).
Maxcy, G.	'The Motor Industry', in P. Cook and R. Cohen, *The Effects of Mergers* (Cambridge Studies in Industry, 1958).
Pomeroy, L. H.	'Automobile Engineering After the War', *PIAE*, IX (1914–15).
Remington, A. A.	'Some Probable Effects of the War on the Automobile Industry', *PIAE*, XIII (1918–19).

Rouch, E. A. — 'The Overseas Automobile Market', *PIAE*, XVIII (1923–24).

Sayers, R. S. — 'The Springs of Technical Progress in Britain, 1919–1939', *Economic Journal*, LX (1950).

Saul, S. B. — 'The Motor Industry in Britain to 1914', *Business History*, V (1962).

Silberston, A. — 'The Motor Industry', in D. L. Burn (ed) *The Structure of British Industry* (Cambridge, 1958).

Smith, D. J. — 'The Need for a Wider Outlook in Automobile Engineering', *PIAE*, XVII (1922–23).

Thomas, H. K. — 'The Fundamentals of Cost Reduction', *PIAE*, XVIII (1923–24).

Thomas, H. K. — 'The Effects of Automobile Manufacture in the Midlands', *PIAE*, XIX (1924).

Woollard, F. G. — 'Notes on British Methods of Continuous Production', *PIAE*, XIX (1924).

Woollard, F. G. — 'Sir Leonard Lord, KBE, A Personal Assessment,' *Motor*, 6 July 1955.

Wyatt, R. J. — 'The Year 1919', *Old Motor*, July 1963.

5. Books

Alford, B. W. — *Depression and Recovery? British Economic Growth 1918–1939* (1972).

Andrews, P. W. S. & Brunner, Elizabeth — *The Life of Lord Nuffield* (Oxford 1955).

Ashworth, W. — *Contracts and Finance* (1953).

Austin Motor Company — *The Coming of Age of the Austin Motor Company 1905–1925* (1926).

Austin Motor Company — *Longbridge Today* (1937).

Austin Motor Company — *History of the Austin Motor Company* (1960).

Austin Motor Company — *How Longbridge Spanned the Years of War, Austin 1939–45* (1946).

Austin Motor Company — *The Story of Longbridge, An Industrial Romance* (1932).

Austin Motor Company — *Austin Through the Years* (1949).

Bellamy, Roland C. & Andrews, Cyrus (eds).	*Who's Who in the Motor Industry* (1952).
Bersey, W. C. & Foucard, W. F.	*A List of Motor Cars, 1908–1914* (1914).
Birmingham Reference Library	*The Nine Days in Birmingham: The General Strike 1926* (Birmingham 1976).
British Commerce and Motor Industry (1934)	
Burn, D. L.	*The Economic History of Steelmaking 1867–1939* (Cambridge 1940).
Butler, H. J.	*Motor Body Work, The Design and Construction of Private, Commercial and Passenger Types* (1924).
Carr, J. C. & Taplin, W.	*History of the British Steel Industry* (Cambridge, Mass. 1962).
Castle, H. G.	*Britain's Motor Industry* (London 1951).
Caunter, C. F.	*The Light Car, A Technical History* (1970).
Clutton, Cecil & Stanford, John	*The Vintage Motor Car* (1954).
Critchley, J. S.	*British Motor Vehicles* (1912).
Darbyshire, L. D.	*The Story of Vauxhall 1857–1946* (Luton, 1946).
Davison, A. G. S.	*At the Wheel* (1931).
Davy, J. R.	*The Standard Car 1903–1963* (1964).
Duncan, H. O.	*The World on Wheels* (Paris, 1926).
Edge, S. F.	*My Motoring Reminiscences* (London, 1934).
Ferrie, William	*The Banned Broadcast of William Ferrie* (1934).
Fletcher & Son Ltd	*The Motor Car Index 1913–1924* (Norwich, 1925).
Fletcher & Son Ltd.	*The Motor Car Index 1928–1939* (reprinted Brighton, 1964).
Georgano, G. N.	*A History of the London Taxicab* (Newton Abbot, 1972).
Haynes, C. E.	*Motor Vehicle Taxation in Foreign Countries*, Trade Information Bulletin 463, US Dept. of Commerce (1927).
Henry, Freddie	*Lord Austin of Longbridge* (n.d.), Montague Motor Museum.
Hornby, William	*Factories and Plant* (1958).

Howitt, W. A. — *Impressions of Lord Austin* (1941), National Motor Museum, Beaulieu.

Imperial Economic Committee (Thirtieth Report) — *A Survey of the Trade in Motor Vehicles* (1936).

Jackson, R. — *The Nuffield Story* (London 1964).

Kingsford, P. W. — *F. W. Lancaster, A Life of an Engineer* (1960).

Lambert, Z. E. & Wyatt, R. J. — *Lord Austin, the Man* (1968).

Maxcy, G. and Silberston, A. — *The British Motor Industry* (London, 1959).

Lord Montague of Beaulieu — *Lost Causes of Motoring* (London, 1960).

Nicholson, T. R. — *The Vintage Car 1919–1930* (London 1966).

Nixon, St. J. C. — *Wolseley, A Saga of the Motor Industry* (1949).

Nixon, St. J. C. — *The Antique Automobile* (1956).

Nixon, St. J. C. — *The Story of the S.M.M.T. 1902–1952* (1952).

Oliver, G. A. — *A History of Coachbuilding* (1962).

Oliver, G. A. — *The Rover* (1971).

Overy, R. J. — *William Morris, Viscount Nuffield* (1976).

Peters, Percy & Thorton, H. (eds) — *Who's Who in the Motor Trade* (1934).

Plowden, W. E. — *The Motor Car and Politics* (1971).

Political and Economic Planning — *Motor Vehicles*, PEP Engineering Report II (London, 1950).

Prest, A. R. — *Consumers' Expenditure in the United Kingdom 1900–1919.*

Reader, W. J. — Imperial Chemical Industries, A History, Vol. II, *The First Quarter Century 1926–1952* (1975).

Red Book of Commerce (1911)

Richardson, K. — *Twentieth Century Coventry* (1972).

Rhys, D. G. — *The British Motor Industry* (1972).

Rostas, L. — *Comparative Productivity in British and American Industry* (Cambridge, 1948).

Sedgwick, M. — *Cars of the 1930s* (1970).

Sedgwick, M. — *Passenger Cars* (London, 1975).

Sargant Florence, P. — *Ownership, Control and Success of Large Companies* (1961).

Scott-Moncrieff, D.	*The Thoroughbred Motor Car 1930–40* (London, 1963).
Skinner, T. (Pubs.)	*Directory of Directors.*
Society of Motor Manufacturers and Traders	*The Motor Industry of Great Britain* (published annually).
Thomas, Sir Miles	*Out On a Wing* (1964).
Turner, Graham	*The Leyland Papers* (1971).
Wilkins, Mira & Hill, Frank Ernest	*American Business Abroad: Ford on Six Continents* (Detroit, 1966).
Wilson, Charles & Reader, William	*Men and Machines: A History of D. Napier & Sons, Engineers, Ltd., 1808–1958* (1958).
Wyatt, R. J.	*The Motor for the Million: The Austin Seven 1922–1939* (1968).

Index

Index